Probate and Settle an Estate in California

Third Edition

Douglas E. Godbe
John J. Talamo

Attorneys at Law

SPHINX® PUBLISHING
AN IMPRINT OF SOURCEBOOKS, INC.®
NAPERVILLE, ILLINOIS
www.SphinxLegal.com

Third Edition, 2007

Published by: **Sphinx® Publishing, A Division of Sourcebooks, Inc.®**

Naperville Office
P.O. Box 4410
Naperville, Illinois 60567-4410
630-961-3900
Fax: 630-961-2168
www.sourcebooks.com
www.SphinxLegal.com

This publication is designed to provide accurate and authoritative information in regard to the subject matter covered. It is sold with the understanding that the publisher is not engaged in rendering legal, accounting, or other professional service. If legal advice or other expert assistance is required, the services of a competent professional person should be sought.

From a Declaration of Principles Jointly Adopted by a Committee of the American Bar Association and a Committee of Publishers and Associations

This product is not a substitute for legal advice.

Disclaimer required by Texas statutes.

Library of Congress Cataloging-in-Publication Data
Godbe, Douglas, 1951-
  Probate and settle an estate in California / by Douglas E. Godbe and John J. Talamo. -- 3rd ed.
      p. cm.
  Rev. ed. of: How to probate and settle an estate in California. 2nd ed. 2004.
  Includes index.
  ISBN-13: 978-1-57248-592-1 (pbk. : alk. paper)
  ISBN-10: 1-57248-592-2 (pbk. : alk. paper)
 1. Probate law and practice--California--Popular works. I. Talamo, John.
II. Godbe, Douglas, 1951- How to probate and settle an estate in California.
III. Title.

KFC205.Z9G63 2007
346.79405'2--dc22
                                                              2007000348

Printed and bound in the United States of America.
SB — 10 9 8 7 6 5 4 3 2 1

Contents

Using Self-Help Law Books

Before using a self-help law book, you should realize the advantages and disadvantages of doing your own legal work and understand the challenges and diligence that this requires.

The Growing Trend

Rest assured that you won't be the first or only person handling your own legal matter. For example, in some states, more than seventy-five percent of the people in divorces and other cases represent themselves. Because of the high cost of legal services, this is a major trend and many courts are struggling to make it easier for people to represent themselves. However, some courts are not happy with people who do not use attorneys and refuse to help them in any way. For some, the attitude is, "Go to the law library and figure it out for yourself."

We write and publish self-help law books to give people an alternative to the often complicated and confusing legal books found in most law libraries. We have made the explanations of the law as simple and easy to understand as possible. Of course, unlike an attorney advising an individual client, we cannot cover every conceivable possibility.

Cost/Value Analysis   Whenever you shop for a product or service, you are faced with various levels of quality and price. In deciding what product or service to buy, you make a cost/value analysis on the basis of your willingness to pay and the quality you desire.

When buying a car, you decide whether you want transportation, comfort, status, or sex appeal. Accordingly, you decide among such choices as a Neon, a Lincoln, a Rolls Royce, or a Porsche. Before making a decision, you usually weigh the merits of each option against the cost.

When you get a headache, you can take a pain reliever (such as aspirin) or visit a medical specialist for a neurological examination. Given this choice, most people, of course, take a pain reliever, since it costs only pennies; whereas a medical examination costs hundreds of dollars and takes a lot of time. This is usually a logical choice because it is rare to need anything more than a pain reliever for a headache. But in some cases, a headache may indicate a brain tumor and failing to see a specialist right away can result in complications. Should everyone with a headache go to a specialist? Of course not, but people treating their own illnesses must realize that they are betting on the basis of their cost/value analysis of the situation. They are taking the most logical option.

The same cost/value analysis must be made when deciding to do one's own legal work. Many legal situations are very straight forward, requiring a simple form and no complicated analysis. Anyone with a little intelligence and a book of instructions can handle the matter without outside help.

But there is always the chance that complications are involved that only an attorney would notice. To simplify the law into a book like this, several legal cases often must be condensed into a single sentence or paragraph. Otherwise, the book would be several hundred pages long and too complicated for most people. However, this simplification necessarily leaves out many details and nuances that would apply to special or unusual situations. Also, there are many ways to interpret most legal questions. Your case may come before a judge who disagrees with the analysis of our authors.

Therefore, in deciding to use a self-help law book and to do your own legal work, you must realize that you are making a cost/value analysis. You have decided that the money you will save in doing it yourself outweighs the chance that your case will not turn out to your satisfaction. Most people handling their own simple legal matters never have a problem, but occasionally people find that it ended up costing them more to have an attorney straighten out the situation than it would have if they had hired an attorney in the beginning. Keep this in mind while handling your case, and be sure to consult an attorney if you feel you might need further guidance.

Local Rules

The next thing to remember is that a book which covers the law for the entire nation, or even for an entire state, cannot possibly include every procedural difference of every jurisdiction. Whenever possible, we provide the exact form needed; however, in some areas, each county, or even each judge, may require unique forms and procedures. In our state books, our forms usually cover the majority of counties in the state, or provide examples of the type of form which will be required. In our national books, our forms are sometimes even more general in nature but are designed to give a good idea of the type of form that will be needed in most locations. Nonetheless, keep in mind that your state, county, or judge may have a requirement, or use a form, that is not included in this book.

You should not necessarily expect to be able to get all of the information and resources you need solely from within the pages of this book. This book will serve as your guide, giving you specific information whenever possible and helping you to find out what else you will need to know. This is just like if you decided to build your own backyard deck. You might purchase a book on how to build decks. However, such a book would not include the building codes and permit requirements of every city, town, county, and township in the nation; nor would it include the lumber, nails, saws, hammers, and other materials and tools you would need to actually build the deck. You would use the book as your guide, and then do some work and research involving such matters as whether you need a permit of some kind, what type and grade of wood are available in your area, whether to use hand tools or power tools, and how to use those tools.

Before using the forms in a book like this, you should check with your court clerk to see if there are any local rules of which you should be aware, or local forms you will need to use. Often, such forms will require the same information as the forms in the book but are merely laid out differently or use slightly different language. They will sometimes require additional information.

Changes in the Law   Besides being subject to local rules and practices, the law is subject to change at any time. The courts and the legislatures of all fifty states are constantly revising the laws. It is possible that while you are reading this book, some aspect of the law is being changed.

In most cases, the change will be of minimal significance. A form will be redesigned, additional information will be required, or a waiting period will be extended. As a result, you might need to revise a form, file an extra form, or wait out a longer time period; these types of changes will not usually affect the outcome of your case. On the other hand, sometimes a major part of the law is changed, the entire law in a particular area is rewritten, or a case that was the basis of a central legal point is overruled. In such instances, your entire ability to pursue your case may be impaired.

Again, you should weigh the value of your case against the cost of an attorney and make a decision as to what you believe is in your best interest.

Introduction

The purpose of this book is:

- ✪ to describe basic probate and death tax law;

- ✪ to guide a layperson through the probate procedure without a lawyer;

- ✪ to point out when a lawyer would be useful or needed;

- ✪ to describe nonprobate procedures to transfer property at death; and,

- ✪ to provide blank forms and samples of completed forms for both the probate and nonprobate transfer of property.

Reading this book and following the instructions will enable you to start and complete a simple probate. This book also warns you when you need to hire an attorney. If you do require an attorney, this book enables you to better understand the probate process, and helps communicate your concerns and wishes to your attorney.

Most assets owned at death do not need to go through probate. This book identifies those nonprobate assets and provides information—including instructions, blank forms, and examples of completed forms—to assist you in transferring those assets without a lawyer.

Chapter 1 outlines some of the issues that need to be addressed when a person dies, and touches on which assets are subject to probate and which are not.

Chapter 2 gives step-by-step instructions and forms for the transfer of nonprobate assets. *This could be the sole reason to buy this book.* Keeping assets out of probate can save a great deal of money. Sometimes lawyers slip up and probate assets unnecessarily. If you read Chapter 2, this probably will not happen to you.

Chapters 3–6 walk you through the probate process of appointing the personal representative and preparing the estate Inventory and Appraisal. You will learn what to do, when to do it, and how to do it. Examples, hints, and warnings will steer you away from problems. Appropriate instructions and explanations for the forms in Appendix B are included.

Chapter 8 explains family protection rights in probate, while Chapter 9 explains the personal representative's rights under the Independent Administration of Estates Act.

The sale of assets is a tricky aspect of probate. Chapter 10 gives details on how to accomplish this, while Chapter 11 provides information on income and estate taxes.

Eventually, the probate process needs to end, and Chapter 12 takes you through the final distribution and discharge of the personal representative.

The end of this book contains a glossary of words that are used repeatedly throughout the text.

There are two appendices. Appendix A provides examples of completed forms, pleadings to the court, and the documents needed to transfer nonprobate assets. Appendix B provides blank court forms.

An Overview

Probate is the court supervision of the distribution of assets of a deceased person (called a *decedent*) to his or her beneficiaries or heirs. Probate occurs only when there is no other way to change the title of a deceased person's assets to the persons entitled to them.

Most property belonging to a decedent never goes through the probate process due to the many exceptions to probate. The exceptions to probate are listed on pages 4 and 5.

If assets must go through the probate process, it should take less than a year from beginning to end.

FINDING THE LAW AND USING COURT FORMS

The law itself is found primarily in the *California Probate Code* (Cal. Prob. Code). The California Probate Code contains all of the statutes (called *code sections*) relating to probate and the probate process. The California Probate Code can be purchased in most law bookstores for about $25, and is also available on several Internet websites.

Besides the California Probate Code, the law of probate is found in case decisions and in local court rules. In a simple probate the case law should not be necessary. However, case law interprets the California Probate Code, so if you want clarification on a part of the probate code, the case law may be useful. Also, an annotated version of the California Probate Code can be found in all county law libraries. *Annotated* versions cite and summarize cases and the legislative intent for each statute.

Local court rules are both written and unwritten. Most counties publish their local rules, and they can be found on the Internet or purchased from the court clerk. In addition, each judge will have his or her own rules or policies. You should inquire with the judge's clerk as to local, unwritten rules and procedures.

Most documents filed with the court are prepared on forms. Most are called *Judicial Council forms* and are used statewide. Other forms, created by a single county, are called *local forms*. Both Judicial Council forms and local forms may be purchased from the county clerk or obtained on the Internet.

Forms use a *fill-in-the-blank* or *fill-in-the-box* format to expedite court review. A properly completed form forces the person completing it to make all necessary allegations and give all necessary facts to the court.

In a simple probate there should only be two documents filed with the court that are not forms:

1.　the *First and Final Account and Report of Personal Representative and Request for Distribution of the Estate* and

2.　the *Order Settling First and Final Account and Report of Personal Representative and Decree for Distribution*.

Examples of these non-form documents are found in Appendix A.

Non-form documents, called *pleadings*, that are filed with the court (e.g., petitions and orders) need to be typed and must be on *pleading paper*, which can be purchased at most stationery stores or selected on most word processing programs. All pleadings must be on recycled paper. The title of the non-form pleading must be typed across the bottom of each page, as shown on the samples in Appendix A.

The information placed on the forms must be typed. (You can usually get away with a few printed words if you need to add them after preparation of the typed form.) Traditionally, forms were attached to the court file at the top and needed a standard two-hole punch (3" from end to end of the holes) at the top. Many counties now scan all court documents into their computer database, and thus no longer require the two-hole punch. As most counties no longer use the two-hole punch system, the use of two-sided court forms with an upside-down back page is not suggested. Check with your county clerk to determine how your county does it.

TYPES OF PROPERTY

In California, property is either separate property or community property. *Separate property* consists of the assets of a single, divorced, or widowed person. It also includes the assets of a married person that were either acquired before marriage or after marriage by gift or inheritance.

Community property, defined in the California Probate Code, Section 28, is property acquired during marriage, unless acquired by gift or inheritance. When a married person living in California acquires property, either *real property* (land, homes, and buildings) situated in California, or *personal property* (things other than land, homes, and buildings) situated anywhere, the law assumes it was acquired by the *community*. This means each spouse owns half the property, even if the title to the property is in the name of only one of the spouses. The spouses may, however, by agreement (in writing if the agreement is after 1985), make the property the separate property of one spouse or the other.

Another aspect of community property is that each spouse may transfer, at death, his or her one-half interest in any community property asset to someone other than the surviving spouse. If that transfer at death by one spouse is by will to someone other than the surviving spouse, probate is likely required for that property interest. The surviving spouse's one-half interest in the community property, regardless of what happens to the deceased spouse's interest, is not probated.

Community property can only exist during the marriage. At the moment of the death of either spouse, the property becomes separate property, one-half owned by the deceased spouse and one-half owned by the surviving spouse. Any property, community or separate, that the surviving spouse inherited from the deceased spouse becomes the separate property of the surviving spouse.

NOTE: *Real property is governed by the law of the state in which it is located. If the decedent owned real property located outside California, get professional advice. Not all states recognize the concept of community property.*

Quasi-Community Property

Quasi-community property is defined by California Probate Code, Section 66, as property acquired by a married person living outside California that would have been community property if the person was living in California. It applies to all personal property situated anywhere and to all real property situated in California.

ASSETS THAT MUST BE PROBATED

As a simple guideline, all assets of the deceased must go through probate unless the law specifically provides otherwise. However, since the exceptions to probate are numerous, most property that belonged to a deceased person does not need to go through probate.

ASSETS THAT DO NOT HAVE TO BE PROBATED

Assets that do not have to be probated include:

- ✪ assets in which the title lists the decedent and at least one living person as *joint tenants*;

- ✪ assets passing *outright* to a surviving spouse (this does *not* include property passing to a trust for the benefit of a surviving spouse);

✪   financial accounts in which the title is in the decedent's name "as trustee for" or "in trust for" a living person;

✪   brokerage accounts in which the title is in the decedent's name with the designation *transfer on death* to a living person;

✪   financial accounts or savings bonds in which the title is in the name of decedent with the instruction to *pay on death* to a living person;

✪   assets in which the title is in the name of the decedent as the trustee of a trust;

✪   assets belonging to the decedent (such as a pension plan, 401(k), annuity, or life insurance) in which the decedent designated a *beneficiary* or payee in the event of death and the payee survived the decedent; and,

✪   assets in which the title is in the name of the decedent, but they have a gross value of $100,000 or less.

Although the above types of properties pass title without probate, they generally do not pass automatically. Chapter 2 of this book explains the nonprobate properties in detail, and provides instructions and forms for the transfer of those types of assets.

NOTE: *A decedent often leaves assets that can be transferred without probate along with assets that must be probated.*

THE PERSONAL REPRESENTATIVE

California Probate Code, Section 58, defines a *personal representative* as:

> *an executor, administrator, administrator with the will attached, special administrator, successor personal representative, or a person who performs substantially the same function under the law of another jurisdiction governing the person's status.*

This is the person who administers the estate going through probate.

NOTE: *For convenience, this book will use only the term personal representative. Remember, the term encompasses all executors, executrixes, administrators, and administratrixes.*

Although a will may nominate someone to act as personal representative, he or she may not be the personal representative until he or she is appointed by the court. If the will does not nominate a personal representative, then California Probate Code, Section 8461, lists the priority of persons entitled to appointment. The person with the highest priority is the surviving spouse, followed by the children of the decedent.

INCOME TAXES

The death of the decedent does not end his or her income tax liability for income received until the date of the decedent's death. Income tax returns must be filed for the year of the decedent's death if the deceased is entitled to a refund or if his or her income was above the minimum for filing. The filing forms and procedures are the same as those for a living person, and there a joint return can be filed with the permission of the surviving spouse.

All of the decedent's prior year's tax returns must be filed. If not, the Internal Revenue Service (IRS) may later look up the beneficiaries and ask them for their share of the decedent's back taxes and penalties (based upon the percentage of the estate that the beneficiary inherited).

ESTATE AND INHERITANCE TAXES

Regardless of whether a decedent's assets pass through probate or not, there are both federal and California estate tax requirements that must be met.

Federal and California estate tax returns must currently be filed for all estates with a gross value over $2,000,000, regardless of whether or not any tax is due. This amount will increase through 2010 and then revert to $1,000,000 in 2011. (see Chapter 11.)

USING A LAWYER

You can, of course, hire a lawyer to handle the estate. If this is your preference, this book will help you to follow what the lawyer is doing and intelligently communicate your desires.

Another way to use a lawyer is for specific problems. If, for example, a piece of real estate is located in another state, you should coordinate the transfer or sale of the property with a lawyer familiar with that state's laws. You can also use a lawyer to check your work. It is a good idea to have someone you can go to when you are not quite sure of what you are doing.

It is *strongly recommended* that you hire a lawyer in the following circumstances:

❂   the will is *contested* (someone attacks the will's provisions);

❂   the will is unclear as to the decedent's intent;

❂   if the decedent had real property in another state or the decedent was a resident of another state;

❂   the decedent left unfinished contract obligations, such as property still in escrow;

❂   the decedent had an interest in a business, such as a partnership or sole proprietorship (simply owning stock in a public corporation is not the concern here);

❂   there is not enough in the estate to pay everyone (either creditors, beneficiaries, or both); and,

❂   when there is anything that you feel is beyond the scope of your knowledge (the *better safe than sorry* rule).

Finding a Lawyer   The California Bar Association certifies specialists in probate. They can give you a list of the certified specialists in your area. A lawyer becomes certified by proof of experience and passing a test. It is no secret that lawyers who are knowledgeable in one area of the law may not know as much about another area, so it makes sense to get a specialist.

As with the choice of anyone you hire, a personal interview, references, costs, and a general feeling of comfort with the person should be your guidelines in finding the right attorney.

FUNERAL ARRANGEMENTS AND OTHER IMMEDIATE TASKS

Regardless of whether or not probate will commence, there are certain immediate tasks to be completed. The first thing is to arrange the funeral. This may be a simple matter if the death was expected and the wishes of the decedent were known. Otherwise, check for burial instructions in the decedent's will, power of attorney for health care, or health care directive. The decedent's health care agent has authority for disposal of the remains if no specific burial instructions have been given.

Notify any pension payors and the Social Security Administration of the decedent's death (by telephone). Social Security checks are received on the third day of each month, but to be entitled to that check, the recipient must have been living on the last day of the prior month.

Example 1:
Bob Smith dies on March 1, 2007. On March 3, 2007 a Social Security check arrives. Bob Smith's estate is entitled to that check, as he was alive on February 28, 2007.

Example 2:
John Jones dies on February 27, 2007. On March 3, 2007, a Social Security check arrives. John Jones' estate is not entitled to that check, as he was not alive on February 28, 2007.

A surviving spouse is entitled to a $255 Social Security death benefit payment.

Finally, be sure to order at least twelve certified copies of the death certificate. These certificates will be attached to various forms throughout the process. In any case, order at least six more certified copies of the death certificate than you believe you will need. Due to antiterrorism legislation, California makes it very difficult to subsequently obtain certified copies of death certificates.

Transferring Nonprobate Assets

Most property titles pass at death without a will (or regardless of the provisions of a will) and without probate. Even when there is a probate proceeding, much of the decedent's estate will pass outside of the probate proceeding. The purpose of this chapter is to identify the property that does not pass through probate and to instruct how to transfer title to that property from the decedent's name to the name of the beneficiary.

JOINT TENANCY AND RIGHT OF SURVIVORSHIP

Joint tenancy may be the most common way that title to property passes at death. In California, property can be held in the names of two or more persons as joint tenants. To be joint tenancy property, the title must say so in writing. (California Civil Code (Cal. Civ. Code), Section (Sec.) 683.) Sometimes the initials JTWROS (joint tenants with right of survivorship) are used to designate joint tenancy property. There is a limited exception to the rule that the words *joint tenancy* must appear on the title—car and boat titles using the words *or* or *and/or* mean, by statute, joint tenancy.

Real property owned by a husband and wife that is held in their names as "husband and wife, as community property, with right of survivorship" will be treated as a joint tenancy even though the words "joint tenancy" or "joint tenants" are not included. (Cal. Civ. Code Sec. 682.1.) Real property is sometimes held in this manner for income tax purposes. (See "Income Tax Basis Adjustment" in Chapter 11.)

Example:

Property with a written title *Bob and Mary, as joint tenants* or *Bob and Mary, husband and wife, JTWROS* is joint tenancy property. Property with a written title *Bob and Mary as husband and wife* or *Bob and Mary as tenants in common* is not joint tenancy property.

Title to joint tenancy property at the death of one of the joint tenants passes to the surviving joint tenant. Accordingly, all the surviving joint tenant has to prove is that he or she survived the deceased joint tenant to acquire the deceased joint tenant's interest. This is done with a certified copy of the deceased joint tenant's death certificate, and if required, a written statement that the person in the death certificate is the same person as the one listed on the joint tenant title.

– Warning –

When community property is held in joint tenancy between a deceased spouse and someone other than the surviving spouse, it becomes, at the death of the deceased spouse, subject to the community property interest claim of the surviving spouse. In that event, contact a lawyer.

Banks/ Brokerage Accounts

To transfer financial institution and brokerage accounts to the surviving joint tenant, give the financial institution or brokerage a certified copy of the decedent's death certificate. A statement identifying the person named in the death certificate as the same person listed on the account should not be required, because the death certificate shows the Social Security number of the decedent. The decedent's Social Security number is usually on file with the financial institution or brokerage.

Stocks/Bonds and Limited Partnership Interests

The *transfer agent* for registered stock certificates and bonds should be contacted. (Many companies' websites list their transfer agents, or the transfer agent's name and phone number can be obtained from the company's stockholder relations department or a stockbroker.) Most transfer agents will send a *transfer package* to be completed and returned with a certified copy of the decedent's death certificate and the original stock or bond certificates. The transfer package usually consists of a W-9 tax withholding form (to show the new owner's Social Security number), an affidavit of the decedent's residence, and an affidavit that the person named in the death certificate is the same person listed on the stock or bond certificates. Original certificates should always be sent by *certified mail* or with an overnight mail service that provides a tracking service.

For private company stocks and limited partnership interests, the procedure through the corporate secretary or general partner is often less formal and might only require a death certificate and a letter asking that the old certificates be reissued in the name of the surviving joint tenants.

The following is an example of a letter to transfer private company stock.

> **Dear Sirs:**
>
> **This is to advise you that John Doe, the person listed in XYZ Corp. stock certificate #113 for 500 shares, common, as a joint tenant with the undersigned, Mary Doe, is the same person as John Doe listed in the enclosed death certificate, issued by Los Angeles County, State of California, as certificate number 04-1222222. The undersigned hereby requests that you reissue said enclosed stock certificate to the name of Mary Doe, Social Security number 555-12-4545, as the surviving joint tenant.**

Having stock or bond certificates reissued in the name of the surviving joint tenant should not require the endorsement of a stock assignment (sometimes labeled *stock power*) either on the back of the stock certificate or on a preprinted form. A stock power is a separate certificate that transfers the ownership of stock.

Autos/Boats   A certificate of ownership (pink slip) for cars and boats with the words *or* or *and / or* between the names of the owners makes the title a joint tenancy. It can be transferred to the surviving joint tenant at the Department of Motor Vehicles office with the certificate of ownership signed by the surviving joint tenant in the appropriate locations. The pink slip must be accompanied by the annual registration, a certificate of smog compliance for cars (spouses, children, parents, and siblings of the decedent are exempted from the requirement of a certificate of smog compliance), and a certified copy of the decedent's death certificate.

Real Property   The **Affidavit—Death of Joint Tenant** for a deed is used by the surviving owner of the real property. Joint tenancy real property is transferred by recording an **Affidavit—Death of Joint Tenant** (form 1, p.263) in the county where the real property is located. At this time, attach a certified copy of the decedent's death certificate and file a **Preliminary Change of Ownership Report** with the county recorder. (see form 2, p.265.)

Deed of Trust   The **Affidavit—Death of Joint Tenant** for a deed of trust (mortgage) is used by a surviving joint tenant beneficiary on the deed of trust (i.e., a person who is owed the money). No **Affidavit—Death of Joint Tenant** for a deed of trust is necessary for a deceased joint tenant *trustor*, the person who owes the money that is secured by the real property. (The **Preliminary Change of Ownership Report** should not be required for an **Affidavit—Death of Joint Tenant** for a deed of trust, but some counties require it anyway.)

Appendix A has a filled-in **Affidavit—Death of Joint Tenant** for a deed. By inserting the term *deed of trust* in lieu of *deed*, the same sample can be used as a guide to prepare an **Affidavit—Death of Joint Tenant** for a deed of trust. A blank form for **Affidavit—Death of Joint Tenant** is in Appendix B. (see form 1, p.263.) Many title companies, through their websites, also offer an **Affidavit—Death of Joint Tenant** form.

The following are some tips in completing the **Affidavit—Death of Joint Tenant**.

✪ The **Affidavit** is usually signed by a surviving joint tenant, but may be signed by anyone who knows that the person named in the death certificate is also the person named in the deed or deed of trust.

✪ The **Affidavit** must be executed in the presence of a notary.

✪ The address inserted in the upper left of the **Affidavit** is the address where the future property tax bills will be sent.

✪ The APN is the assessor's parcel number. If not found on the prior deed or deed of trust, it can be located on the property tax bill or obtained from the customer service department of a title insurance company or from the county assessor's office. (Although the APN is not legally required in order to file the **Affidavit**, it is useful for the county recorder and is required for the **Preliminary Change of Ownership Report**.)

✪ If the prior deed or deed of trust recorded does not have an *instrument number* (usually deeds recorded before the mid-80s) near the recording date, then use the book and page number listed near the recording date on the prior deed or deed of trust.

✪ If the legal description is lengthy, it might be easier to list it on a separate sheet and state: *See Exhibit A for legal description.* In that event, listing the common street address and assessor's parcel number becomes more important. If the legal description was listed on an exhibit on the prior deed or deed of trust, it may be copied and used as the exhibit on the **Affidavit**. In that event, remove all prior recording information from the legal description exhibit (be creative with a copy machine), and be sure that the legal description exhibit is very legible (the county recorder will reject documents that it deems illegible).

✪ Identify the decedent in the death certificate by the exact name used in the death certificate, and identify the same decedent in the prior deed or deed of trust by the exact name used in the prior deed or deed of trust.

Example:

If the death certificate says *John Baylor Jones,* then the **AFFIDAVIT** must also say *John Baylor Jones* when referring to the person in the death certificate. If the prior deed or deed of trust says *J. Baylor Jones*, then the **AFFIDAVIT** must say *J. Baylor Jones* when referring to the person in the prior deed or deed of trust.

A **PRELIMINARY CHANGE OF OWNERSHIP REPORT** (form 2, p.265) must be filed along with the **AFFIDAVIT—DEATH OF JOINT TENANT** for a deed. The purpose of this form is to advise the county assessor whether the real property transfer (from the decedent to the surviving joint tenant) is a *change of ownership*, which causes a reassessment of the real property. The *transferor* is the decedent and the *transferee* is the surviving joint tenant.

Complete the **PRELIMINARY CHANGE OF OWNERSHIP REPORT** as follows.

→ Obtain the assessor's parcel number from the county assessor's office, from the prior deed or deed of trust, or from the customer service department of a title insurance company.

→ Part I: If the surviving joint tenant is the decedent's spouse, then answer A "yes" and answer B through H, and J through L, "no." Then skip to Parts II and IV and sign at the bottom of the second page. If the surviving joint tenant is a child, stepchild, parent, stepparent, daughter- or son-in-law, or grandchild of the decedent, then A through F, H, K, and L will be answered "no" and J will be answered "yes." All other surviving joint tenants will answer A through F, H, and J through K as "no." G is answered "yes" only if the prior deed was a transfer from the surviving joint tenant to the surviving joint tenant and the decedent. I is answered "yes" only if the real property is subject to a thirty-five year or longer lease.

If the **PRELIMINARY CHANGE OF OWNERSHIP REPORT** is for an **AFFIDAVIT—DEATH OF JOINT TENANT** for a deed of trust (*deed of trust* is a mortgage document—not a deed showing ownership) and is only being filed because the county recorder is demanding it, then at the bottom of Part I insert the following.

The property interest being transferred is an interest in personal property only (i.e., a promissory note). No interest in real property is being transferred. The transferor was the beneficiary on a deed of trust.

◈ Part II: If the answer to A, G, or I was "yes" in Part I, then Parts II–IV are ignored and the form is signed at the bottom of page 2. Otherwise (and this includes surviving joint tenants who are children or grandchildren), Part II is completed as follows. A is the date of the decedent's death. At B, the box "inheritance" is checked and the date of death entered. C is answered with a "yes," and the interest of the decedent is entered. The interest of the decedent is the number 1 divided by the number of joint tenants. For example, if there were two joint tenants, then the percentage transferred would be 1 divided by 2, or 50%.

◈ Part III is not answered if the transfer was an inheritance.

◈ Part IV, if answered, is self-explanatory.

◈ A surviving joint tenant signs the form at the bottom.

◈ If J of Part I of the **Preliminary Change of Ownership Report** is answered "yes," then the surviving joint tenant, if he or she is a parent or child of the deceased joint tenant, may be exempt from a reassessment of the property tax on the real property. (Prop. 13 Reassessment Exclusion for Parent-Child Transfers.)

This exclusion from a Prop. 13 reassessment of the property value is not automatic. The surviving joint tenant must file a **Claim for Reassessment Exclusion for Transfer between Parent and Child** in a timely manner (form 3, p.267) to be entitled to the parent-child transfer exclusion. (There is a sample, filled-in form in Appendix A.) This claim must be filed within three years of the decedent's death.

The exclusion can apply to the decedent's residence no matter what the value, as well as the first $1,000,000 of the property tax assessed value of the decedent's nonresidence real property. Other real property that is exempt because it passes to a surviving spouse of the decedent does not reduce the $1,000,000 nonresidential real property exclusion for parent-child transfers. To be exempt at the time of the transfer, it must be between:

- parent and child;

- stepparent and stepchild only if the parent of the child and the stepparent are married, or the parent married to the stepparent is deceased and the stepparent has not remarried;

- child and parent;

- parent and son-in-law or daughter-in-law, unless the relationship ended due to a divorce of the child and the son-in-law or daughter-in-law, or unless the relationship ended due to the death of the child and the son-in-law or daughter-in-law remarried; or,

- grandparent and grandchild if the parent of the grandchild, who is also the child of the grandparent, is deceased and the other parent of the child is also deceased or remarried.

The claim form is not difficult to complete. At Item A4, only the date of death is applicable. Item A5 is not applicable. Answer Item B6 "yes" and insert the applicable percentage. Answer Item B7 "yes." If Item C3 applies, a lawyer should be consulted.

P.O.D. BANK ACCOUNTS AND T.O.D. BROKERAGE ACCOUNTS

Payable on death (P.O.D.) bank accounts and *transfer on death* (T.O.D.) brokerage accounts are transferred simply by presenting a certified copy of the decedent's death certificate. (Cal. Prob. Code, Sec. 5100 through 5512.)

– Warning –

Sometimes community property is held in a P.O.D. or T.O.D. account in the name of a deceased spouse, and someone other than the surviving spouse is the named beneficiary of the account. In this case, the surviving spouse has a claim for his or her community property interest in the account. In that event, contact a lawyer.

LIFE INSURANCE, ANNUITIES, PENSIONS, IRAS, AND PRIVATE RETIREMENT ACCOUNTS

Life insurance, annuities, pensions, individual retirement accounts (IRAs), and private retirement accounts are all examples of property that passes at death based upon a contract. The owner of the contract (i.e., the insured, the annuitant, the owner of the employee contracts), along with the insurer, employer, or plan administrator, pay the benefits, property, or proceeds to a beneficiary that the owner of the contract designated as the recipient in the event of his or her death. In the event the owner of the contract fails to designate a beneficiary, some contracts will designate a *default* beneficiary, such as the spouse or children of the owner of the contract. The beneficiary need only execute the appropriate claim forms and submit a certified copy of the decedent's death certificate to claim the benefits, property, or proceeds.

– Warning –

When the contractual property benefits are community property (such as employment benefits) or the premiums that paid for the benefits are community property, and someone other than the surviving spouse is the named beneficiary of the benefits or property, then the surviving spouse has a claim for his or her community property interest in the benefits or property. In that event, contact a lawyer.

TOTTEN TRUST ACCOUNT

A financial institution account can be held in the name of an individual *as trustee for* or *in trust for* a named beneficiary. In that situation, the *trustee* is the owner of the account and has created a mini revocable trust for the account proceeds, commonly called a *Totten trust*. In the event of the death of the account owner, the named beneficiary need only bring a certified copy of the account owner's death certificate. If the account is held in the name of two persons as joint tenants *as trustees for* or *in trust for* a named beneficiary, and one of the account owners dies, the surviving account owner, as the surviving joint tenant, owns all of the account and can revoke the account or change the named beneficiary.

– Warning –

When the Totten trust account contains community property and someone other than the surviving spouse is the named beneficiary of the account, then the surviving spouse has a claim for his or her community property interest in the account. In that event, contact a lawyer.

LIVING TRUST

Property titled in the name of a living trust is not subject to probate. The title to property in a living trust might read something like: *John Smith, Trustee of the Smith Family Trust dated 4/2/07*. One of the main purposes of creating a living trust is to avoid probate. Upon the death of the trustor, the successor trustee administers and distributes the living trust estate pursuant to the written instructions in the living trust document. (The rights of the living trust beneficiaries and the obligations of the trustees are beyond the scope of this book.)

If the *trustor* (the person that created the trust) declares in the living trust that certain property is part of the living trust, but fails to actually change the title of the property to the name of the living trust, an action can be brought in the probate court to have such property declared to be part of the living trust. In that event, that property can be ordered by the court to be exempt from probate under the *Estate of Heggstad*. (A lawyer should be consulted if these facts exist.)

PROPERTY PASSING TO A SURVIVING SPOUSE OR DOMESTIC PARTNER

NOTE: *Under California law, a registered domestic partner has basically the same property rights as a spouse. In this chapter, the term "spouse" can be interchanged with "domestic partner" and is applicable for registered domestic partnerships.*

Any property left outright to a surviving spouse or domestic partner—either by will or by intestate succession—passes without probate. (Cal. Prob. Code, beginning with Sec. 13500.) The estate could be ten million dollars and if the deceased spouse's or domestic partner's will says *all to my spouse (domestic partner)*, it will all pass to the spouse or domestic partner without probate in California. However, if there are any restrictions on the use of the property passing to the surviving spouse or domestic partner, such as a bequest to a spouse or domestic partner *in trust* or to a spouse or domestic partner *for his or her lifetime use*, then the property does not pass outright to the surviving spouse or domestic partner and is subject to probate.

The one-half community property interest of a surviving spouse or domestic partner does not pass to the surviving spouse or domestic partner as a result of the death of the deceased spouse or domestic partner, because the surviving spouse or domestic partner owned his or her one-half interest in the community property all along.

Property Petition

Sometimes it is difficult for a surviving spouse or domestic partner to convince third parties—such as banks, title insurance companies, or stock transfer agents (especially when there is no will)—that he or she is entitled to the deceased spouse's or domestic partner's interest in the property. It is also often difficult to convince the third parties that the surviving spouse or domestic partner has a community or quasi-community property interest in the property if the property is held in the sole name of the decedent. Other times there is a general dispute as to the provisions in favor of a surviving spouse or domestic partner in the decedent's will, or a dispute as to the community or separate property character of assets.

To help the surviving spouse or domestic partner in this situation, the California Probate Code provides a procedure for the surviving spouse or domestic partner to file a **SPOUSAL/DOMESTIC PARTNER**

PROPERTY PETITION. (see form 5, p.271.) (There is also a sample, filled-in form in Appendix A.) With this form, the surviving spouse or domestic partner can ask the court to make an order:

- ✪ determining what property held by the deceased spouse or domestic partner or the surviving spouse or domestic partner is community or quasi-community property and confirming to the surviving spouse or domestic partner his or her one-half interest therein, and/or

- ✪ confirming what property owned by the deceased spouse or domestic partner passes to the surviving spouse or domestic partner without probate.

To the extent property is determined not to pass to a surviving spouse or domestic partner or is not community property, the **SPOUSAL/DOMESTIC PARTNER PROPERTY PETITION** may also determine what property is going to pass through probate.

Complete the **SPOUSAL/DOMESTIC PARTNER PROPERTY PETITION** as follows.

- ◈ Complete the caption, which is above the title *Spousal/Domestic Partner Property Petition*. The petitioner's name, address, and phone number are inserted in the first box. The court county, address, and branch (*Probate*) belong in the second box. The decedent's name is inserted in the "Estate of" box.

- ◈ Item 1: Insert the name of the person filing the petition and check the appropriate boxes. Box a is for a determination of what property passes from the deceased spouse or domestic partner to the surviving spouse or domestic partner. Box b is checked for a confirmation that the surviving spouse or domestic partner owns a community property interest in certain property even if the deceased spouse or domestic partner gave his or her one-half community property interest to someone else. Box c would normally not be checked, as it infers either a litigation issue or a request to value certain property to fulfill a cash bequest in the decedent's will to the surviving spouse or domestic partner.

❖   Item 2: Check which is the petitioner.

❖   Item 3: Insert the date of the decedent's death.

❖   Items 4, 5, and 6 are completed so the court will be able to determine to whom the petitioner must give a written notice of the hearing.

❖   Item 7: Attachment 7 must be prepared. Attachment 7 contains the reason for the surviving spouse's or domestic partner's claim to property under boxes 7a and 7b. If only box 7a is checked and the decedent's will leaves everything to the surviving spouse or domestic partner, then Attachment 7 might only say the following.

> *Paragraph 3 of decedent's will, dated 8/1/05 and attached as Attachment 3 to this petition, says: "I bequeath to my wife [domestic partner], Jane Jones, all of estate, real, personal, and mixed, or whatsoever kind and wheresoever situated."*

If there is no will, but everything is community property, then Attachment 7 might read something like the following.

> *Decedent and petitioner were married thirty years. At the time of the marriage, neither spouse owned any assets. During the marriage, neither spouse inherited or received by gift any assets of value. Everything listed in Attachments 7a and 7b represents the community property of decedent and petitioner.*

(If you are uncertain as to how Attachment 7 should be worded, consult a lawyer.)

Check box 7a if box 1a was checked, and check box 7b if box 1b was checked. An example of an Attachment 7a is provided in Appendix A (form 5).

❖   Fill in the appropriate box for Item 8.

◈   Item 9: List all persons named as beneficiaries under any will of the decedent and all persons who are identified in Items 4 and 5. If there are more than six or so names, it will be easier to list them on a separate sheet titled Attachment 9. (The sample in Appendix A shows the format when listing the individuals at Item 9.)

If the persons listed are not relatives of the decedent, they can each be identified as a *friend*.

NOTE: *Under "Age," state either "Adult" or "Minor." Under "Residence or Mailing Address," beware—most courts do not permit the use of post office boxes as a mailing address.*

Finally, the petitioner's name and address need not be listed at Item 9.

◈   Item 10: List any nominated executors in the decedent's will or any court-appointed personal representatives if the decedent's estate is being probated. One of the boxes must be checked. Persons whose name and address would be in Item 10 can be omitted if they are already listed in Item 9. In that event, check either the first or second box. (The first box should then read "are listed above" and the second box should read "are listed in Attachment 9.")

◈   Item 11: Check if the petitioner is the trustee of a trust that is a beneficiary under the decedent's will.

◈   Item 12: Check the appropriate box.

◈   Item 13: Count the actual attachment pages and insert that number.

◈   The **SPOUSAL/DOMESTIC PARTNER PROPERTY PETITION** is dated and signed at the bottom of page 2. (Only sign the second signature line entitled "signature of petitioner.")

File the **Spousal/Domestic Partner Property Petition** with the clerk of the court in the county where the decedent resided, or in any county in which the decedent owned property if the decedent was not a resident of California. The filing fee will be approximately $350. The clerk will set the **Spousal/Domestic Partner Property Petition** for a court hearing about forty days from the date it is filed. After learning the hearing date, someone other than the petitioner must mail a **Notice of Hearing** (form 34) to all persons listed in Items 8–11 at least fifteen days before the court hearing date. (See Chapter 4 regarding the review of probate notes, preparation of any supplements, and attendance of the hearing.)

After the court grants the **Spousal/Domestic Partner Property Petition**, the petitioner presents the court clerk with a completed **Spousal/Domestic Partner Property Order**. (see form 6, p.273.) A sample, filled-in form is in Appendix A. It is prepared as follows.

◈ Complete the caption as directed for **Spousal/Domestic Partner Property Petition** on page 20.

◈ Item 1 should be easy to complete, and Items 3 and 4 can be copied from the **Spousal/Domestic Partner Property Petition**.

◈ Item 5a should be checked if Items 1a and 7a were checked on the **Spousal/Domestic Partner Property Petition**. Attachment 5a will mirror Attachment 7a, if all of the property on Attachment 7a was approved.

◈ Item 6 is generally not addressed. If creditors appeared in the action, consult a lawyer.

◈ Item 7a should be checked if Items 1b and 7b were checked on the **Spousal/Domestic Partner Property Petition**. Attachment 7a will mirror **Spousal/Domestic Partner Property Petition** Attachment 7b, if all of the property was approved.

◈ Insert at Item 10 the number of pages of the Attachments.

Order a certified copy of the **Spousal/Domestic Partner Property Order** for each county in which there was real property listed in the **Spousal/Domestic Partner Property Order**, and for each third party holding assets to be delivered to the surviving spouse or domestic partner.

Delivery of a certified copy of the **SPOUSAL/DOMESTIC PARTNER PROPERTY ORDER** to each third party holding title to a personal property asset should suffice to have the title changed by the third party to the name of the surviving spouse or domestic partner.

As to real property, the **SPOUSAL/DOMESTIC PARTNER PROPERTY ORDER** must be recorded in each county for which real property is listed in it. For each property listed on Attachment 6a, a **PRELIMINARY CHANGE OF OWNERSHIP REPORT** will have to be filed with the recording of the **SPOUSAL/DOMESTIC PARTNER PROPERTY ORDER**. (Some counties may incorrectly require a **PRELIMINARY CHANGE OF OWNERSHIP REPORT** to be filed for each property in Attachment 7a as well. Instructions for completing a **PRELIMINARY CHANGE OF OWNERSHIP REPORT** are given on page 14.)

In a **SPOUSAL/DOMESTIC PARTNER PROPERTY ORDER** situation, box A on Part I of the **PRELIMINARY CHANGE OF OWNERSHIP REPORT** is answered "yes." Accordingly, Parts II, III, and IV can be ignored.

Informal Personal Property Transfers

Most transfer agents will not require a **SPOUSAL/DOMESTIC PARTNER PROPERTY ORDER** to transfer title to a surviving spouse or domestic partner. For most personal property, a declaration by the surviving spouse or domestic partner that he or she is entitled to the decedent's property is sufficient. This declaration must be made forty days after the death of the deceased spouse or domestic partner and be accompanied by a certified copy of the decedent's death certificate. Many financial institutions, brokerages, and some stock/bond transfer agents provide affidavit or declaration forms to transfer property under their control. A **SPOUSAL/DOMESTIC PARTNER DECLARATION** is found in Appendix B. (see form 43, p.335.)

Real Property and Secured Note Transfers

When the passing of title to the surviving spouse or domestic partner is not disputed by another person, real property and notes secured by real property (i.e., deed of trust) do not need a **SPOUSAL/DOMESTIC PARTNER PROPERTY ORDER**. An **AFFIDAVIT—DEATH OF SPOUSE OR DOMESTIC PARTNER** for a deed or a deed of trust can be recorded forty days after the death of the spouse. (see form 4, p.269.) Appendix A has a sample, filled-in form.

SMALL ESTATE DISTRIBUTION

If all of the nonprobate transfers discussed above are excluded, then what is left should go through probate. However, if the *gross value* of real property and personal property that should go through probate is under $100,000, then those properties may also pass without probate. On the other hand, if the gross value of those properties that should go through probate is over $100,000, then all of the property that should go through probate must go through probate. (Cal. Prob. Code, beginning with Sec. 13100.)

Personal Property under $100,000

The personal property of a decedent can be obtained by an affidavit or declaration filed at least forty days after the death of the decedent. Many banks and brokerages will have their own form of the declaration. In case the third party does not have a form, a sample **Declaration for Transfer of Personal Property of Decedent** is found in Appendix B. (see form 7, p.275.) (A filled-in sample is in Appendix A.) If there is more than one beneficiary or heir entitled to the asset, all beneficiaries or heirs must sign the declaration, and it should be modified accordingly. A certified copy of the decedent's death certificate should accompany any such declaration.

The declaration does not need to allege that all creditors of the decedent have been paid, although the persons receiving property pursuant to a declaration are liable for the decedent's debts up to the value of the property received. (Cal. Prob. Code, Sec. 13156.)

Real Property under $20,000

If there is no probate proceeding; all of the decedent's funeral expenses and debts have been paid; and the total value of the decedent's real property to be transferred under California Probate Code, Section 13050; is under $20,000; then there is an expedited court procedure to obtain title for the beneficiary or heir. This procedure is useful for transferring small vacant lots, time-shares, and mineral rights.

At least six months after the death of the decedent, the person claiming the property as beneficiary or heir may file an **Affidavit re Real Property of Small Value ($20,000 or less)** with the clerk of the court, along with a $35 fee. (see form 8, p.277.) The beneficiary or heir will receive back, without a court hearing, a certified copy of the filed **Affidavit re Real Property of Small Value ($20,000 or less)**, which can be recorded with the appropriate county recorder.

Complete the **AFFIDAVIT RE REAL PROPERTY OF SMALL Value ($20,000 OR LESS**) as follows.

⬧ All persons entitled to an interest in the property must be petitioners and sign the affidavit. The affidavit must cover all of the decedent's interest in the subject property.

⬧ An **INVENTORY AND APPRAISAL** must be attached to the affidavit, and thus, should be prepared first. (see form 24, p.305.) (See Chapter 6 for instructions on preparing an **INVENTORY AND APPRAISAL**.) It must be sent to a *probate referee* appointed for the county in which the property is located. Obtain the name and address of a probate referee for the appropriate county from the court clerk. The probate referee should be advised that the **INVENTORY AND APPRAISAL** is for an **AFFIDAVIT RE REAL PROPERTY OF SMALL VALUE ($20,000 OR LESS**). (Items 6–8 of the **INVENTORY AND APPRAISAL** can be ignored.)

⬧ The **AFFIDAVIT RE REAL PROPERTY OF SMALL VALUE ($20,000 OR LESS**) will be filed in the county of the decedent's *domicile* (residence) unless the decedent was a nonresident of California. In that case, the affidavit is filed in the county in which the real property is located.

⬧ See page 20 to complete the caption (everything above the title "Affidavit Re Real Property of Small Value ($20,000 or less)").

⬧ Insert at Item 1 the decedent's name and date of death as it appears on the deed.

⬧ At Item 2, insert the city and state where the decedent died.

⬧ Attach a certified copy of the decedent's death certificate.

⬧ Check Item 4a if the decedent lived in the county where the **AFFIDAVIT RE REAL PROPERTY OF SMALL VALUE ($20,000 OR LESS**) is being filed. Check Item 4b if the decedent was a nonresident of California leaving real property in the county where the **AFFIDAVIT RE REAL PROPERTY OF SMALL VALUE ($20,000 OR LESS**) is being filed.

◈ At Item 5a the legal description of the property is listed. The assessor's parcel number (APN) and the street address should also be included. At Item 5b, the decedent's interest in the real property is listed.

Example:

If the decedent was the only owner of the property, his or her interest would be 100%. If the decedent only owned 10% of the property, the legal description under 5a would be for 100% of the property and the decedent's 10% interest would be reflected under 5b.

◈ Check Item 6a if the beneficiary's interest is derived from the decedent's will (and a copy of the will is then attached as Attachment 6a). Item 6b is checked if the heir's interest is derived from intestate succession. (Cal. Prob. Code, Secs. 6401–6402.5.)

◈ At Item 7, list the name and address of any guardian or conservator of the decedent at the time of the decedent's death. A copy of the **AFFIDAVIT RE REAL PROPERTY OF SMALL VALUE ($20,000 OR LESS)** (with attachments) must also be mailed to each person, if any, listed in Item 7, before it is filed with the court clerk.

◈ On page 2, the notarized signature of each petitioner must be affixed.

Real Property under $100,000

If the total value of the decedent's real property to be transferred under California Probate Code, Section 13050, is over $20,000 but under $100,000, there is a different expedited court procedure to obtain title for the beneficiary or heir entitled to the property.

At least forty days after the death of the decedent, the persons claiming the property as beneficiaries or heirs may file a **PETITION TO DETERMINE SUCCESSION TO REAL PROPERTY (ESTATES $100,000 OR LESS)** with the clerk of the court to be set for a court hearing. (see form 9, p.279.) (There is a sample, filled-in form in Appendix A.)

Complete the **PETITION TO DETERMINE SUCCESSION TO REAL PROPERTY (ESTATES $100,000 OR LESS)** as follows.

◈ All persons entitled to an interest in the property must be petitioners and sign the petition. (Unfortunately, some courts will charge each petitioner a separate filing fee of about $350.)

◈ An **INVENTORY AND APPRAISAL** must be attached to the petition, and thus, should be prepared first. (See Chapter 6 for instructions on preparing an **INVENTORY AND APPRAISAL**.) Send it to a probate referee appointed for the county in which the property is located. Obtain the name and address of a probate referee for the appropriate county from the court clerk. The probate referee should be advised that the **INVENTORY AND APPRAISAL** is for a **PETITION TO DETERMINE SUCCESSION TO REAL PROPERTY (ESTATES $100,000 OR LESS)**. Items 6–8 of the **INVENTORY AND APPRAISAL** can be ignored.

◈ The petition will be filed in the county of the decedent's domicile (residence) unless the decedent was a nonresident of California. In that case, the petition is filed in the county in which the real property is located.

◈ See page 20 to fill in the caption of the petition (everything above the title "Petition to Determine Succession to Real Property (Estates $100,000 or less)").

◈ List at Item 1 each petitioner's name. If the petitioners want an order that they are entitled to some personal property as well, then check the box at Item 1 as well as the box in the title of the petition. At Item 2, insert the decedent's name as it appears on the deed to the real property, along with the decedent's date of death and the city and state where the decedent died.

◈ A certified copy of the decedent's death certificate does not have to be attached.

◈ Check Item 4a if the decedent lived in the county where the petition is being filed. Check Item 4b if the decedent was a nonresident of California, and is leaving real property in the county where the petition is being filed.

◈ The box *intestate* at Item 5 is checked if the decedent died without a will, and the box *testate* is checked if the decedent died with a will. A copy of the will is attached as Attachment 5.

◈ In Item 7, check box a if no probate proceedings have commenced and box b if probate proceedings have been commenced. If b is checked, then list the state, county, court, and case number. It is unlikely that a California probate would have been commenced.

◈ At Item 9a, check the appropriate boxes. At 9b, the box "is" should be checked if the decedent is survived by a stepchild, and the stepparent (or foster parent) to stepchild (or foster child) relationship began when the stepchild was a minor and continued until the death of the stepparent.

For example, if there was no divorce between the stepparent and parent of the stepchild, and if the stepparent would have adopted the stepchild but for a legal bar (such as no parental consent) to the adoption, check the box "is." (Cal. Prob. Code, Sec. 6454.) The box "is not" is checked if there is no stepchild (or foster child) to stepparent (or foster parent) relationship as defined above.

◈ Item 10 is self-explanatory. Remember, only the first applicable box is checked.

◈ At Item 11, the box *personal property* is checked as long as it is checked in Item 1 and Attachment 11 is attached with the legal description of the property. The assessor's parcel number and the street address must be included and the decedent's interest in the property described.

For example, if the decedent was the only owner of the property, his or her interest would be 100%. If the decedent only owned 10% of the property, the legal description would be for 100% of the property and the decedent's 10% interest would be reflected separately at the end of Attachment 11.

◈   Check Item 12a if the beneficiary's interest is derived from the decedent's will (and a copy of the will is attached as Attachment 5). Item 12b is checked if the heir's interest is derived from intestate succession. (Cal. Prob. Code, Secs. 6401–6402.5.)

◈   Item 13 describes the interest of each petitioner.

Example:

Joe's will leaves Bob 25%, Mary 50%, Mel 10%, and Sue 15%. Attachment 13 would read:

Bob as to an undivided 25%; Mary as to an undivided 50%; Mel as to an undivided 10%; and, Sue as to an undivided 15%.

◈   At Item 14, list all persons named as beneficiaries under any will of the decedent, all heirs at law, and all persons who are identified in Items 1, 9, and 10. If there are more than six names it will be easier to list them on a separate sheet titled Attachment 14. (The filled-in, sample form in Appendix A shows the format when listing the individuals at Item 14.)

If the person listed is not a relative of the decedent, he or she can be identified as a *friend*.

NOTE: *Under "Age," state either "Adult" or "Minor." Under "Residence or Mailing Address," most courts do not permit the use of post office boxes as a mailing address.*

Finally, the petitioner's name and address should also be listed under Item 14.

◈ List in Item 15 any nominated executors in the decedent's will. One of the boxes must be checked. Persons whose name and address would be in Item 15 can be omitted if they are already listed on Item 15 and if the second box is checked.

◈ Item 16 is only checked if the petitioner is the trustee of a trust that is a beneficiary under the decedent's will. If checked, the names, addresses, and relationships of all beneficiaries of the trust must be listed on Attachment 16.

◈ Item 17 is only checked if there was a guardian or conservator of the decedent at the time of decedent's death. Check the appropriate boxes, if any, and list any said persons.

◈ At Item 18, list the number of pages attached to the petition.

◈ On page 2, the petitioners (if more than two petitioners, the excess petitioners can sign on an attached signature page) must sign where indicated.

File the **PETITION TO DETERMINE SUCCESSION TO REAL PROPERTY (ESTATES $100,000 OR LESS**) with the clerk of the court in the county where the decedent resided, or in any county in which the decedent owned property if the decedent was not a resident of California. The clerk will set the **PETITION TO DETERMINE SUCCESSION TO REAL PROPERTY (ESTATES $100,000 OR LESS**) for a court hearing about forty days from the date the petition is filed. After learning the hearing date, someone other than the petitioner must mail a **NOTICE OF HEARING** to all persons listed in Items 14, 15, 16, and 17, and file a **PROOF OF SERVICE** with the mailing at least fifteen days before the court hearing date. (See Chapter 4 regarding the mailing of the **NOTICE OF HEARING** and filing of the **PROOF OF SERVICE**. Also see Chapter 4 regarding the review of probate notes, preparation of any supplements, and attendance of the hearing.)

After the court grants the **PETITION TO DETERMINE SUCCESSION TO REAL PROPERTY (ESTATES $100,000 OR LESS**), the petitioner presents the court clerk with a completed **ORDER DETERMINING SUCCESSION TO REAL PROPERTY (ESTATES $100,000 OR LESS**). (see form 10, p.281.) A filled-in, sample form is in Appendix A, and is prepared as follows.

◈ See page 20 under **SPOUSAL/DOMESTIC PARTNER PROPERTY PETITION** to fill in the caption.

◈ Item 1 should be easy to complete, and Item 3, 5, 7, and 9 can be taken from the **PETITION TO DETERMINE SUCCESSION TO REAL PROPERTY (ESTATES $100,000 OR LESS)**.

◈ Item 9 can be taken from Item 13 (or Attachment 13) of the **PETITION TO DETERMINE SUCCESSION TO REAL PROPERTY (ESTATES $100,000 OR LESS)**.

A certified copy of the **ORDER DETERMINING SUCCESSION TO REAL PROPERTY (ESTATES $100,000 OR LESS)** should be recorded in each county where real property is affected by the order. A **PRELIMINARY CHANGE OF OWNERSHIP REPORT** will have to be filed with the recording of the order for each real property listed.

In an **ORDER DETERMINING SUCCESSION TO REAL PROPERTY (ESTATES $100,000 OR LESS)** situation, the only likely "yes" on Part I of the **PRELIMINARY CHANGE OF OWNERSHIP REPORT** would be J if the decedent was a parent, child, grandparent, mother-in-law, father-in-law, or stepparent. If J is checked "yes," a **CLAIM FOR REASSESSMENT EXCLUSION FOR TRANSFER BETWEEN PARENT AND CHILD** might be appropriate. (see form 3, p.267.)

chapter 3

Starting Probate Proceedings

California Probate Code, beginning with Section 8000, sets out the rules for filing the **PETITION FOR PROBATE**. (see form 11, p.283.) The petition may be filed by any interested party at any time after the decedent's death. An *interested party* may be someone who takes under the will (beneficiary), an heir, or even a creditor. Most often, the party filing the petition is the person who requests to be named the *personal representative* (PR) to handle the estate.

The **PETITION FOR PROBATE** has three purposes.

1. It asks the court for an order determining the date of death and the residence of the decedent at his or her date of death.

   The date is necessary to establish who is entitled to the estate. For example, say a will left property to a friend of the decedent. If the date of death of the decedent is after the date of death of the friend, the gift to the friend might *lapse* (not go to the friend's estate).

   The place of death establishes in what county the probate should be handled. It is the residence of the decedent and not the place of the decedent's death that determines the correct county. A question could arise if the decedent died in a care facility in a county different from the decedent's last home address. Was the facility also the residence or only place where the decedent was temporarily living? *Residence,* for purposes of determining the proper county, means the place where the decedent intended to permanently live. (If there is genuine uncertainty as to the date of death or the residence of the decedent, consult a lawyer.)

2. The petition asks the court to appoint a personal representative for the estate.

3. The petition asks the court to probate the will if the decedent made a will.

WAIVER OF RIGHT TO ACT AS A PERSONAL REPRESENTATIVE

A person named in a will as the personal representative (PR) has thirty days after learning of being named the PR to file the **PETITION FOR PROBATE**. Failure to do so without an acceptable reason for the delay is a waiver of the right to be the PR.

PREPARING THE PETITION FOR PROBATE

California Probate Code, Section 8002, sets forth the requirements of the contents of the **PETITION FOR PROBATE**. (see form 11, p.283.) The person who files the **PETITION FOR PROBATE** is called the *petitioner*. (A filled-in, sample form is in Appendix A.) Complete the petition as follows.

◈ Caption: At the top left of the **PETITION FOR PROBATE**, the petitioner inserts his or her name, address, and telephone number where indicated. In the box below that, the petitioner inserts the county of the court where the probate is being filed and the street and mailing address of that court. In the box below that, the petitioner inserts the name of the decedent and any aliases by which the decedent was known. It is wise to review the title in which the decedent held his or her property to correctly identify any aliases.

Example:
Estate of Robert Jones Smith, aka, R. J. Smith, aka, Bob Jones, aka, Robert Smith.

◈ Under *Petition for*, if there is a will and the petitioner is asking the court to appoint a person nominated in the will as the PR, then the petitioner checks the box *Probate of Will and for Letters Testamentary*. If there is a will but the person the petitioner is asking to be appointed as the PR is not nominated in the will, then the petitioner should check the box *Probate of Will and for Letters of Administration with Will Annexed*. If there is no will, the petitioner checks the box *Letters of Administration*. One and only one of those three choices must be checked on a **PETITION FOR PROBATE**.

> **NOTE:** *Regardless of whether there is a will or not, the estate may need immediate attention (e.g., ongoing business, assets in peril, completion of sales transaction—but not funeral bills or last illness expenses) that cannot wait approximately forty days. The court can be petitioned to immediately appoint a special administrator to act until the appointment of the PR by checking the "Letters of Special Administration" box. This is done on a separate* **PETITION FOR PROBATE**, *which is filed simultaneously with a regular* **PETITION FOR PROBATE**. *If the decedent's estate needs immediate attention requiring the appointment of a special administrator, it is time to consult an attorney.*

The last two boxes are both optional. The first box, if checked, tells the court that the PR is requesting authority to administer the estate under the *Independent Administration of Estates Act* (IAEA). (See Chapter 9 for a detailed analysis of the IAEA.) Generally, the PR will want those powers.

The last box, if checked, requests the IAEA powers with *limited authority*. If this box is checked, the PR will not have the power to sell real property unless the sale is confirmed by the court at a scheduled, noticed hearing. Unless the beneficiaries object to the PR having full authority, or if having full authority increases the bond a PR will have to post with the court, the PR will not want limited power.

Even if the PR has *full power,* the PR must obtain the consent of the beneficiaries for most sales of estate property. If any beneficiary objects to a sale, it must then be confirmed by the court at a scheduled, noticed hearing before the sale can proceed, even if the PR has IAEA powers.

◈ The areas to the right of the *Petition for* boxes (*Case Number, Hearing Date, Dept.,* and *Time*) will be filled in by the court clerk upon filing of the **PETITION FOR PROBATE**. Insert the case number on all subsequent court documents filed in the case.

◈ Item 1: Before filing the **PETITION FOR PROBATE**, the petitioner should arrange for the mandatory newspaper publication of the **NOTICE OF PETITION TO ADMINISTER ESTATE**. The petitioner should contact local newspapers and ask if they do legal publications. If so, the petitioner asks if they are a newspaper of general circulation in the city where the decedent last resided, or the city in which the decedent owned real property if the decedent is not a California resident. If there is no newspaper of general circulation in the city where the decedent last resided, then the publication is in a newspaper of general circulation in the county in which the decedent last resided.

The petitioner should also ask the publication cost and if the newspaper will give the mailed **NOTICE OF PETITION TO ADMINISTER ESTATE** (the notice to all heirs, beneficiaries, and nominated fiduciaries listed in the will of the **PETITION FOR PROBATE** and its hearing date). Most newspapers charge their fee based upon their total circulation. Accordingly, a major metropolitan daily newspaper is likely to charge more than a local weekly newspaper. The petitioner is only concerned about the publication being legal, and the local weekly newspaper is generally sufficient. Expect to pay up to $300 for the publication.

After the arrangements have been made for the newspaper to publish, the petitioner will mark Item 1a, *Publication Requested*, and insert the name of the newspaper.

NOTE: *Remember to leave a copy of the* **PETITION FOR PROBATE** *with the clerk for pick-up by the newspaper.*

◈ Item 2: Insert the name of the petitioner. If there are multiple petitioners, each petitioner must pay a separate filing fee (about $350).

◈ Item 2a: Check this box if a will is being offered for probate.

◈ Item 2b: Insert the name of the proposed PR and indicate either (1) executor if he or she is nominated in will as executor; (2) administrator with will annexed if he or she is not nominated in will; or, (3) administrator if there is no will (if a special administrator is requested, the assistance of a lawyer is recommended).

◈ Item 2c: If you requested in the *Petition for* box for powers under the IAEA, then this item must be checked and further checked as to whether the request is for full or limited authority.

◈ Item 2d: One of the three boxes must be checked. The first box indicates that bond will not be required (because either the will waives the bond requirement or because all heirs or beneficiaries are adults and have waived bond). The second box will be checked when a bond is required. The amount is determined from the total at Item 3c plus the value of real property if the PR is requesting the IAEA powers with full authority. The third box is checked when a bond may be reduced or eliminated by the placing of the estate monies into bank accounts over which the PR will have no access without a specific court order. (It is much easier to post the bond than to deal with the hassles involved in blocking accounts. *Blocking* only relates to the cash in the estate, and therefore, may not eliminate the bond requirement.)

◈ Item 3a: Check the appropriate box as the estimated size of the probate estate (do not include assets passing outside of probate, such as joint tenancies, life insurance, etc.). The box checked will determine the filing fee. The larger the estate, the larger the filing fee. If you underestimate the actual value of the estate the court will subsequently require the additional filing fee to be paid before the estate can be closed.

Item 3b: Check if your **PETITION FOR PROBATE** is *not* the first **PETITION FOR PROBATE** filed. In this event, your filing fee will be the amount charged by the court for an estate with a value of less than $250,000.

◈ Item 4a: Insert the date, street address, city, and state of the decedent's death, and check the appropriate box regarding state residency.

◈ Item 4b: Insert the street address, city, and county of the decedent's residence.

◈ Item 4c: (1) Insert the estimated value of personal property (e.g., securities, bank accounts, notes, CDs, cars, etc.). (2) Insert the estimated annual gross income from real property and personal property. Then add items (1) and (2) for the total. The value of real property, less debt on the real property, need only be completed if the petitioner is requesting the IAEA powers with full authority. (Some judges prefer that the real property value be stated anyway.)

◈ Item 4d: This item explains to the court why a bond is not necessary. The first box, *Will waives bond,* is checked if the will states that the PR may serve without bond. The second box is only applicable to special administrators. The third box, *All heirs at law are adults and have waived bond*, is checked if there is a will that does not state that the PR must be bonded, all beneficiaries under the will are adults, and all, in writing, waive the requirement of bond. In that event, the waivers of the beneficiaries must be attached to the **PETITION FOR PROBATE** as Attachment 4d. The last box, *Sole personal representative is a corporate fiduciary,* is only used when a bank or trust company is acting as the PR.

◈ Fill in the name of the decedent (aliases can be omitted) at the top of the second page.

◈ Item 4e: If there is no will, the petitioner marks the box *Decedent died intestate*. If there is a will, the petitioner marks the box *Copy of decedent's will dated* and indicates the date of the will. If there is more than one will (and the subsequent wills do not revoke the prior wills) or any *codicils* (amendments to a will), the petitioner also marks the box *codicils dated* and fills in the date of all subsequent wills/codicils. If there are multiple wills, the last will's date is used under *Copy of decedent's will dated*. Copies of all wills and codicils must then be marked at the bottom of each page, Attachment 4e, and attached to the **PETITION FOR PROBATE**.

NOTE: *If the will is handwritten (a* **holographic will**)*, a typed version must also be attached (and identified as a typed copy). If the will is in a foreign language, an English language translation must be attached (and identified as an English translation).*

◈ The last box, *The will and all codicils are self-proving,* is only marked if in the *attestation clause* (the clause just before the witnesses' signatures) the witnesses attest under penalty of perjury that the will was properly executed. Following is an example of a self-proving attestation clause.

Example:

The foregoing instrument, consisting of 3 pages, including the page on which this attestation clause is completed and signed, was at the date hereof by Jane Jones signed as and declared to be her Will, in the presence of us who, at her request and in her presence, and in the presence of each other, have subscribed our names as witnesses thereto. Each of us observed the signing of this will by Jane Jones, and by each other subscribing witnesses and knows that each signature is the true signature of the person whose name was signed. Each of us is now an adult and a competent witness and resides at the address set forth after his or her name. We are acquainted with Jane Jones. At this time, she is over the age of eighteen (18) years, and to the best of our knowledge, she is of sound mind and is not acting under duress, menace, fraud, misrepresentation, or undue influence. We declare under penalty of perjury that the foregoing is true and correct.

If the will is witnessed by at least two persons but is not *self-proving,* the petitioner will need to locate one of the witnesses and have him or her sign the **Proof of Subscribing Witness**. (see form 16, p.293.) If the witnessed will is self-proving, the petitioner does not have to locate one of the witnesses to the will to execute a **Proof of Subscribing Witness**.

NOTE: *A witnessed will or codicil can be typed or handwritten. The will or codicil must have either the testator's signature, or the testator's name signed by another at the testator's direction. The will or codicil must also be witnessed by at least two **competent** witnesses, meaning over the age of 18 and mentally competent to testify at the time the will was witnessed. Both witnesses must be present when the decedent either signs, directs another to sign, declares that he or she or another at his or her direction signed, or declares the document to be his or her will or codicil. The witnesses themselves need not sign at the same time, in the presence of the testator, or even in the presence of each other. (Cal. Prob. Code, Sec. 6110.)*

A holographic will, on the other hand, is not witnessed, but has all material parts of the will in the testator's own handwriting and is signed by the testator. The testator could title the document "Will of Bob Jones" and the words "Bob Jones" could be his signature.

NOTE: *Holographic wills are **never** self-proving, as they are not witnessed by two or more persons. A holographic will needs a **Proof of Holographic Instrument** filed to prove the handwriting of the decedent. (see form 17, p.295.)*

⬧ Item 4f(1): One of these boxes will be checked if there is a will. Box (a) is checked if the proposed PR is named in the will and consents to act. If the proposed PR is not the first nominated

PR, then box (d) must also be checked and the reasons explained in Attachment 4f(1)(d). Box (b) is checked when there is a will that fails to nominate any PR. Box (c) is checked when the proposed PR is the nominee of a person entitled, under the will, to nominate a PR.

❖ Item 4f(2): One of these boxes will be checked when there is no will. Box (a) is checked if the person nominated as the PR is a person entitled to Letters of Administration. Under California Probate Code, Section 8461, the order of priority of appointment is: spouse or domestic partner, children, grandchildren, other lineal descendants, parents, siblings, lineal descendants of siblings, grandparents, lineal descendants of grandparents, children of predeceased spouse or predeceased domestic partner, other lineal descendants of predeceased spouse or predeceased domestic partner, etc. If two or more persons of the same priority ask to be appointed, both may act as co-PRs. Box (b) will be checked if the person nominated as the PR is nominated by a person entitled to act, under California Probate Code, Section 8461, as the PR. The nominee of a person entitled to priority supercedes a person with less priority. For example, the nominee of the decedent's spouse supercedes a request for appointment by the decedent's child. Box (c) is always checked in conjunction with box (a) or box (b), and the relationship of the petitioner to the decedent is specified.

❖ Item 4f(3): This box is checked only if the **PETITION FOR PROBATE** is requesting the appointment of a *special administrator* to act as the PR pending the appointment of a regular PR (e.g., emergency appointment to run a business, etc.). It is recommended that you consult with a lawyer in this instance.

❖ Item 5: If there is a will and if the will (or codicil) specifically prohibits the administration of the estate under the Independent Administration of Estates Act powers, this box is *not* checked. Item 5 will nearly always be checked, as wills and codicils rarely prohibit those powers.

❖ Item 6a: Check at least one box for (1) through (4).

◈ Item 6b: Check the box that applies. Obviously, if the decedent had no stepchildren or adopted children, then the second box is checked. If the decedent had either a stepchild or a foster child and the relationship between the child and the decedent began when the child was a minor and continued during the lifetime of the decedent (a stepchild's relationship continues if the parent of the stepchild who is the spouse of the decedent predeceases the decedent) and the decedent would have adopted the stepchild or foster child but for a legal barrier (e.g., the nonconsent of the biological parent), then the first box is checked. If there is a stepchild or foster child, you should review California Probate Code, Section 6454, carefully. Generally, the failure of an adoption to take place after the stepchild or foster child attains 18 years of age is sufficient to refute any argument that said child would have been adopted but for a legal barrier, as the biological parent would then not have the right to withhold consent to the adoption.

◈ Item 7: This item is self-explanatory.

◈ Item 8: Complete only if no spouse or *issue* (lineal descendants, such as children and grandchildren) survived the decedent.

◈ Item 9: List everyone named in the decedent's will or codicils, including all nominated PRs, trustees, guardians, etc., and all heirs of the decedent (and the heirs of the decedent's predeceased spouse if there are no issues—children, grandchildren, etc.—of the decedent living), with their ages (*adult* is okay if over age 17), their relationships to the decedent (*friend* is okay if not a relative), and their addresses. A lot of people think they have no *heirs*. Everyone has heirs. California Probate Code, Sections 6400 through 6414, describe *heirship*. Generally, your heirs are your spouse and children. If your children are deceased, then their lineal descendants take the place of your children. If you have no surviving spouse and no lineal descendants, then your parents become your heirs. If they are both deceased, then their lineal descendants become your heirs (i.e., your siblings or their lineal descendants if the siblings are also deceased) and so on. If the decedent dies without a surviving spouse, but has a predeceased spouse and no lineal descendants *and* the predeceased spouse died no more than five years before the decedent (if there is no real property at decedent's death) or no more than fifteen years before decedent (if there is real property at decedent's death), then the heirs of the predeceased spouse must also be listed on Item 9. In many cases, you will have to continue Item 9 on an Attachment.

➲ Item 10: Insert the number of pages attached to your **PETITION FOR PROBATE**, which will include your attachments and a copy of any will and codicil.

PROOF OF SUBSCRIBING WITNESS FORM AND PROOF OF HOLOGRAPHIC INSTRUMENT

If **PROOF OF SUBSCRIBING WITNESS** (form 16, p.293) must be filed with the court before the hearing on the petition, it is filled in as follows.

➲ Caption: See instructions on page 34 for **PETITION FOR PROBATE** (be sure to include the case number).

➲ Item 1 (only check one box for the six choices): If the witness saw the decedent sign his or her name on the will or codicil in the presence of both witnesses, box 1a(1) is checked. If the decedent instead instructed another to sign the decedent's name to the will or codicil in the presence of the decedent and the witness, 1a(2) is checked. If the witness did not see the decedent sign the will or codicil, but instead the decedent acknowledged in the presence of the witnesses that his or her name was signed by the decedent personally, the witness will check 1b(1). If the witness did not see the decedent sign the will or codicil, but instead the decedent acknowledged in the presence of both witnesses that his or her name was signed by another in the presence of the decedent at the decedent's direction, then box 1b(2) is checked. (Ascertain which occurred before the witness is asked to sign, and have the correct box pre-checked.)

Item 1c is appropriately checked when neither 1a or 1b applies, but the decedent, in the presence of at least two witnesses, declares the will or codicil to be his or her will or codicil.

◈ Item 2 must be checked for the witness's statement to be effective. The box cannot be checked if the statement is untrue.

If the attorney's certification to the will or codicil is not being used, a *certified* copy (certified by the county clerk) will have to be attached to the **PROOF OF SUBSCRIBING WITNESS**.

If a witness to the will cannot be located, then contact a lawyer.

If a **PROOF OF HOLOGRAPHIC INSTRUMENT** must be filed before the hearing on the **PETITION FOR PROBATE** (form 11, p.283), it must be completed by a person who can testify that the handwriting on the holographic will or codicil is in the handwriting of the decedent, and should be filled in as follows.

◈ Caption: See instructions on page 34 for **PETITION FOR PROBATE** (be sure to include the case number).

◈ Item 1: Insert the number of months or years the person who can testify about the decedent's handwriting knew the decedent.

◈ Item 2: Check the box and state the relationship of the person who can testify about the decedent's handwriting to the decedent. If not a relative, write *friend*.

◈ Item 3: One or more of the four boxes under Item 3 must be checked. Check only the boxes that apply.

◈ Item 4: Please note that a copy of the holographic will or codicil must be attached to the **PROOF OF HOLOGRAPHIC INSTRUMENT** and labeled as Attachment 4.

If the attorney's certification to the holographic will or codicil is not being used, a certified copy (certified by the county clerk) will have to be attached as Attachment 4 to the **PROOF OF HOLOGRAPHIC INSTRUMENT**.

The Hearing

After preparing the **PETITION FOR PROBATE**, file it with the court clerk who will set it for a hearing in court. In most larger counties there is a specific place to file court documents. Some courts call it a *filing window.* Give the **PETITION FOR PROBATE** to the court clerk along with a check for the filing fee (from $300 on up, depending on the size of the estate), an extra copy of the petition (for the newspaper publication), and the original will. Bring a second copy of the **PETITION FOR PROBATE**. It will be date-stamped and returned to the person filing the **PETITION FOR PROBATE**. The date-stamped copy should have the hearing date, department, and time, as well as the court case number that will be assigned to the probate matter at that time.

NOTE: *Normally, the clerk will set the hearing date approximately forty days away.*

NOTICE OF THE HEARING

The petitioner must serve a **NOTICE OF HEARING**. (Cal. Prob. Code, Sec. 8003(b).) (see form 34, p.327.) In a few counties the notice is mailed by the court clerk. In other counties the newspaper doing the publication will prepare and mail the **NOTICE OF PETITION TO ADMINISTER ESTATE**. (see form 13, p.287.) The **NOTICE OF PETITION TO ADMINISTER ESTATE** is prepared as follows.

◈ Complete the caption like the **PETITION FOR PROBATE**, and insert the case number. (see page 34.)

◈ Insert any names the decedent was known by at Item 1.

◈ Insert the name of the petitioner and the county in which the petition was filed at Item 2.

◈ Insert the name of the proposed personal representative at Item 3 (likely the petitioner).

◈ Check Item 4 if any wills or codicils have been filed with the court.

◈ Check Item 5 if the petitioner is requesting that the personal representative be given the *Independent Administration of Estates Act* (IAEA) powers. (The **PETITION FOR PROBATE** should have requested the IAEA powers.)

◈ At Item 6, insert the date, time, and department or room for the hearing, and insert the address of the court (the box *same as noted above* will be checked if the court address is given in the caption of the document).

◈ At Item 10, check the box *Petitioner* and insert the petitioner's name, address, and telephone number. Sign where indicated, and check the box *Petitioner* under the signature.

On page 2 is a separate document called a **PROOF OF SERVICE**. (see form 13, p.287.) The **PROOF OF SERVICE** is completed to prove that the notice was mailed. Complete the **PROOF OF SERVICE** as follows.

◈ Insert the information at the top. Aliases of the decedent may be omitted.

◈ At Item 2, insert the residential or business address of the person who mails the notice. The petitioner may not mail the notice. Be sure that the person who mails the notice could later be available to testify that he or she did mail the notice.

❖ At Item 3, check a if the notice is mailed in a mailbox or directly in the post office. Check b if the notice is placed in a private mail room, etc. to be taken to the post office.

❖ At Item 4, insert the date and city of mailing.

❖ A copy of the **Petition for Probate** need not be sent with the notice. However, if it is, check the box at Item 5.

❖ Under Item 5, the date is inserted. The name of the person (not the petitioner) who mails the notice (and the **Proof of Service** that is attached to the notice) is typed or printed. The person who does the mailing then signs.

❖ The name and address of each person or entity to whom a **Notice of Petition to Administer Estate** is mailed is listed where indicated on the bottom half of the **Proof of Service**. The persons and entities who receive notice are those who were listed on Attachment 9 of the **Petition for Probate**. If a beneficiary is a charity or trust without a resident trustee, the attorney general in Sacramento must also be mailed a **Notice of Petition to Administer the Estate** and added to the **Proof of Service**. If there is insufficient room on the **Proof of Service** to list everyone, check the box on the lower left side and add the names and addresses of the remaining persons or entities receiving notice on a separately attached sheet of paper.

❖ Make enough copies of the **Notice of Petition to Administer Estate and Proof of Service** to send one to each person listed on the **Proof of Service**, plus two. Each person on the **Proof of Service** is then mailed a copy of the **Notice of Petition to Administer Estate** and the **Proof of Service**. If the attorney general in Sacramento receives notice, send him or her a copy of any will and a copy of the **Petition for Probate** as well. The original **Notice of Petition to Administer Estate** and the **Proof of Service** is then promptly filed with the clerk of the court. (Another copy should be file-stamped by the court clerk and returned to the petitioner to verify that the original was filed.)

Correcting Errors before the Hearing

Many counties send the petitioner what are commonly referred to as *probate notes* before the hearing. (In some counties, you must call in or check a website for the probate notes.) The purpose of the probate notes is to assist the petitioner in clearing up procedural problems in the **PETITION FOR PROBATE** before the hearing.

Before the hearing, each matter in probate is reviewed by a court employee or the judge. In the larger counties, the court employee is called a *probate examiner* or *probate attorney*. His or her job is to review the probate matters for the judge and make recommendations based upon his or her review. If everything is in order and the matter submitted is routine, the probate examiner or probate attorney may recommend a matter for approval. The judge will usually follow the recommendation unless there is an objection filed. Other times, the probate notes will summarize the defects on the pending matter. Reviewing the probate notes permits the petitioner to correct errors, via the **SUPPLEMENT TO THE PETITION FOR PROBATE**, before the hearing to avoid a continuance or dismissal of the matter. (There is a filled-in, sample form in Appendix A, but since this document is unique to each matter, there is no blank form in Appendix B.)

When preparing a supplement or an amendment, be sure to use *pleading* paper, which can be purchased at a stationery store or selected in most word processing systems.

California requires that pleadings be on recycled paper. Please note that the beginning of the caption begins at line 8, that the title of the pleading is required at the bottom of each page, and that all pleadings must be *verified* at the end.

THE HEARING

Probate hearings held in the courthouse are open to the public. If the matter is continued before the hearing date (by agreement with the court) or is recommended for approval, the petitioner need not appear. Otherwise, the judge will likely have a question and the petitioner must appear. In that event, the petitioner should dress appropriately, quickly approach *the bar* (usually a desk in front of the judge) when the case is called, announce his or her name, state that he or she is acting *in pro per* (without an attorney), and address the judge as "Your Honor."

Example:

Good morning, Your Honor. My name is John Smith. I am the petitioner in pro per.

Although the petitioner is entitled to argue with the judge, the petitioner must remain civil and courteous. Remember, the judge makes the final decision.

When the judge approves the **PETITION FOR PROBATE**, he or she will make a statement such as "the petition is approved as filed," which means that the petitioner was granted everything he or she requested. Sometimes, however, the judge will modify the petitioner's request. For example, the judge might say "the petition is approved except that the bond shall be $100,000 and the request for the Independent Administration of Estates Act powers shall be with limited authority." The **ORDER FOR PROBATE** must be prepared reflecting any modifications made by the judge at the hearing.

After the court approves the **PETITION FOR PROBATE**, the petitioner can submit the **ORDER FOR PROBATE, DUTIES AND LIABILITIES OF PERSONAL REPRESENTATIVE**, the bond (if required), and the **LETTERS TESTAMENTARY** (or of **ADMINISTRATION**). (Some counties have additional or special requirements, so check with the court clerk.)

ORDER FOR PROBATE

Prepare the **ORDER FOR PROBATE** (form 18, p.297) as follows.

◈ Complete the caption (as on page 20 under the **SPOUSAL/DOMESTIC PARTNER PROPERTY PETITION**). Check the appropriate box as to *Executor, Administrator with Will Annexed*, or *Administrator*. Check the box *Order Authorizing Independent Administration of Estate*, if requested in the petition and granted by the court. Insert the case number.

◈ At Item 1, insert the date, time, department, or room of the court and the name of the judge.

◈ At Item 2b, insert the decedent's date of death and check whether the decedent was a resident of California (box 1) or not (box 2).

◈ At Item 2c, check if the decedent died without a will (box 1, Intestate) or with a will (box 2, Testate). If a will was admitted to probate, indicate the date of the will and the date of any codicils admitted to probate.

◈ At Item 3, insert the name of the PR and check the appropriate box as to executor, administrator with will annexed, or administrator, as requested in the petition.

◈ At Item 4, if the Independent Administration of Estates Act powers were granted, check whether the powers are with *full* or *limited* authority.

◈ At Item 5, check box a if bond was waived, or check box b if bond was ordered and insert the amount of the ordered bond. (It is unlikely that box c or d would be checked.)

◈ Leave Item 6 blank. The court will insert the name of the appointed probate referee. (Some counties, like Los Angeles, require a separate county form for the appointment of the probate referee. The petitioner should check with the court clerk and the local rules to determine if a separate form for the appointment of a probate referee is required.)

◈ At Item 7, insert the number of pages attached to the order, if any.

DUTIES AND LIABILITIES OF THE PERSONAL REPRESENTATIVE

A few years ago, the courts got fed up with PRs mishandling estates. Personal representatives were being brought into court saying, "Nobody ever told me I could not do those things." As a result, the courts created the **DUTIES AND LIABILITIES OF PERSONAL REPRESENTATIVE**, which forces the personal representative, as a condition to receiving his or her **LETTERS TESTAMENTARY OR LETTERS OF ADMINISTRATION**, to acknowledge having read the list of things a personal representative cannot do. The proposed personal representative must read the **DUTIES AND LIABILITIES OF PERSONAL REPRESENTATIVE** carefully. Then, on the last page, he or she must acknowledge in writing that he or she has read the form and kept a copy of the form. The original **DUTIES AND LIABILITIES OF PERSONAL REPRESENTATIVE** is filed with the court. (see form 14, p.289.)

BOND

If a bond was ordered by the judge, it must be filed (by the bond company) with the court before **LETTERS TESTAMENTARY** or **LETTERS OF ADMINISTRATION** can be issued.

LETTERS

LETTERS TESTAMENTARY (for an executor) or **LETTERS OF ADMINISTRATION** (for an administrator) prove to the world outside of the courthouse that the PR has been given the legal authority to act on behalf of the decedent's estate. (see form 20, p.301.) Until the Letters are actually issued by the court, there is no acting PR of an estate even if the **ORDER FOR PROBATE, DUTIES AND LIABILITIES OF PERSONAL REPRESENTATIVE**, and the bond have all been filed. A PR will want to have several certified copies of his or her Letters at all times. A certified copy costs about $10, and many times the bank, title insurance company, securities broker, and so on will want a certified copy dated within sixty days of the time being used. Accordingly, new certified copies should be periodically obtained from the court clerk.

NOTE: *The personal representative should be prepared to leave a stamped, self-addressed envelope when ordering certified copies of* **LETTERS***, as they cannot usually be processed on the spot by the court clerk.*

Complete the **Letters Testamentary/of Administration** as follows.

⬦ Complete the caption (as on page 20 under **Spousal/Domestic Partner Property Petition**), including the case number. Check *Testamentary*, *of Administration*, or *of Administration with Will Annexed*. Check only one box.

⬦ In the left column, if a will was admitted to probate, check the first box at Item 1. Check box a if *executor* or box b if *administrator with will annexed.*

⬦ In the left column, if no will was admitted to probate, at Item 2 check the first box and box a if administrator. (Box b relates to special administrators, a situation not covered by this book.)

⬦ In the left column, at Item 3, check the first box if the Independent Administration of Estates Act powers were granted. Check the appropriate box for *limited authority* or *full authority*.

⬦ In the left column, Item 4 is not checked unless the **Order for Probate** so orders.

⬦ In the right column, check the box at Item 2.

⬦ At Item 4, insert the date and place where executed and sign. However, do not sign the **Letters** until after filing the **Petition for Probate**.

NOTE: *File the* **Duties and Liabilities of Personal Representative**, **Order for Probate**, *any bond, and the* **Letters** *at the same time. If filed separately, there can be delays in processing.*

Personal Representative's Initial Steps

chapter 5

Now the work begins. The personal representative (PR) needs to immediately:

❂ take control of the estate assets;

❂ take steps to preserve the estate assets;

❂ obtain a tax identification number for IRS purposes;

❂ set up an accounting system;

❂ file tax returns;

❂ give a notice to the California Director of Health Services if the decedent or the decedent's predeceased spouse received any Medi-Cal benefits; and,

❂ give notice to the Director of the California Department of Corrections if any heir or beneficiary of the estate is in jail or prison in California.

UNDERSTANDING FIDUCIARY DUTY

Fiduciary duty is a duty to act for the welfare of others before the welfare of yourself. Accordingly, although the PR has the power to administer the estate, he or she must wield that power in such a manner as to benefit the estate instead of the PR personally. The PR must be fair to all persons interested in the estate, such as the estate creditors and the estate beneficiaries. The PR cannot prefer any beneficiary over another and cannot place the PR's interests above those of the estate.

The PR must keep the estate monies and assets separate from his or her own, cannot borrow money from the estate, cannot buy property from the estate without prior court permission, and cannot use estate property personally (e.g., live rent-free in a residence owned by the estate or use a car owned by the estate). Although entitled to fees for administering the estate as the PR, the PR cannot earn any other commissions or fees from the estate (e.g., realtor fees, sales commissions, labor wages, or repair fees). The PR cannot pay him- or herself or his or her attorney any fees without an express court order for the fees.

The PR has limitations on his or her right to invest any surplus estate monies. Unless the estate is going to stay open more than two years, all surplus estate monies should be placed into insured (no more than $100,000 in any single FDIC-insured institution) savings, money market, or CD accounts. Get a court order for any investment beyond direct obligations of the U.S. or State of California maturing within one year from the date of making the investment, certain money market funds, and certain common trust funds described in California Financial Code, Section 1564. (Cal. Prob. Code, Sec. 9730.)

NOTE: *The PR also has a duty to diversify the estate in certain conditions.*

Example:

The decedent's estate is valued at $2,000,000, of which $1,950,000 of that value is in XYZ Company, a very risky technology stock. The PR has a duty to minimize the estate's exposure to a sudden price drop by selling a substantial amount of the estate's XYZ Company stock.

The PR should play the investment game very conservatively. The PR gets no reward for a successful investment strategy, but may be personally held liable for an unsuccessful investment strategy.

The court will remove a PR from office if it believes the PR has, or is about to, waste estate assets, is guilty of self-dealing, or is hostile to the estate beneficiaries. The court further has the power to *surcharge* the PR for any losses incurred by the estate due to the PR's improper administration. The *losses* could include a beneficiary's attorney's fees as well as any decrease in the estate value.

Although the PR can hire family members to do estate work such as repairs on real property owned by the estate, that fact must be reported in detail to the court in the **PERSONAL REPRESENTATIVE'S FINAL ACCOUNT** and will be scrutinized by the court. (See Appendix A, form 36, paragraph IX.)

MARSHALING ESTATE ASSETS

One of the most important responsibilities of the PR is to get the assets of the estate accounted for and get them ready to pass to the beneficiaries.

Decedent's Mail

The PR should go to the post office with a certified copy of his or her **LETTERS** and arrange for the decedent's mail to be redirected to the PR's address. The PR should carefully monitor the decedent's mail for evidence of the decedent's assets and liabilities.

NOTE: *A review of the decedent's prior year income tax returns and checkbook register is also helpful in discovering assets and determining income and payments.*

Securing Property

The PR must take steps to ensure that the real and personal property of the estate is preserved. This may require garaging vehicles, changing locks to residences, or even hiring property managers. No one should be driving any estate vehicles, as they expose the estate to liability. If practical, all residential real property should be rented (month to month is preferred, but no lease longer than one year). Valuable personal property, such as coin collections or jewelry, should be placed in a safe-deposit box rented in the name of the estate.

The PR must confirm or acquire adequate property insurance (real property, cars, etc.) to protect the estate against loss.

Federal Tax Identification Number for the Estate

The PR should obtain a federal employer's tax identification number (EIN) for the estate. An EIN is like a Social Security number for the estate. It is used by financial institutions to identify the estate to the IRS for tax reporting purposes. The PR will use the estate's EIN on any estate income tax returns. (IRS Form 1041, California Form 5410.) The EIN is obtained by completing **IRS FORM SS-4** online at **www.irs.gov**, or by faxing the completed form to the IRS at 559-443-6961, or by submitting the application over the telephone at 888-829-4399. (see form 19, p.299.) (A filled-in, sample form is in Appendix A.) If the application is faxed, the IRS will usually fax back the EIN within forty-eight hours or mail it within ten days. If the EIN does not arrive, the IRS phone number is 559-452-3201.

Transferring Decedent's Assets to the Estate

After obtaining the tax identification number, the PR should transfer the title to the decedent's bank and brokerage accounts to the name of the PR, using the estate's tax identification number.

Example:
John Smith, Executor of the Estate of Joe Smith, deceased.

The PR should order new checks under the new title of the checking account. He or she should withdraw any uninsured financial accounts and may wish to consolidate the estate assets into fewer banks and brokerages.

Recordkeeping

The PR has a duty to account for all financial transactions and must record each estate receipt and disbursement. Receipt information includes the day the payment was received, the amount received, the name of the payor (including any account number if the payor, such as a bank, is paying interest on different accounts in the name of the estate), the reason for payment, and whether it was income or principal receipt. Rents, dividends, and interest are typical income receipts. Refunds are typical principal receipts. Some investment returns (especially with mutual funds) and typical mortgage payments have both income and principal components. The sale of an estate asset is a profit or loss to the estate. The profit or loss is measured by the gross amount received subtracted from the **INVENTORY AND APPRAISAL** value of the asset. (see form 24, p.305.) Costs of a sale such as real estate commissions are listed as disbursements. All disbursements must be listed as to date paid, amount paid, name of payee, and purpose of the payment.

The PR must keep all vouchers, receipts, invoices, cancelled checks, bank and brokerage statements, and so on. Although the beneficiaries can waive an accounting by the PR, the PR cannot count on that occurring. Besides, keeping excellent financial records and preparing a court accounting assists in the preparation of the estate income tax returns and provides a permanent record that can be reviewed long after the PR and beneficiaries have forgotten the details.

Decedent's Income Tax Return
The PR must file the decedent's income tax returns. If the decedent died early in the calendar year, he or she may not have filed the prior year's income tax returns and it may be necessary to obtain an extension if possible.

Notice to Medi-Cal Director
If the decedent or the decedent's predeceased spouse was receiving California Medi-Cal benefits, then the PR must give notice to the California Director of Health Services within ninety days of the issuance of the PR's **LETTERS**. To avoid making a mistake, the PR should consider simply giving the notice to start the four-month period in which the Director can make a claim against the estate. (A sample of such notice is form 22 in Appendix A.)

Notice to Department of Corrections
If any heir of the decedent is in jail or prison in California, then the PR must give notice to the Director of the California Department of Corrections within ninety days of the issuance of the PR's **LETTERS**. (A sample of such notice is form 22A in Appendix A.) Although California Probate Code, Section 9202(b), refers only to *heirs*, it is wise to also send the notice if any *beneficiaries* of the estate are in jail or prison in California.

Change in Ownership Statement
For each parcel of real property, you must file a **CHANGE IN OWNERSHIP STATEMENT** (form 26, p.309) with the county assessor's office of that county. If the beneficiary of the property is a child, parent, son- or

daughter-in-law, or grandchild when the grandchild's parent is deceased, determine if a **Claim for Reassessment Exclusion for Transfer Between Parent and Child** (form 3, p.267) should also be filed.

REQUEST FOR SPECIAL NOTICE

Any interested person (beneficiary, heir, or creditor) may directly or through his or her attorney file a **Request for Special Notice**. (see form 21, p.303.) If the PR receives a **Request for Special Notice**, he or she must send a copy of each document specified in Item 1 or 2 of the request within fifteen days of filing (for an Inventory and Appraisal) or more than fifteen days before the hearing (for matters that are set for a hearing). The PR must also mail a Notice of Hearing at least fifteen days before any hearing to the person requesting special notice. The PR must prepare and file with the court a Proof of Service showing that the Notice of Hearing or a copy of the Inventory and Appraisal was mailed to the person requesting the special notice.

Inventory and Appraisal

The personal representative (PR) must report an inventory of the estate assets with their fair market values with the court within four months of the PR's appointment. This report is done on an **INVENTORY AND APPRAISAL**. (see form 24, p.305.) Appendix A has a filled-in sample. Before it is filed with the court, the **INVENTORY AND APPRAISAL** must be submitted to the probate referee for appraisal. The personal representative should have the **INVENTORY AND APPRAISAL** (without values for noncash items) ready within three months of his or her appointment as the PR by the court.

The **ORDER FOR PROBATE** appointed the probate referee (some courts require a separate, local form to be filed for the appointment of the probate referee). The probate referee appraises all assets on Attachment 2 of the **INVENTORY AND APPRAISAL** and the personal representative appraises the assets on Attachment 1 of the **INVENTORY AND APPRAISAL**. The probate referee is entitled to a fee equal to 0.1% of the value of the assets that he or she appraises plus costs, which runs about $30 for each real property appraised.

TYPES OF INVENTORY AND APPRAISALS

There are several types of **INVENTORY AND APPRAISALS**.

✪ A *final* Inventory and Appraisal lists all of the assets of an estate or is the last *partial* Inventory and Appraisal filed.

✪ A *partial* Inventory and Appraisal lists some of the assets of an estate. Partial Inventory and Appraisals are numbered sequentially. This might be done when the PR is having difficulty ascertaining some assets of the estate, but wants to file a partial Inventory and Appraisal to appraise the known assets.

✪ A *supplemental* Inventory and Appraisal is filed when the personal representative (PR) discovers assets after the filing of the final Inventory and Appraisal.

✪ A *correcting* Inventory and Appraisal is filed to correct a description or value of an asset listed on a prior Inventory and Appraisal.

✪ A *reappraisal for sale* Inventory and Appraisal is filed when real property is being sold subject to court confirmation more than one year after the decedent's death.

PREPARING THE INVENTORY AND APPRAISAL

The **INVENTORY AND APPRAISAL** is completed as follows, starting with the summary page. (see form 24, p.305.)

◈ Prepare the caption as indicated on page 20 under **SPOUSAL/DOMESTIC PARTNER PROPERTY PETITION**. Indicate if the **INVENTORY AND APPRAISAL** is a partial (and number the partial), final, supplemental, correcting, or reappraisal for sale. Check the box *Property Tax Certificate* if the **INVENTORY AND APPRAISAL** contains real property.

◈ At Item 1, insert the value of the items on Attachment 1.

◈ Skip Item 2. The probate referee will insert that amount and the total of Items 1 and 2.

◈ At Item 3, check box *all* if the **INVENTORY AND APPRAISAL** is a final, otherwise check the box *a portion*.

◈ Item 4 is checked only if all of the assets are listed on Attachment 1 (and thus, appraised by the PR).

◈ At Item 5, box a or box b must be checked. Check box a if there is no real property on the **INVENTORY AND APPRAISAL**. If there is real property, then check box b. The PR must file a **CHANGE IN OWNERSHIP STATEMENT** for each parcel of real property in the county in which the real property is located before the filing of the **INVENTORY AND APPRAISAL**. The purpose of the **CHANGE IN OWNERSHIP STATEMENT** is to advise the county assessor whether or not a change of ownership, which triggers an assessment value for property tax purposes, has occurred. (see form 26, p.309.) Some counties use a **PRELIMINARY CHANGE IN OWNERSHIP REPORT** instead. (see form 2, p.265.) Call the county assessor's office to determine the correct form.

◈ Insert the date and the PR's signature after Item 5.

◈ Check Item 6 if there is no bond because it was waived.

◈ Check Item 7 if there is a bond and insert the amount of the bond. Check the box *sufficient* if the bond amount, based upon the values of all completed **INVENTORY AND APPRAISALS**, is sufficient. Otherwise, the box *insufficient* is checked.

◈ Check Item 8 if, in lieu of a bond, estate monies have been placed into a blocked account at a financial institution. In that event, insert the total amount of the financial institution receipts for the money in the blocked accounts.

◈ The attorney for the PR, or if the PR is acting without an attorney, signs the *Statement About the Bond* after Item 8.

If the **INVENTORY AND APPRAISAL** values show that the bond is insufficient, the PR must file an additional bond. This additional bond covers the value of the assets subject to the bond (all personal property plus real property if the PR has IAEA powers with full authority), plus one year's estimated income from the estate assets. Some bond companies will issue an additional bond without a court order. If necessary, a PR can obtain a court order for an additional bond without a formal, noticed court hearing. In that event, the PR files an **EX PARTE PETITION TO INCREASE BOND AND ORDER THEREON** with the court clerk. The **EX PARTE PETITION** is then approved by the judge and given to the bond company. (There is a filled-in, sample form in Appendix A.)

Attachment 1   Attachment 1 of the **INVENTORY AND APPRAISAL** lists all of the assets that the PR can appraise in the estate, modified at the top where it should indicate Attachment 1. (see form 25, p.307.) Attachment 1 lists the following assets.

- ✪ Cash and all instruments that can be immediately converted to funds, such as checks; drafts; money orders issued before the decedent's death; and certain checks issued after the decedent's death, such as paychecks, refund checks for taxes and utilities, and medical reimbursements. Coin and currency would be listed as a single lump sum. Each check should be listed with the payor, date of the check, check number, and the amount of the check. If the decedent is a co-owner of any asset, then only the decedent's interest is listed.

Example:
Decedent's undivided 10% interest in check no. 1333356, issued on January 12, 2007, by ABC Annuity Company in the amount of $250 would be valued at $25.

- ✪ All deposit accounts in banks, savings and loans, credit unions, and other financial institutions. Each account should be listed with the name of the financial institution, type of account (e.g., checking or savings), account number, principal balance, and accrued interest at time of death. The accrued interest is the amount of interest earned but unpaid at time of death.

Example:

Decedent died on January 15, 2007. He owned a savings account with a January 15, 2007, principal balance of $10,000. The savings account earns 3% paid monthly on the last day of the month. The accrued interest would be $10,000 times 3%, divided by 365 times 15 days, or $12.33.

- ✪ Proceeds of insurance policies, retirement plans, and annuities that are payable in a lump sum.

NOTE: *If a check or any other asset normally listed on Attachment 1 is not worth its face value or is not collectible, then it is listed on Attachment 2 instead of Attachment 1.*

The PR is required to state whether the assets listed are the separate property or community property interest of the decedent. If all of the property is separate property, then a simple statement to that effect can be made after the listing of the last asset. If all of the property is the community property interest of the decedent, then a simple statement to that effect can be made after the listing of the last asset.

Attachment 2   Any property in which the decedent had an interest that is not listed on Attachment 1 is listed on Attachment 2. Use the same form 25 as Attachment 1, but put *Attachment 2* at the top. Only the probate referee can appraise those assets. Those assets would include the following.

- ✪ Stocks (although *ex dividends* will need to be listed, they are inserted on the **INVENTORY AND APPRAISAL** by the probate referee), bonds (including accrued interest separately listed), and mutual funds. Descriptions generally will include the name of the security, the number of shares owned, the CUSIP number, whether *common* or *preferred*, and the exchange where they are listed (e.g., NYSE), if any. However, more information may also be provided. Generally, the per share appraised value will be included for stocks.

Example 1:

For a stock: 100 shares, common, ABC Corp, CUSIP #22222-333, NYSE. Per Share $.

Example 2:

For a mutual fund: 100 shares, ABC Tax Free Class B fund, CUSIP #222-44401. Per Share $.

Example 3:

For a bond: $25,000 Orange County General Revenue Bond, due 2/15/10, 6%, CUSIP: #4444-55555. Accrued Interest: $231.33.

- ✪ Notes. The description of a note should include the original and date of death amount, the date, the interest rate, the term or due date, and the names of the obligor(s). If the note is secured by a deed of trust or a mortgage, then the note should also have a description of the property secured as well as the date of the deed of trust or mortgage, the recording date of the deed of trust or mortgage, and the instrument number (or book and page) assigned by the county recorder on the deed of trust or mortgage.

Example:

A note in the original amount of $20,000 ($6,735 was owed at decedent's date of death), dated 3/4/95, interest rate 7%, owed by Jack Smith and secured by a first deed of trust dated 3/4/95 and recorded on 3/5/95 as Instrument No. 1995-333576 in the Orange County Recorder's office and securing real property located at 1211 Iris, Irvine, CA.

- ✪ Real property, including leasehold interests. Descriptions should include a general description (e.g., single family residence or unimproved land); interest owned (e.g., 100% interest); street, city, and county location of the property; the assessor's parcel number; and, a complete legal description of the property. Real property outside of California is not listed, as California has no jurisdiction over that real property.

Example:

A single family residence located at 1222 Iris, Irvine, CA, and more accurately described as Lot 2 of Tract No. 4422, Miller's Subdivision as recorded in the Orange County Recorder's Office. APN: 844-34-1167.

○ Partnership interests. Give as much information as possible, such as name of partnership, percentage and units held, name of the general partner, date of partnership agreement, and any business interests not in the partnership name (e.g., sole proprietorships). The personal representative should, in a letter, advise the probate referee of additional information to help the probate referee determine a value. The PR may want to supply partnership K-1s or tax returns.

Example:

Undivided 25% percent limited partnership interest in ABC Properties, Bob Smith, general partner.

○ Any causes of actions (lawsuits pending) or any accounts receivable.

○ Personal, tangible property (e.g., cars, artwork) and all items specifically given by will (e.g., my diamond ring with the rubies) may be specifically itemized on Attachment 2. Personal, tangible property not specifically bequeathed should be grouped together as a single item, listed as *household furniture and furnishings*.

Example 1:

For car: 1994 Pontiac LeMans, Lic. 1ABC 229.

Example 2:

For specifically devised ring: Wedding ring with 1-carat diamond and two heart-shaped rubies.

Example 3:

For tangible, personal property not specifically bequeathed: Household furniture and furnishings and personal effects.

However, if there are items of personal, tangible property for which the beneficiary may later need to prove the source of title, such as a valuable painting, said items should be individually identified and listed. Finally, if there is a potential or actual dispute as to entitlement of an item of personal, tangible property, it should be individually identified and listed.

SUBMITTING THE INVENTORY AND APPRAISAL TO THE PROBATE REFEREE

A cover letter to the probate referee should help explain the contents of the **INVENTORY AND APPRAISAL**. The following is an example letter.

Dear Probate Referee:

Enclosed please find the Final Inventory and Appraisal for the Estate of Mary Smith, deceased. As to Item 1, Attachment 2, the single family residence at 10 Maple St. was recently sold to a disinterested party, after exposure to the market for 2 months on the multiple listing service, for $180,000. As to Item 3, Attachment 2, an appraisal of the 1-carat diamond ring listed, appraising it at $2,000, is enclosed for your review. As to Item 4, Attachment 2, the decedent's flower shop, a sole proprietorship, was closed after her death. The store location was rented on a month-to-month basis. At the time of the decedent's death, the store inventory and fixtures were sold for $200,000. However, the accounts receivable of $10,000 have proved difficult to collect, and so far only $2,300 has been received despite diligent efforts to collect all of the accounts receivable. As to Item 5, Attachment 2, the commercial real property is entirely occupied by one tenant who has 30 years left on the lease. A copy of the lease is enclosed for your review. As to Item 6, Attachment 2, the decedent's household furniture and furnishings and personal effects are believed to be worth $1,000.

Thank You.

FILING THE INVENTORY AND APPRAISAL

After the probate referee returns the **INVENTORY AND APPRAISAL**, his or her appraisals should be reviewed. If the personal representative (PR) disagrees with an appraisal, he or she should telephone the probate referee to discuss the matter or write a letter to the probate referee explaining the disagreement before the PR files the **INVENTORY AND APPRAISAL** with the court. Most probate referees are extremely accommodating and will seriously consider the PR's position. (Pay the probate referee's bill immediately.)

When the PR is satisfied that the **INVENTORY AND APPRAISAL** is correct, he or she should file it with the court clerk and have an additional copy file stamped by the court clerk.

Handling Creditors' Claims

One of the purposes of probate is the payment of the decedent's debts. In many ways the rights of a creditor are superior to the rights of an estate beneficiary. Accordingly, it is the job of the personal representative (PR) to determine the decedent's debts, notify known and potential creditors, and pay the debts if the estate has sufficient funds.

This chapter deals with debts incurred by the decedent before the date of death, as well as funeral expenses. All expenses (other than funeral expenses) incurred after death are not *creditor's claims* as discussed in this chapter, but instead are *expenses of estate administration*.

DUTY TO ASCERTAIN CREDITORS

The PR must, by law, make a diligent search to ascertain creditors of the decedent. The PR must give actual notice of the estate proceedings to all known or reasonably ascertainable creditors of the decedent. (Cal. Prob. Code, Sec. 9050.) The PR should review the decedent's files for records of bills, monitor the mail of the decedent, check the decedent's most recent income tax returns, review the decedent's cancelled checks and checkbook register, check courthouse records to determine the existence of any pending lawsuits in which the decedent was a party, and check with the county recorder's office to determine if any judgments have been recorded against the decedent. Such a review will usually uncover all of the decedent's unpaid medical, utility, and credit card bills, as well as unpaid taxes, mortgages, and promissory notes. The PR should also ascertain if the decedent was a cosigner on a note or a potential defendant in a legal action, such as a personal injury lawsuit.

After determining the known and potential creditors, the PR should make a list of the creditors and the amounts likely owed.

INFORMAL PAYMENT OF DEBTS

If the estate is solvent, some bills can be paid without the necessity of the creditor filing and presenting a formal claim for payment. The PR may pay written invoices if they are presented within four months of the date the PR's LETTERS are issued (Cal. Prob. Code, Sec. 9154), if all of the following are true:

- ✪ the debt was justly due;

- ✪ the debt was paid in good faith;

- ✪ the amount paid was the true amount of the indebtedness over and above all payments and offsets; and,

- ✪ the estate is *solvent* (there will be money to distribute after payment of all debts and expenses of estate administration).

Besides being more expedient, this informal method of debt paying has practical considerations, such as the avoidance of late charges, interest charges, foreclosures, and discontinuance of utilities.

GIVING WRITTEN NOTICE TO CREDITORS

The PR must give the remaining known and potential creditors written notice of their right to file a creditor's claim. California Probate Code Section 9053 sets forth the liability of a PR who fails to give the necessary notice. Notice must be given within four months after the date of the issuance of **Letters**. (Cal. Prob. Code, Sec. 9051.) If the PR first learns of a creditor after the four-month period, he or she must give notice within thirty days of learning about the creditor. The PR should be sure to give notice to all creditors on an obligation where the decedent is a *guarantor* (cosigner), as well as to the IRS or Franchise Tax Board (FTB). Technically, all secured mortgage lenders should be given notice, but as a practice, this is rarely done if the debts are adequately secured by the real property.

The written notice is given by a **Notice of Administration**. (see form 27, p.311.) (There is a filled-in sample in Appendix A.) The creditor then has sixty days after service of the **Notice of Administration** or four months after the issuance of **Letters** to file his or her claim, whichever date is later. If the creditor files after those dates, his or her claim will likely be barred as untimely. Accordingly, to give a creditor as little time as possible to file his or her claim, the **Notice of Administration** should be mailed to known creditors within two months after the issuance of **Letters**.

Complete the **Notice of Administration** (form 27) as follows.

⬦ Item 1: Insert the name of the PR, address, and phone number.

⬦ Item 2: Insert the county of estate administration, address of court, branch name of court (if applicable), and the estate case number.

⬦ Item 3: Insert the date the **Letters** were issued (the filing date on the top right side of the **Letters**) and the date this notice is being mailed.

> **NOTE:** *The PR does not have to mail a blank creditor's claim form as stated at the bottom of form 27.*

⬦ The PR should also have page 2 of the form, entitled *Proof of Service*, completed. All potential creditors and their addresses to whom notice is being mailed should be listed where indicated at the bottom of page 2.

If the **Proof of Service** is to be valid, the PR cannot personally mail the **Notice of Administration**. Instead, some other person must do so on the PR's behalf. That other person will complete the **PROOF OF SERVICE** by listing his or her address at Item 2, checking box a at Item 3, inserting the date at Item 4a, printing the name of the person who is signing the form at 4b and, finally, signing the **PROOF OF SERVICE** where indicated. (see form 27, p.311.)

The person signing the **PROOF OF SERVICE** must place the **NOTICE OF ADMINISTRATION** in an addressed, postage-paid envelope, and directly deposit the envelope at either a U.S. Post Office or into a U.S. Post Office mailbox on the date he or she entered at Item 4.

CLAIMS NOT COVERED BY THE REGULAR RULES

Certain claims receive special treatment and are handled in a different manner than general claims. Some of the most common claims follow.

Tax Claims

Both IRS and FTB claims for taxes are not affected by the general rules stated in this book. The PR may have personal liability for claims, so the PR should review the decedent's income tax records to verify that all returns were filed and all income taxes paid.

Medi-Cal Claims

If the decedent or the decedent's predeceased spouse received health care under the *Medi-Cal Act* or the *Waxman-Duffy Prepaid Health Care Plan*, the PR must notify the director of health services of the decedent's death within ninety days after **LETTERS** are issued. (Cal. Prob. Code, Sec. 9202). The director has four months thereafter to file a claim.

Claims Secured by Property

Creditors whose claims are secured by property need not file a creditor's claim if the creditor is only looking at the secured property for payment. Although a secured creditor may file a creditor's claim, it is limited to the terms of the note itself (e.g., the mortgage payments). Accordingly, most creditors will not file a creditor's claim unless there is doubtful equity in the property.

Unknown Claims

Creditors not discovered by the reasonable efforts of the PR are put on notice by the original publication of **NOTICE OF PETITION** to probate the decedent's estate, and have four months after **LETTERS** are issued to file their claims.

Other Claims   There are other types of claims that are beyond the limits of this book. If the PR receives claims to which he or she is uncertain as to what action should be taken, it is time to speak to a lawyer. Claims within this category could include claims for damages covered by the decedent's insurance, claims not matured at the decedent's death, spousal support, and child support.

FILING THE CREDITOR'S CLAIM

Most creditors' claims must be filed with the court within four months of the date that **LETTERS** are issued or within sixty days of receiving the **NOTICE OF ADMINISTRATION**, whichever date is later. A copy must be delivered to the PR. (Cal. Prob. Code, Sec. 9050.) The claim must be supported by an affidavit (on the reverse side of the form). If the claim is based on a written document, such as a note, the original or a copy must be attached to the claim form. If a copy is attached because the original is lost or destroyed, it must be so stated on the claim form. If the claim is based on a recorded instrument, such as a mortgage, the recording information rather than a copy of the instrument itself is sufficient. (Cal. Prob. Code, Sec. 9152.)

The PR may be a creditor of an estate. This could be the case if the PR paid, from personal funds, any debts of the decedent or the decedent's funeral expenses. If so, the PR must timely file a claim like any other creditor. A **CREDITOR'S CLAIM** form is in Appendix B. (see form 28, p.313.)

ALLOWING OR REJECTING A CREDITOR'S CLAIM

Once a claim is filed, the PR has several options. The PR may allow the claim, reject the claim, or allow part and reject part.

If the PR wishes to negotiate the amount of the claim, it might be wise to discuss it with the creditor informally before preparing written allowance or rejection of the claim. For example, credit card companies and banks are sometimes willing to forgive all or part of the *post-mortem* (after death) interest on credit card debt or unsecured loans.

Although there is no requirement that the PR act promptly on claims, it is a good idea for several reasons. First, a creditor may *deem* a claim rejected if not allowed within thirty days of its filing and file a lawsuit to collect the monies owed. (Cal. Prob. Code, Sec. 9256.) This could cause additional time and expense to the estate and may hinder efforts to negotiate the claim amount. Second, a claim that the PR intends to reject should be done immediately to start the ninety-day period that the creditor has after notice of rejection to file a civil suit. (Cal. Prob. Code, Sec. 9250(c)(8).) In allowing or rejecting the claim, an **ALLOWANCE OR REJECTION OF CREDITOR'S CLAIM** is used. (see form 29, p.315.) Complete the form as follows.

◈ Fill in the caption as described on page 20 under **SPOUSAL/DOMESTIC PARTNER PROPERTY PETITION**.

◈ Item 1: Insert the name of the creditor.

◈ Item 2: Insert the date the claim was filed with the court.

◈ Item 3: Insert the date the **LETTERS** were issued by the court to the PR.

◈ Item 4: Insert the date the PR mailed **NOTICE OF ADMINISTRATION** if the claim is from a creditor who received notice.

◈ Item 5: Insert the date of the decedent's death.

◈ Item 6: Insert the estimated gross value of the decedent's estate.

◈ Item 7: Insert the amount of the claim.

◈ Item 8: If any portion of the claim is allowed, check the box and insert the amount of the claim allowed.

◈ Item 9: If any portion of the claim is rejected, check the box and insert the amount of the claim rejected.

◈ Item 10: If Item 9 is checked and the PR has the Independent Administration of Estates Act (IAEA) powers, insert the date that the notice of rejection was mailed to the creditor. The PR should use this **ALLOWANCE OR REJECTION** itself as the notice of rejection form. The insertion of the date that the notice of rejection is mailed requires that the notice of rejection be mailed the same day as the date inserted. The **PROOF OF SERVICE** of the notice of rejection is on the back side of the **ALLOWANCE OR REJECTION**. (Please note that a copy of the creditors' claim must be attached to the notice of rejection.)

⟡ Item 11: If the PR has the IAEA powers, this box is checked and the court need not separately approve or reject the claim (Items 12 and 13). The printed or typed name of the PR is then inserted where indicated, and the PR signs the form.

⟡ Items 12 and 13: This part of the form is left blank. If Item 11 was not checked, Items 12 and 13 will be completed by the court. If Item 11 was checked, Items 12 and 13 will be ignored by the court. If Items 12 and 13 must be completed, this fact should be brought to the attention of the clerk when filing (give the clerk a note that the court must approve or reject the claim). If the court must act on the claim, the PR should give the clerk a self-addressed, stamped envelope to mail a confirmed copy of the claim back to the PR after the court acts on the claim.

Upon receipt of the court rejection or allowance of the claim, a copy of **ALLOWANCE OR REJECTION** must be mailed to the creditor along with a copy of the claim. The **PROOF OF SERVICE** on the back of another copy of form 29 should be completed and an original **PROOF OF SERVICE** filed with the court. The creditor gets a copy of the **PROOF OF SERVICE** only, not the original.

PR or Attorney as Creditor

If a creditor's claim is filed by the PR or his or her attorney, the claim must be submitted to the court for approval regardless of whether or not the PR has the IAEA powers. (Cal. Prob. Code, Sec. 9252.) In that event, the creditor's fiduciary status (executor) should be typed at Item 1 of form 29. The court, before acting on the claim, may require the PR to file a separate petition for approval of the claim.

CONTESTING ALLOWANCE OR REJECTION OF CLAIM

As stated above, a creditor may contest the rejection of any claim or any partial rejection of a claim. In addition, any *interested party* (usually a beneficiary) may contest the allowance or partial allowance of any claim. In either case, the PR needs to consult with an attorney. A creditor must file a civil suit on a rejected claim within ninety days of notice of the rejection (ninety days plus five days if the **ALLOWANCE OR REJECTION OF CREDITOR'S CLAIM** was mailed) to contest the PR's rejection.

If the PR or the court fails to allow a claim within thirty days after the claim is filed, the creditor may deem the claim rejected and file a civil suit (but the ninety-day period to file a civil suit does not begin to run until the creditor has actual, written notice of rejection by the PR).

INFORMAL RESOLUTION OF REJECTED CLAIMS

Although a creditor may file a civil suit on a rejected claim, the creditor and PR may enter into a written agreement to do any of the following instead. (Cal. Prob. Code, Secs. 9620-9621.)

- ✪ Submit the matter to a designated temporary judge (lawyer or court commission). The written agreement is then submitted to the clerk, who refers the matter to a temporary judge who hears the matter without pleadings or discovery. (The decision of the temporary judge is binding.)

- ✪ Submit the matter on the same basis as above, but to a judge rather than a temporary judge (the judge must consent to act).

- ✪ Submit the matter to arbitration.

The above resolution methods should be more expedient and less costly than a civil lawsuit.

JUDGMENTS

Judgments against the decedent or the PR while representing the estate must be filed as creditor's claims and have the same status as other claims. (Cal. Prob. Code, Sec. 9300 (b).) However, once a money judgment becomes final, the creditor no longer has to prove the claim is valid, and must be paid when there is money available in the estate. (Cal. Prob. Code, Sec. 9301.) If there are attachment liens and unresolved lawsuits, the PR should consult an attorney.

Family Protection

This chapter concerns family protection laws that can be invoked through the probate court to protect surviving spouses and minor children of the decedent regardless of the terms of a will, the laws of intestate succession, or the rights of certain creditors. Petitions to the court for family protection should not be attempted without the assistance of a competent lawyer. However, this chapter will outline the law and its opportunities.

TEMPORARY FAMILY PROTECTION

When a person dies and leaves a surviving spouse and/or minor children, the law requires that provisions be made for the immediate care of those survivors. Regardless of the provisions of the decedent's will or the laws of intestate succession, the spouse and any minor children are entitled to remain in the family home and keep its furnishings plus any other property exempt from a money judgment. (California Code of Civil Procedure (Cal. Code of Civ. Pro.) beginning with Sec. 704.010.) This temporary family protection is in effect for a maximum of sixty days after the **INVENTORY AND APPRAISAL** of the estate is filed. (Cal. Prob. Code, Sec. 6500.)

EXEMPT PROPERTY

Regardless of the solvency of the estate, the will terms, or intestate laws, *exempt property* may be set aside by the court and given to the surviving spouse or minor children of the decedent. (Cal. Prob. Code, Sec 6510, and Cal. Code of Civ. Pro., beginning with Sec. 704.010.) This includes up to $1,900 in equity in motor vehicles, all household furniture and furnishings, jewelry, heirlooms, certain life insurance, vacation credits, child support judgments, personal injury claims or proceeds, wrongful death claims or proceeds, and workers' compensation claims or proceeds.

Example:

If the decedent died having $100,000 in personal injury proceeds that could be identified, then his or her surviving spouse and/or minor children could receive all of those monies, even if the decedent specifically bequeathed them to someone else or if the decedent's estate was insolvent (lacking money).

PROBATE HOMESTEAD

Regardless of the provisions of a will, the laws of intestate succession, or the solvency of the estate, a probate homestead may be set aside by the court and given to the surviving spouse and/or minor children of the decedent. (Cal. Prob. Code, beginning with Sec. 6520.) A *probate homestead* is basically the right to remain in possession of a residence in which the decedent owned an interest. The property need not have been the decedent's personal residence. The duration of a probate homestead is within the discretion of the judge, but cannot last longer than the lifetime of the surviving spouse or when the minor children attain the age of majority, whichever time ends last.

During the period of the probate homestead, the property is absolutely exempt from the claims against the surviving spouse or minor children. Creditors of the decedent who are secured (mortgage holders) or have filed liens against the property are not affected by the probate homestead, except that the person holding the probate homestead is entitled to assert his or her *homestead exemption* against any execution by lien holders. Unsecured creditors of the decedent may require a sale of the residence to satisfy their claims against the estate. However, the buyers of the probate homestead residence take the property and are subject to the rights of the probate homestead. Beneficiaries or heirs to the probate homestead property also take the property and are subject to the rights of the probate homestead.

NOTE: *To avoid any subsequent confusion, it is wise to have the court specify what obligations or conditions the homestead is subject to. For example, is the person enjoying the probate homestead going to be required to make necessary repairs on the property, pay the property taxes, or make any mortgage payments?*

FAMILY ALLOWANCE

The court must grant a surviving spouse, minor children of the decedent, and adult children of the decedent who are physically or mentally incapacitated and were dependent upon the decedent for their support a *family allowance* (a sum of money paid to them from the estate, usually on a monthly basis, for a discretionary period of time decided by the court). In addition, the court may grant a family allowance to other adult children or parents of the decedent who were dependent upon the decedent for support and do not have other resources for their reasonable support. (Cal. Prob. Code, Sec. 6540.)

The family allowance is paid as an *expense of administration,* which means that the family allowance is paid *off the top* of the estate and not specifically from the share of any beneficiary or heir of the estate. (Cal. Prob. Code, Sec. 6544.)

A request for a family allowance for a spouse, minor children, or qualifying incapacitated adult children may be made to the court *ex parte* (without the normal notice requirements) if made before an **INVENTORY AND APPRAISAL** is filed. All other requests for a family allowance require a hearing.

The duration and the amount of the family allowance is within the discretion of the court. The court will consider the size of the estate as well as the assets, income, and expenses of the person requesting the family allowance in making its decision. Most counties will require that the person requesting the family allowance detail his or her expenses. Those expenses may include tax payments, savings, gifts, and entertainment, as well as rent, utilities, food, clothing, and car payments.

SMALL ESTATE SET ASIDE

The court may *set aside* an entire estate to a surviving spouse or minor when it can be shown that the *net* value of the probate estate, as determined by the **INVENTORY AND APPRAISAL**, less encumbrances and creditor claims, is $20,000 or less. In that event, the surviving spouse or minor children take the probate estate subject to the estate's debts. (Cal. Prob. Code, beginning with Sec. 6600.)

Independent Administration of Estates Act

Unless the will prohibits it, the personal representative (PR) may petition the court for the *Independent Administration of Estates Act* (IAEA) authority to manage the estate without prior court approval for certain actions the PR takes. (Cal. Prob. Code, Sec. 10450.) Normally, the PR requests this authority in the **PETITION FOR PROBATE**.

The IAEA authority, if granted by the court, may be full or limited. If the IAEA authority granted is *limited,* the PR may not sell, exchange, grant an option to buy, or borrow against real property without prior court approval. (Cal. Prob. Code, Sec. 10403.) If the authority granted is *full,* the PR may.

Actions that can be taken without court approval under the IAEA—whether with limited or full authority—may require prior notice to *interested* parties. An interested person is defined in California Probate Code, Section 48. Basically, anyone who has a financial interest in the estate or has filed a *Request for Special Notice* is an interested person. If a written prior notice is required, any interested person can stop the action with an *objection* filed with the court. The IAEA powers can be revoked by the court. (Cal. Prob. Code, Sec. 10454.) If the PR takes action under the IAEA, it can be challenged by an interested party at a later time unless the interested person signs a written consent to the action before it is taken.

Finally, even if the PR has the IAEA, the PR may request prior court approval for any act, especially when the PR believes that he or she cannot obtain the prior consent of all interested parties.

ACTIONS THAT CANNOT BE TAKEN UNDER THE IAEA

Court supervision is required for some acts even if powers of the IAEA are granted. (Cal. Prob. Code, Sec. 10501.) Those actions include:

- ✪ fees to the PR or the attorney for the estate;

- ✪ settlement of estate accountings;

- ✪ petitions to distribute estate property to the beneficiaries or heirs; and,

- ✪ any action between the PR or the attorney for the PR and the estate.

ACTIONS THAT CAN BE TAKEN UNDER THE IAEA

Certain actions can be taken under the IAEA as long as notice is given, while others can occur with no notice given.

With Notice   The PR who has the IAEA may proceed with the following actions after giving a **NOTICE OF PROPOSED ACTION** (form 30):

- ✪ sell, exchange, or encumber real property (Cal. Prob. Code, Secs. 10511, 10514) (requires IAEA with full authority);

- ✪ sell or incorporate a business (Cal. Prob. Code, Sec. 10512);

- ✪ abandon personal property (Cal. Prob. Code, Sec. 10513);

- ✪ grant an option to purchase real property (Cal. Prob. Code, Sec. 10515) (requires IAEA with full authority);

✪   complete a contract made by the decedent transferring real or personal property (Cal. Prob. Code, Sec. 10517);

✪   transfer property subject to an option to purchase granted in the decedent's will (Cal. Prob. Code, Sec. 10516);

✪   allow, compromise, or settle claims by third parties to property held by the decedent or claims by the estate to any property held by third parties (Cal. Prob. Code, Sec. 10518);

✪   make disclaimers (Cal. Prob. Code, Sec. 10519);

✪   make certain, limited, preliminary distributions, after the time for creditor's claims has expired, if the distributions will not affect the rights of any creditors. Such distributions are limited to estate income, specific cash bequests not to exceed $10,000 to any one person, and household furniture and furnishings not to exceed $50,000 in total;

✪   sell or exchange personal property (except for publicly traded securities and bank obligations that can be sold without notice) (Cal. Prob. Code, Sec. 10537);

✪   make the first payment of a reasonable family allowance, payment of any increase in the family allowance monthly payments, and the first monthly payment made more than twelve months after the death of the decedent (Cal. Prob. Code, Sec. 10535);

✪   continue the decedent's business for a period exceeding six months (Cal. Prob. Code, Sec. 10534);

✪   enter into leases and other contracts for a period exceeding two years (Cal. Prob. Code, Sec. 19532 and 10536);

✪   invest estate monies in direct obligations of the U.S. or State of California that have a maturity date of more than one year (Cal. Prob. Code, Sec. 10533); and,

✪   enter exclusive contract to list property for sale for a period exceeding ninety days (Cal. Prob. Code, Sec. 10538).

Notice of proposed action. All of the actions described above can only be taken after a **NOTICE OF PROPOSED ACTION** is mailed to all persons whose interest in the estate would be affected by the action, or who have requested *special notice* (Cal. Prob. Code, Sec. 10581)—in other words, every beneficiary, heir, and any person requesting special notice. You do not have to send a **NOTICE OF PROPOSED ACTION** to a creditor unless it has requested special notice. (see form 30, p.317.) (A filled-in sample is in Appendix A.)

Prepare the form as follows.

- ◈ Fill in the caption as directed on page 20 under **SPOUSAL/DOMESTIC PARTNER PROPERTY PETITION**.

- ◈ Under the caption there are two boxes, marked *Objection* and *Consent*. These boxes are marked if the person receiving the **NOTICE OF PROPOSED ACTION** makes a decision, so leave it blank.

- ◈ At Item 1, list the name of the PR.

- ◈ At Item 2, check the box reflecting whether the PR's Letters specify that the IAEA powers are with *full authority* (necessary to sell real property with a **NOTICE OF PROPOSED ACTION**) or with *limited authority* (same as full authority, except the PR does not have the power to sell real property, even with a **NOTICE OF PROPOSED ACTION** or the consent of all interested persons).

- ◈ At Item 3, insert the date of the proposed action. That date must be at least fifteen days after the date the **NOTICE OF PROPOSED ACTION** is mailed to the interested persons. Next, describe the contemplated action in detail.

Example:

If the action is the sale of real property, insert the street address, the legal description, and a description of the property sold (e.g., a single family residence). Name the buyer; the sales commission to be paid; to whom it will be paid; the sales price; any terms of the sale (including amount, payment, interest rate, whether secured, and if secured, the address of the property securing the note and the priority of the deed of trust securing the note); allocation of taxes; escrow costs; and, whether the seller is paying any points or monies back to buyer.

– Warning –

Failure to disclose a material term of the sale could result in liability for the PR.

◈ Complete Item 4 if the action to be taken is the sale, lease, or option of real property. Item 4b requires the asset's value on the **INVENTORY AND APPRAISAL** to be listed unless the **INVENTORY AND APPRAISAL** has not yet been received back from the probate referee.

◈ On the back side of the **NOTICE OF PROPOSED ACTION**, print the PR's name. The PR signs where indicated. The remainder of the back side is for use by the person receiving it.

The mailing of the **NOTICE OF PROPOSED ACTION** may be by the PR. A **PROOF OF SERVICE** listing the date the **NOTICE OF PROPOSED ACTION** was mailed, to whom it was mailed, and signed by the person mailing the **NOTICE OF PROPOSED ACTION**, may be filed with the court. (The second page of form 34 is the **PROOF OF SERVICE** to use.)

By law, if no person who is mailed the **NOTICE OF PROPOSED ACTION** obtains a court order preventing the taking of the action or sends the PR an objection to the proposed action, the PR may take the action on or after the date specified in Item 3. However, to avoid a dispute over whether an objection was received or not, it is recommended that the PR obtain each person's consent to the proposed action via the return of the **NOTICE OF PROPOSED ACTION** with their written consent on the back of page 2.

With No Notice   The following actions can be taken under the IAEA without giving a **NOTICE OF PROPOSED ACTION**:

❂ sale or redemption of publicly traded securities on an established exchange and bank obligations (Cal. Prob. Code, Sec. 10537);

- ✪ make the monthly payments after the first payment of a reasonable family allowance (if payment amount is not increased) and payments after first monthly payment made more than twelve months after the death of the decedent (Cal. Prob. Code, Sec. 10535);

- ✪ continue the decedent's business for a period not exceeding six months (Cal. Prob. Code, Sec. 10534);

- ✪ enter into leases and other contracts for a period not exceeding two years (Cal. Prob. Code, Secs. 10532 and 10536);

- ✪ invest estate monies in securities on a national board, certain common trust funds, money market mutual funds, insured bank accounts, and direct obligations of the U.S. or State of California that have a maturity date of one year or less (Cal. Prob. Code, Sec. 10533 and 10537); and,

- ✪ enter exclusive contract to list property for sale for a period not exceeding ninety days (Cal. Prob. Code, Sec. 10538).

Having the right to perform an action without prior court permission and without giving a **NOTICE OF PROPOSED ACTION** does not necessarily mean that the PR should exercise that right. If there is any chance that an interested person may later object to the action taken, the PR should consider giving a **NOTICE OF PROPOSED ACTION**, requesting that all interested persons sign a written consent or seeking prior court approval of the action.

If an action taken without prior court approval or without consent turns sour, the PR may be liable. Giving a **NOTICE OF PROPOSED ACTION**, even when unnecessary, eliminates unnecessary risks.

Sales

Sales are the most complicated and risky aspect of a personal representative's (PR) duties. The PR does not have the absolute right to sell property of the estate. (Cal. Prob. Code, Sec. 1000.) A sale of estate property is not permitted unless:

- ✪ it is necessary to pay debts, bequests, expenses of administration, taxes, or family allowances;

- ✪ it is to the advantage of the estate and in the best interest of the interested persons (if all beneficiaries or heirs agree and no creditors object, a sale is said to be in the best interest of the interested persons); or,

- ✪ the will directs or authorizes it.

Although a beneficiary can object to a sale, he or she has no statutory right to stop a sale. With that being said, the beneficiary can ask the court to deny sale on the grounds that the sale is unnecessary or not in the best interest of the estate.

If the PR refuses to sell property, any interested person may petition the court for an order directing the PR to sell based on the reasons mentioned above.

If property is specifically bequeathed in the will, the PR cannot generally sell that property without the consent of the beneficiary of the specifically bequeathed property.

If the will provides for specific property to be sold or a specific method of sale, the PR must follow those directives. If the PR convinces the court that the directives are not in the best interest of the estate or the interested parties, the court can permit the PR to abandon the will's directives regarding a sale. (Cal. Prob. Code, Sec. 1002.)

The PR does have the right to:

- ✪ select which estate property to sell first;

- ✪ decide to sell estate property at public auction or private sale; and,

- ✪ decide whether to sell estate property separately or as a unit (e.g., whether the estate furniture should be sold piecemeal or as a group, or whether two real property lots should be sold together or separately).

All sales of real property must be for a price within 90% of the appraised value of the property. The *appraised value* is the value determined by the probate referee on the estate **INVENTORY AND APPRAISAL**. Further, if the sale occurs more than one year after the decedent's death, the property must be *reappraised* by the probate referee for the proposed sale.

The PR or his or her attorney may not purchase estate property unless the court approves, and either all beneficiaries of the estate who are affected by the sale agree in writing or the will of the decedent permits the purchase. (Cal. Prob. Code, beginning with Sec. 9880.)

PUBLISHED NOTICE OF SALE

California Probate Code, Section 10250, requires a published notice of the sale of *personal property,* and Section 10300 requires a published notice of the sale of *real property*. The published notice of the sale is an invitation to potential buyers of the PR's intent to sell certain property. The notice must run for a specific period of time, identify the property to be sold, specify the date after which offers to buy can be accepted, and specify any deposits or terms of the sale. The first date that offers can be accepted cannot be more than one year after the date specified in the published notice of sale.

Example:

If the published notice states that a deposit of 10% of the sales price is required, the PR cannot accept less. For that reason, the PR should attempt to minimize deposits or terms of the sale in the published notice.

If the sale needs to be published, you should contact a legal newspaper as described in Chapter 3, regarding publication of the **NOTICE OF PETITION TO ADMINISTER ESTATE**.

Exceptions Following are exceptions to the requirement of a prior published notice of sale.

- ✪ If the will authorizes or directs the sale without a published notice of sale. (*I give my Executor the power to sell property with or without notice* is an example of authorization in a will to dispense with the published notice. (Cal. Prob. Code, Sec. 10252.)) However, an *Administrator with Will Annexed* cannot utilize the authorization in the will to dispense with the notice to interested persons.

- ✪ If the property is perishable, will lose value if not disposed of promptly, will cause a loss or expense to the estate if kept, or the sale is necessary to pay a family allowance. (Cal. Prob. Code, Sec. 10252.)

Example:

A newer model automobile that depreciates over time and has the expense of insurance and storage is property that will lose value if not disposed of promptly.

- ✪ If the PR has the Independent Administration of Estates Act (IAEA) powers (see Chapter 9), except when those powers are limited.

- ✪ If the PR is selling publicly traded securities on an established exchange, CDs, and money accounts. (Cal. Prob. Code, Secs. 10200 and 10201.)

COURT APPROVAL OF SALES

Regardless of whether a prior published notice of the sale was required, a sale must be confirmed by the court before the sale can be consummated, unless there is a specific statute waiving this requirement. A **REPORT OF SALE AND PETITION FOR ORDER CONFIRMING SALE** is used. (see form 33, p.325.) Completing form 33 is detailed later in this chapter.

Example:

After a published notice of sale, the PR agrees to sell a secured note belonging to the estate to Bob Smith for $50,000 and executes a sales agreement to do so. The actual consummation of the sales transaction must first be confirmed by the court.

Exceptions   Exceptions from the requirement of court confirmation include the following types of sales:

- ✪ publicly traded securities (however, such sales must be approved before the date of sale) (Cal. Prob. Code, Sec. 10200);

- ✪ perishable property that will lose value if not disposed of promptly, will cause a loss or expense to the estate if kept, or the sale is necessary to pay a family allowance (Cal. Prob. Code, Sec. 10259);

- ✪ property sold under the IAEA, except real property where the PR's IAEA rights are limited (however, the PR needs prior court approval if an interested person objects to an IAEA sale);

✪   CD and money accounts (Cal. Prob. Code, Sec. 10200 and 10201); and,

✪   personal property sold at auction (Cal. Prob. Code, Sec. 10259).

PERSONAL PROPERTY SALES

Cars and personal, tangible property—like household furniture and furnishings—can generally be sold as perishable property. *Perishable property* is property that if not disposed of promptly, will cause a loss or expense to the estate. This disposal can be made without a prior published notice and does not need a court confirmation. (Cal. Prob. Code, Sec. 10252.)

However, any interested person may later request the court to surcharge the PR if the sale is, after the fact, determined to be improper. Accordingly, the personal representative should make serious efforts to obtain the best price and to adequately expose the property to the market.

Example:

If the PR is selling a car, he or she should determine the value and run ads—and not just sell the car to a friend or beneficiary of the estate.

– Warning –

Before selling such estate property, the PR should invite the estate beneficiaries to make an offer for the property to be sold or to overbid the best non-beneficiary offer. If possible, the PR should obtain written consents from the beneficiaries to sell the property at a certain price.

Often beneficiaries will want to receive certain estate assets before the estate is in a condition to be closed and its assets distributed. As preliminary distributions require a court preapproval, the personal representative may wish to sell such property to the beneficiaries rather than make a distribution. If the beneficiary cannot pay cash, the PR can sell the assets for a promissory note executed by the beneficiary and secured by a lien on his or her share of the estate.

If more than one beneficiary wants to buy a particular asset, the PR should consider having the competing beneficiaries submit sealed bids for the property and then open the bids in the presence of the competing beneficiaries. After the estate beneficiaries have bought household furniture, furnishings, or other personal effects, the PR should sell the remainder of the items at a garage sale handled by a professional third party or to a single buyer (the phone book lists people who will buy estate property) for a single price.

Simply because no prior published notice or court confirmation is required, the PR may elect to publish a prior notice of sale or ask the court to confirm the sale before its consummation. In addition, a PR with the IAEA powers may elect to give a **NOTICE OF PROPOSED ACTION**. The more valuable the asset or the more litigation-minded the beneficiaries, the more consideration the PR should give to a prior published notice, court confirmation of the sale, or a **NOTICE OF PROPOSED ACTION** (even if not required by law).

Publicly Traded Securities

No prior published notice or court confirmation is required for the sale of *securities* (stocks, bonds, mutual funds) that are sold on an established stock or bond exchange (including NASDAQ), through a registered broker, during the regular course of business (including Internet trading through an established broker).

If the PR has the IAEA powers, the sale can occur without prior court approval and does not require a **NOTICE OF PROPOSED ACTION**. However, if the PR does not have the IAEA powers, then an **EX PARTE PETITION FOR AUTHORITY TO SELL SECURITIES AND ORDER** must be secured from the court. (see form 32, p.323.) There is a filled-in sample in Appendix A. The form is completed as follows.

◈ Item 1: Insert the name of the PR and check *Personal Representative*.

◈ Item 2: Check either box b, c, or d. Only one of those boxes need be checked and the box checked should be the first one applicable. If box c is checked, then one or more of the boxes numbered (1) through (6) should be checked. If box number (6) is checked, then the reason must be specified. (Box 2c(6) would be an unusual situation and should be avoided if possible.)

⟡ At the bottom of page 1, the PR dates the petition, prints his or her name, and signs.

⟡ On page 2, the PR lists the number of shares to be sold, the name(s) of the securities to be sold, the name of the exchange (only if required by local rule), the recent bid asked (only if required by local rule), and the minimum selling price (only if the security is not listed on an established exchange).

⟡ The **Ex Parte Petition** is then simply delivered to the clerk of the court to be reviewed, and if proper, signed by the judge at the bottom of page 2 as the *Order Authorizing Sale of Securities.*

⟡ Some courts may require that a three- to five-day written notice and copy of the **Ex Parte Petition** be given to all interested parties. Check with the clerk of the court before filing. The original will stay in the court file. The PR only needs a confirmed copy of the petition showing the signed *Order Authorizing Sale of Securities.*

Other Personal Property

Other personal property, such as promissory notes, industrial equipment, short-term leaseholds, or business interests may be sold in one of the following three manners.

1. The PR can sell the property at an auction. Auctions are rarely used. The PR should read California Probate Code, Sections 10253–10254, if an auction is contemplated. A newspaper published notice of an auction must be given unless the will disposes of the requirement of notice. If the PR employs an auctioneer, the fee agreement is reviewable by the court and may be reduced by the court. (Cal. Prob. Code, Sec. 10255.)

2. If the PR has the IAEA powers, the property may be sold without a prior published notice or a court confirmation. In this situation, the PR discloses all pertinent terms of the pending sale to the interested parties via a **Notice of Proposed Action** (form 30).

3. Personal property may be sold at a *private sale,* or any sale that is not an auction sale, with a prior published notice (unless the will waives the requirement of a published notice of sale). It is then confirmed by the court before the sale is consummated. In

this situation, upon accepting an offer, the PR files a **REPORT OF SALE AND PETITION FOR ORDER CONFIRMING SALE OF PERSONAL PROPERTY** to the court requesting a confirmation of the sale by the court. Most courts will permit the use of form 33, entitled **REPORT OF SALE AND PETITION FOR ORDER CONFIRMING SALE OF REAL PROPERTY**, modified by crossing out "real" and inserting "personal" in the caption and checking the box for *sale of other property*. (see form 33, p.325.)

After filing the petition with the court clerk, a hearing is scheduled for about forty days later. A written **NOTICE OF HEARING** and **PROOF OF SERVICE** on the confirmation of the sale must be mailed to all interested parties at least fifteen days before the court hearing. At the court hearing, persons wishing to bid a higher amount for the property may do so. However, any higher bid must be at least 10% higher than the sale price that the PR is asking the court to confirm.

Example:

If the **REPORT OF SALE AND PETITION FOR ORDER CONFIRMING SALE OF PERSONAL PROPERTY** lists the sale price as $10,000, then any person can come to court and bid a higher price for the same property. The first overbid amount must be at least 10% higher, or $11,000.

REAL PROPERTY SALES

The probate sale procedure is very much like that of any private sale of real estate. Usually, the PR will hire a realtor to assist in marketing and selling the property. Upon finding a buyer, an escrow will be opened. However, there are some significant differences, which must be remembered.

Reasons for Sale

The first thing to determine in selling real property is the reason why. A sale can occur only if the decedent's will directs or authorizes the sale; there is a need to sell the property to pay taxes, debts, or expenses of the estate; the probate administration needs to be settled; or the sale is in the best interest of the estate.

Example:

All of the beneficiaries live in New York. Owning the home in California may not be convenient or the beneficiaries simply do not want to co-own a single-family residence. In such a situation, the beneficiaries may agree that the decedent's home should be sold. Such a sale is then in the best interest of the estate. However, if one of the beneficiaries objects, the court may agree that the sale is not in the best interest of the estate and may refuse to confirm such a sale.

Auctions The PR could sell the real property at an auction. (Cal. Prob. Code, Secs. 10300–10305.) The requirements of an auction are very specific and must be followed. Auctions require a prior publication of notice of sale *and* confirmation by the court.

Employing a Real Estate Agent If an auction is not used, the PR will likely employ a real estate agent. Although *for sale by owner* is allowed, a PR concerned about personal liability for errors will hire a real estate agent. The PR will usually enter into an exclusive listing with a real estate agent. Having the property listed on the *multiple listing service* assures that the property will be exposed to the greatest number of real estate agents, and therefore, the greatest number of potential buyers.

An *exclusive listing* agreement simply hires the real estate agent as the exclusive agent to list the property for sale. This assures the real estate agent one-half of the sales commission. The PR should hire a real estate agent who is advertising and selling properties in the same neighborhood as the estate property to be sold.

In negotiating the listing agreement, the PR should be aware that some courts will only permit a 5% commission, that the listing agreement should state that the sale is a probate sale, and that the listing agreement cannot be for more than ninety days (it can be renewed). Unless the PR has the IAEA powers, an ex parte order from the court is necessary to enter into an exclusive listing agreement. The PR should also negotiate for minimum market exposure of the property where the real estate agent agrees to have a certain number of open houses, newspaper advertisements, and so on.

– Warning –

Be sure to read Chapter 9 carefully if you have IAEA powers with full authority. Such powers will affect the PR's rights of sale.

Court Confirmed Sales

All sales of real property must be *confirmed* by the court before they can be consummated unless the PR is acting under the IAEA powers with full authority, in which case the PR may be able to consummate the sale without prior court confirmation. (see Chapter 9.) Following is a description of the necessary steps leading up to the court hearing to confirm the sale, preparing the petition asking the court to confirm the sale, the court hearing to confirm the sale, and the steps after the court hearing necessary to consummate the sale.

Prior published notice of sale. A prior published notice of the sale in a newspaper publication is required unless the will permits the executor to sell property without notice. The prior published notice takes about three weeks, and thus, the sale date listed in the notice should be accordingly determined. Administrators with will annexed must publish notice regardless of terms of the will or if the court confirmation is a result of an objection to a **NOTICE OF PROPOSED ACTION** given under an IAEA with full authority sale.

Be careful about using language in the published notice of sale that might limit your chances for a sale. For example, if the notice states that a 10% cash deposit is required, the PR is bound by those terms and the court will not confirm a sale with different terms.

Exposure to the market. To satisfy the requirements of adequately exposing the property to the market, the PR should begin marketing the property at the time the newspaper-published notice of sale occurs and should document all showings of the property to prospective purchasers by real estate agents, all open house showings, and all advertising of the property.

The real estate purchase agreement. If there was a prior published notice of sale, the real estate purchase agreement cannot be signed until after the date specified in the notice. Upon accepting an offer, the PR should be certain that the terms of the purchase agreement state the following:

- that the sale is a probate sale and is subject to court confirmation;

- all rules of the probate code relating to the sale of real property;

- that all contingencies (including any loan contingencies) must be removed before the court confirmation hearing date;

- that the seller will NOT provide a disclosure statement per California Civil Code, Section 1102 (probate sales are exempt from making a disclosure statement, but the PR should disclose all known defects);

- that the real estate commission is subject to court review; and,

- that the property is being sold *as is, except as to title.*

As the seller, the PR can agree to pay the costs of the sale including escrow, points, allowances (e.g., a $4,000 carpet allowance to buyer), title policy, repairs, and pest correction costs. However, as there can be no contingencies at the time of the court confirmation hearing, have the bids for any work/pest control done immediately and put caps on those amounts in your real estate purchase agreement.

Example:

If the termite inspector indicates the corrective work will cost $1,200, the seller might agree to pay the cost of the termite corrective work in an amount not to exceed $2,000. (The PR should provide a cushion in such a case.)

In the event the buyer backs out after the court confirmation hearing, he or she is liable for damages resulting from his or her failure to complete the sale. (Cal. Prob. Code, Sec. 10350.) Those damages could include the cost of republishing the notice, obtaining an order vacating the sale, or reducing the price on resale. For that reason, the PR should attempt to collect a deposit from the prospective buyer. Generally, a $5,000 deposit paid to the estate and placed into the estate account (not the escrow) before the court confirmation hearing is sufficient.

Petition the court. The next step is to petition the court to approve the sale by completing a **Report of Sale and Petition for Order Confirming Sale of Real Property** as follows. (see form 33, p.325.)

◈   Fill in the caption (see page 20 under **Spousal/Domestic Partner Property Petition**).

◈   Check the box *And Sale of Other Property Sold as a Unit* only if the sale includes personal property with the real property.

◈   At Item 1, list the name of the personal representative and check the appropriate box. Check box 1b if the estate is selling some personal property as well as the real property. Check Item 1c if there is a commission to be paid, and list the percentage as well as the commission amount. (Some local court rules put limits on the amount of the commission.)

Item 1d is always checked. Check the first box if a new bond will be required after the sale. (Remember, the PR is not bonded for real property unless he or she has the IAEA with full authority. Therefore, an additional bond will be required to cover the net proceeds of the sale.) Check the second box if the current bond amount is sufficient after the sale or if the bond requirement has been waived.

◈   Item 2a lists whether the estate owns 100% of the property sold or less. Item 2b lists whether the property is raw land (unimproved) or has structures (improved). Item 2c is checked if the real property is being sold with personal property (e.g., house sold with furniture). If Item 2c is checked, the personal property must be described on a separate sheet that will be attached to this **Report of Sale**. The description should include any **Inventory and Appraisal** value of the personal property being sold with the real property.

At 2d, list the street address and city of the property sold. If the property has no street address (e.g., vacant land in the desert), identify the location by reference to major cross streets. Item 2e instructs that the entire legal description be placed on a separate sheet and identified as Attachment 2e. (Several attachments can be placed on a single sheet of paper.) The legal description must be the complete legal description, and must include all common areas in condominium or planned unit developments, and any exclusions, such as oil rights. Check the title company's *Preliminary Title Report* for the exact legal description, and include the county tax assessor's parcel number (APN).

⬥ At Item 3a, insert the decedent's date of death. At Item 3b, insert the appraised value at date of death. If the **INVENTORY AND APPRAISAL** is not yet completed by the probate referee, verbally advise the probate referee that this value is necessary to complete your **REPORT OF SALE**. Item 3c can be skipped if the sale of the property occurs less than twelve months after the decedent died (as per Item 4c below). If the sale occurs more than twelve months after the decedent died, a reappraisal **INVENTORY AND APPRAISAL** must be prepared, appraised by the probate referee, and submitted to the court before the hearing date. (The probate referee will be paid another appraisal fee.) Remember, the sale price must be at least 90% of the **INVENTORY AND APPRAISAL** value.

The box to the right of Item 3c must be checked if personal property is being sold with the real property. If applicable, the value at Item 3b and 3c must be adjusted upwards for the personal property being sold with the real property.

⬥ At Item 4a, the names of the buyers and the manner of vesting title (e.g., *Rob Smith and Terri Smith as joint tenants*) is inserted. It is essential that the title selected be correct, as no subsequent changes can be made. Be sure that the title vesting selected accommodates any lender involved by the buyers. Item 4b will only be checked if the buyer is the PR.

At Item 4c, check whether the sale was private or public. A *private* sale is any sale not obtained at auction. Be sure to include, at Item 4c, the date of the written real estate purchase sales agreement. That date must not be before the permitted date stated in the published notice of sale. At Item 4d, the sales price and amount of cash deposit is stated.

At Item 4e, the personal representative reports if the sale is cash or credit. *Cash* means *all cash to seller.* If the estate will receive all cash, then it is checked even if the buyer is obtaining a mortgage to buy the property. *Credit* means that the seller (the estate) is taking back a promissory note, and the terms of that note must be described in Attachment 4e. Terms to be disclosed on Attachment 4e include: amount of note, interest rate, due date, payment amounts, whether unsecured or secured, by what property if note is secured, and position of deed of trust securing note (whether the note is secured by a first or second deed of trust).

Item 4f is where additional sale terms are disclosed—Item 4f should always be checked. Attachment 4f should list the buyer or seller responsibility for costs of escrow, title, property taxes, transfer taxes, maximum cost of any seller-paid termite work or repairs, other important terms, and—unless otherwise agreed upon between buyer and seller—that the sale is *as is, except as to title.*

Item 4g is only checked if the will directs the manner of sale. If so, the second box under Item 4g might be checked if the personal representative is not selling the property per the terms directed in the will. Item 4h is not applicable to probate estates.

◈ Check Item 5a if there is no real estate agent involved. Check Item 5b if a written contract with a broker was entered into. If the purchaser was procured by a broker, check the box at Item 5c and list the name of the broker (not the real estate agent) who represents the buyer. At Item 5d, the box is checked if a commission is being paid to the broker(s), and the division, if any, is stated.

◈ List the amount of any existing bond at Item 6a, or check the box *none*. Item 6b requires the PR to state the additional amount of bond necessary. If bond is waived or if the proceeds are going into a blocked account, check the box *none*. Otherwise, the PR must compute the amount of additional bond required. That amount will be the amount *netted* from the sale (the sales price less cost of sale and cost of any liens or mortgages paid off at time of sale).

If Item 6c is checked, the PR will likely need to complete a local form called **ORDER TO DEPOSIT MONEY AND RECEIPT OF DEPOSITORY**. This creates a record, is filed with the court, and indicates where the blocked monies will be. If Item 6c is checked, then escrow will send the sale proceeds directly to the financial institution indicated, which then sends a receipt for the money deposited to the court.

❖ Check one of the boxes at Item 7. If a published notice of sale was waived, then check Item 7b.

❖ Check one subitem at Items 8a, b, and c where appropriate.

❖ If Item 7b or 7c is checked, then Item 9 is skipped. Otherwise, either Item 9a or 9b must be checked (or both can be checked). For Item 9a, multiple boxes can be checked, but no box needs to be if the will authorizes or directs the sale of the property and Item 7b or 7c.

❖ Item 10 computes the first overbid amount. (The first overbid is 5% of the sales price, plus $500.)

❖ At Item 11, the amount on Item 10d is inserted.

❖ Most successful objections to a sale relate to insufficient exposure of the property to the market. Item 12 should detail (use attachment if necessary) all efforts to expose the property to the market.

Example:

Item 12 might read something like:

On multiple listing service for the following local realtor boards: Long Beach, South Bar, N. Orange County. Advertised 15 times in LA Times, 1 realtor caravan, 5 open houses, shown by appointment 7 times, listed on Internet at www.wesellu.com for 3 months.

❖ At Item 13, the number of attachment pages are listed. The PR signs, dates, and prints his or her name at the bottom of the REPORT OF SALE AND PETITION FOR ORDER CONFIRMING SALE OF REAL PROPERTY.

Filing the Report of Sale and Petition for Order Confirming Sale of Real Property. The PR should then make as many copies as persons who have filed special notice or who are estate beneficiaries, plus two. When the PR files the original **REPORT OF SALE AND PETITION FOR ORDER CONFIRMING SALE OF REAL PROPERTY** (including all attachments) with the court, be sure to have a copy confirmed that shows that the original was filed, indicating the hearing date, time, and department.

NOTE: *If the* **INVENTORY AND APPRAISAL** *(original or reappraisal) was not on file when the* **REPORT OF SALE AND PETITION FOR ORDER CONFIRMING SALE OF REAL PROPERTY** *was filed, the PR needs to be certain he or she files it with as much time as possible before the hearing.*

Giving notice of hearing. The PR must have someone else mail a **NOTICE OF HEARING** with a copy of the **REPORT OF SALE AND PETITION FOR CONFIRMING SALE OF REAL PROPERTY** to the buyer, each person who requested special notice or is a specific devisee of the property sold, and each beneficiary of the estate at least fifteen days before the court hearing. The **PROOF OF SERVICE** regarding the notice must be filed at least a week before the actual hearing. The PR should verify that all contingencies of buyers (e.g., financing contingency or sale of buyer's residence) have been removed before the hearing. The PR should advise the real estate agents and the buyer to attend the hearing.

Attending the hearing. The PR must attend the hearing. Before the hearing, the PR should approach the court clerk in the department where the hearing will take place and check in with the clerk. Some courts will place the court files on a desk in the courtroom and want the PR to hold the court file for his or her case until the matter is called. Check with the clerk to see if this is the local practice.

When the matter is called, the PR walks up to the judge and says:

> *Good morning your honor. I am John Smith, personal representative and petitioner today appearing in pro per.*

The judge may ask the PR some questions about the sale. If satisfied that the sale confirmation hearing should go forward, the judge will announce that the property listed in the petition is for sale, announce the first minimum overbid amount, ask if there are any persons interested in bidding on the property, and ask about the commission to be paid. Most often there will be no overbidders and the court will simply confirm the sale at hand. After confirming the sale, the judge will ask what the new bond amount will be. The PR should have that answer ready and be able to explain why that amount is necessary.

Example:

"Your honor, the additional bond should be $50,000. The sale proceeds of $105,000 will be reduced by costs of sale and the payoff of a $55,000 mortgage on the property, resulting in about $47,000 actually being received by the estate. That amount, plus one year's income on that amount, is $50,000."

After the hearing, the PR presents the **ORDER CONFIRMING SALE OF REAL PROPERTY** to the clerk (sometimes in the courtroom, sometimes at a separate filing window), and requests that the **ORDER CONFIRMING SALE OF REAL PROPERTY** be signed and a certified copy be sent to the PR. (Give the clerk a pre-addressed, stamped envelope and a check for the cost of certifying the **ORDER**, about $20.) (see form 35, p.329.)

The certified copy of the **ORDER CONFIRMING SALE OF REAL PROPERTY** is given to escrow. The PR should also confirm that escrow will prepare the deed. (Some title companies will also require a certified copy of the PR's **LETTERS** dated within sixty days of the date delivered to escrow.)

If someone overbids at the hearing. If overbidders appear, the judge will essentially act as an auctioneer to determine the highest amount to be paid for the property. If the last remaining overbidder is not the original buyer, the PR should ask the judge to *trail* the matter until the end of the court's calendar (about fifteen minutes) to permit the PR to ascertain that the new buyer is qualified to make the purchase. Outside of the courtroom, the PR should ask the unsuccessful bidders to remain until the PR can ascertain that the new buyer is qualified.

The PR must ascertain that the new buyer has no sales contingencies, has a certified check for 10% of the first overbid amount, and either has the money to complete the transaction or adequate credit to get a loan. In addition, the PR must verify that the buyer is able to either complete the transaction on the same terms (except for the higher price) or on terms that are acceptable to the PR. The check for 10% of the first overbid amount goes to the estate and not to escrow.

If satisfied, the PR should take the buyer's certified check, return to the courtroom, and advise the judge that the buyer is satisfactory. The judge will confirm the sale and ask about the bond, as previously discussed. If the new buyer is unsatisfactory, the PR should advise the judge and be prepared to explain why. If the PR appropriately refuses the overbidder's offer, the judge will start the confirmation of sale procedure over again.

Preparing the order. The **Order Confirming Sale of Real Property** (form 35) is completed as follows.

- ❖ Complete the caption. (See page 20 under **Spousal/Domestic Partner Property Petition**.)

- ❖ At Item 1, insert the date, time, and department or room number.

- ❖ Check Item 3a or 3b depending on how you checked this item on the **Report of Sale and Petition for Order Confirming Sale of Real Property**.

- ❖ If the sale was a private sale, check Item 6.

- ❖ Item 7 is always checked. The box checked in Item 7 depends on whether the original offer was overbid in court or not.

- ❖ The Item 9 boxes are self-explanatory—insert the name and vesting of the buyers and the sale price.

- ❖ Items 10–12 are self-explanatory and are completed as per the **Report of Sale and Petition for Order Confirming Sale of Real Property**.

- ❖ At Item 13, additional information should be affixed (or put on the reverse) with the terms listed on Attachment 4f of the **Report of Sale and Petition for Order Confirming Sale of Real Property**.

- ❖ If any attachment is on a separate page, Item 13 is completed and Item 15 is checked if applicable.

- ❖ Item 16 is checked if used.

Taxes

This chapter discusses the issues relating to a decedent (regardless of whether there is probate or not) and taxes. There are three tax issues to be concerned with: income taxes to the estate and beneficiaries; income tax basis adjustments as a result of the decedent's death; and, inheritance or estate taxes.

INCOME TAXES

An income tax return for the decedent must be filed for the year of death. For example, if the decedent died on March 1, 2007, then 2007 personal income tax returns for the decedent are due by April 15, 2008 (federal and state). The PR signs the returns. Depending on the date of death, the fact that the decedent died partway through the calendar year often results in an income tax refund. In that event, the PR must file IRS Form 1310 (claim for refund) with the decedent's personal income tax return. Any income tax refunds are assets of the estate and must be listed on Attachment 2 of the **INVENTORY AND APPRAISAL**. Besides customary income items, the PR should be aware of the following.

- ✪ Federal Savings Bonds have certain elections regarding the reporting of income upon the death of the owner. A tax preparer should be consulted if the decedent owned savings bonds.

- ✪ If there is a surviving spouse, a joint return for the year of death may be filed at the election of the PR and surviving spouse.

Estate An estate must file income tax returns and pay income tax on income received unless that income is distributed to estate beneficiaries. Estates file a federal Form 1041 and a state Form 541. The estate income tax return is similar to a personal income tax return, with a couple of differences.

- ✪ An *estate year* does not have to be a calendar year (January 1 through December 31).

- ✪ The estate's first taxable year begins with date of death, and its final taxable year ends when all of the assets are distributed.

- ✪ The estate's first and final taxable year (which can be the same year if less than twelve months in duration) can be *short years* (less than twelve months long).

Example:

Decedent dies on March 15, 2007. The first estate fiscal (non-calendar) year could be March 15, 2007 through April 30, 2007. The second fiscal year of the estate could be May 1, 2007, through April 30, 2008. The final fiscal year would then be May 1, 2008, through whatever date the estate assets were distributed.

Accordingly, good tax planning via short fiscal years for the estate minimizes income taxes.

- ✪ An estate is entitled to a $600 income tax exemption.

✪   Estate income tax rates are steeply progressive. At $7,500 of net income, an estate reaches the maximum federal income tax bracket of 35%.

✪   An estate is entitled to deduct the costs of administration paid during the tax year (court costs, referee fees, attorney's fees, etc.) in addition to customary deductions.

✪   An estate's income is reduced by the payment of nonspecific bequests to beneficiaries.

Example:

The estate has $1,000 of income. The decedent's will leaves $500 to Bob. This is a specific bequest, and if paid during the estate's tax year, is *not* an income tax deduction to the estate. However, if the decedent's will simply leaves one-half of the decedent's estate to Bob, and Bob is distributed $500 from the estate during the taxable year, the estate will then receive an income tax deduction for the distribution and Bob will declare the $500 distribution on his income tax return as income. If Bob's marginal income tax rate is lower than the estate's marginal income tax rate, such a distribution would save income taxes.

✪   To the extent the estate has excess deductions in its last taxable year (deductions it cannot use because they exceed the estate's income for the final year) the excess deductions are distributed to the residual beneficiaries of the estate, who can use them to the extent they exceed 2% of their own *adjusted gross income*. Depending on the number of residual beneficiaries and the estate income, this may be an advantage to the residual beneficiaries.

Example:

If the excess deductions total $2,000, and there are two equal beneficiaries of the estate, each beneficiary will receive a $1,000 excess deduction from the estate that can be used to the extent that his or her adjusted gross income is less than

$50,000. If the adjusted gross income of the residual benefi-
ciary is $40,000, then he or she would use $200 of the $1,000
excess deduction as a deduction against his or her income.

Beneficiary

Estate income or deductions distributed to estate beneficiaries are
reported to the beneficiary on a federal or state form called a
Schedule K-1.

Except for the estate's income, what a beneficiary receives from an
estate is *not* subject to income taxes on his or her estate, with one
exception—any estate pre-tax assets, such as pension plans, would be
income taxable to the beneficiary who receives it, as it would have
been to the decedent (however, pension plans usually pass by contract
to the named beneficiary outside of probate).

INCOME TAX BASIS ADJUSTMENT

If you buy ABC Corp. stock for $10 per share and then sell it for $25 per
share, you have a $15 per share profit, called a *capital gain*. If you sell
your ABC Corp. stock for $2 a share, you have a $8 per share loss, called
a *capital loss*. In either situation, your purchase cost of $10 per share is
called your *basis* for income tax purposes. Capital gains are subject to
income taxation and capital losses are generally income tax deductions.

**Decedent's
Assets**

However, in the event of death, a decedent's assets receive a new
income tax basis, regardless of the original cost basis, equal to the
date of death value. (Internal Revenue Code (I.R.C.), Sec. 1014.) If
the decedent's assets increase in value from his or her date of acquisition to his or her date of death, this new basis is an income tax
advantage to the estate or a beneficiary of the estate who inherits
the property. Obviously, if the decedent's assets decrease in value
from the date of acquisition to the date of death, the new basis is an
income tax disadvantage to the estate or beneficiary of the estate
who inherits the property.

**Community
Property**

Community property held by a decedent and his or her spouse
receives a basis adjustment at the decedent's death on both the decedent's one-half interest, in the community property and on the
surviving spouse's one-half interest, *unless the property was held in*

joint tenancy. The property can be held in one spouse's name or both spouses' names, but not in joint tenancy. (I.R.C., Sec. 1014(b)(6).)

Example 1:

Husband and wife buy rental property for $100,000 using community property funds, and hold title in the husband's name only. The wife dies four years later. At her death, the property is worth $300,000. The new income tax basis of the property is stepped up to the wife's date of death value of $300,000. The new basis value would be used to restart depreciation, or to measure capital gain or loss in the event of eventual sale.

Example 2:

Same facts as previous example, except that title is held in the name of husband and wife as joint tenants. At the wife's death, the new income basis would be (assuming no prior depreciation) $200,000 (wife's one-half interest would receive a basis adjustment step up from $50,000 to $150,000, and husband's one-half interest would remain at $50,000, for a total of $200,000).

On the other hand, if husband and wife have a community property asset (not held in joint tenancy) that goes down in value, then a double step down in the income tax basis would occur.

– Warning –

From an income tax standpoint, a husband and wife should not hold title to community property that has appreciated in value in joint tenancy, and should hold title to community property that has depreciated in value in joint tenancy.

Exceptions   Some types of properties for which the decedent had not paid income taxes do not receive the basis adjustment at date of death. Annuities, IRAs, pension plans, installment sales notes, and savings bonds do not receive a basis adjustment equal to the date of death value.

ESTATE TAXES

The federal government imposes a tax upon estates called the *estate tax*. The estate tax applies to all of the decedent's property whether it goes through probate or passes by contract (IRAs, pension plans, annuities, life insurance), via a living trust, by survivorship (joint tenancy, Totten trust, payable on death accounts), or by operation of law (property passing to a surviving spouse). A common misconception is that if the decedent's estate avoids probate, then it avoids the federal estate tax.

In addition to applying to all the property in which the decedent had an interest at time of death, the federal estate tax also applies to all the gifts made by the decedent during his or her lifetime after 1976 that exceeded the *annual exclusion* amount for gifts. The annual exclusion amount prior to 1982 was $3,000, and prior to 2002 was $10,000. It is now adjusted for inflation, so between 2002 and 2005, the amount was $11,000 and for 2006 and 2007, it is $12,000. For gifts made after 2007, verify with your tax advisor or the IRS the current annual exclusion amount. All gifts made by the decedent to anyone in any calendar year to the extent the gift exceeded the annual exclusion amount are added to the decedent's date of death assets to compute the federal estate tax.

Example:

If the decedent, in 2007, gave Bob Smith $13,000 and Mary Jones $9,000, then the $1,000 excess gift to Bob Smith would be added to the decedent's estate at time of death for purposes of computing the federal estate tax. The first $12,000 of Bob Smith's gift is not included, nor is any of the gift to Mary Jones, as said gift was under $12,000.

Even some property that the decedent did not own can be included in his or her estate for purposes of computing the federal estate tax. For example, life insurance policy proceeds from a policy on the life of the decedent given away by the decedent within three years of the decedent's death are wholly included in the decedent's estate. Also included are assets from which the decedent retained the right to income.

Example:

A decedent gives away his IBM stock during his lifetime but retains the right to the dividends on the gifted stock. In that event, the full value of the stock is included in his estate for purposes of computing the federal estate tax.

Furthermore, assets in which the decedent was a joint tenant are presumed to wholly belong to the decedent (unless the joint tenancy is held with the decedent's spouse, in which case the presumption is that one-half of the joint tenancy belonged to the decedent).

Example:

Computing decedent's federal estate tax:

Assumption: Decedent unmarried at time of death:

Assets Included in Decedent's Estate:

Assets in decedent's estate at date of 5/1/07 death	$2,400,000
Life insurance proceeds paid on decedent's life	$125,000
Decedent's joint tenancies	$30,000
Decedent's IRA	$10,000
Excess gifts made by decedent during lifetime	$25,000
Total estate subject to federal estate tax:	$2,590,000

Deductions:

Gifts to charity	$100,000
Mortgages (date of death principal amount plus accrued interest)	$225,000
Property taxes	$6,000
Debts (including credit cards, utility bills, medical expenses, and unpaid income taxes)	$7,000

Expenses of administration (attorney fees, accountant fees, executor fees, appraisal fees)	$10,000
Funeral expenses	$12,000
Total deductions:	$360,000
Net estate:	$2,230,000
Federal estate tax exemption (for 2007):	$2,000,000
Estate subject to federal estate taxes:	$230,000
Amount of federal estate taxes (46% of $230,000):	$105,800

Several points to remember about the federal estate tax include the following.

✪ Nothing passing outright to a U.S. citizen surviving spouse is subject to federal estate taxes. A decedent could leave one billion dollars outright to a U.S. citizen surviving spouse free of any federal estate taxes.

✪ Nothing passing to a qualified charity is subject to federal estate taxes. Certain types of trusts in which the charities have an interest are not subject to federal estate taxes.

✪ Property passing into certain types of trusts for the benefit of a surviving spouse is not subject to immediate federal estate taxes. Common names of trusts for a surviving spouse that defer the federal estate tax until the death of the surviving spouse are *marital trust*, *QTIP trust*, and *marital deduction trust*.

✪ Every decedent is entitled to a federal estate tax exemption amount. The exemption for decedents who die in 2007 is $2,000,000. There are scheduled increases in the exemption through the year 2010, at which time the federal estate tax is abolished until 2011, when it returns with an exemption of $1,000,000.

With proper planning, a husband and wife who die in 2007 could leave up to $4,000,000 federal estate tax free to their children.

✪ The federal estate tax is due nine months after the death of the decedent. Extensions to pay the federal estate tax *for good cause* can be granted. However, interest will be charged on the federal estate tax not paid nine months after the death of the decedent.

✪ Although the federal estate tax exemptions are significant, the federal estate tax rate starts and ends at basically 46%.

A federal estate tax return (called Form 706) must be filed if the gross value of the estate (value before deductions such as debts, mortgages, and amounts passing to spouse or charity are deducted) exceeds the federal estate tax exemption in the year of the decedent's death.

Example:

If the decedent dies in the year 2007 owning $2,700,000 in assets and $800,000 in debts, mortgages, and other deductions, a federal estate tax return would have to be filed, as the gross value of the decedent's estate exceeded $2,000,000 (although no federal estate taxes would be due, as the net value of the decedent's estate was less than $2,000,000).

The preparation of a federal estate tax return is best left to an attorney or CPA who specializes in preparing returns. If a federal estate tax return is due, it must be filed before a probate estate can be closed.

NOTE: *The term* **inheritance tax** *refers to a State of California death tax that was abolished in 1982.*

CONCLUSION

If you read this chapter, you should realize that the vast majority of decedents' deaths result in a *significant* tax advantage to the beneficiaries of the estate. This is because the exemptions and permitted deductions to an estate mean that 98% of decedent's estates pay no federal estate taxes at all. Yet, most decedents' estates contain appreciated assets that receive a *free* income tax basis step-up of decedent's property at death.

Final Distribution

The goal in probate is to distribute the assets and close the estate. California law assumes that an estate can be completed in twelve months from the date that **LETTERS** are issued if there is no federal estate tax return due, and eighteen months if a federal estate tax is due. (Cal. Prob. Code, Sec. 12200.) If the estate cannot be completed in that time frame, the court expects a *status report* to be filed and set for a noticed hearing. (An attorney should be consulted to prepare the status report.)

FINAL DISTRIBUTION AND CLOSING THE ESTATE

The following is a checklist to use to determine if the estate is in a condition to be closed.

❑   Have at least four months passed since **LETTERS** were issued?

❑   Has a **NOTICE OF ADMINISTRATION** of the estate been mailed to all suspected creditors at least two months ago?

❑   Have all creditors' claims been resolved (that is, resolved and paid, or rejected with the **NOTICE OF REJECTION** being given at least ninety days ago with no lawsuit being filed by the rejected claimant)?

❑ Have all **INVENTORY AND APPRAISALS** been filed with the court?

❑ Have any ownership disputes been resolved?

❑ Have all estate sales been consummated?

❑ Was a **NOTICE TO THE DIRECTOR OF HEALTH SERVICES** given at least four months ago and any claim filed thereon resolved?

❑ If required, was a notice to the Director of the California Department of Corrections given at least four months ago and any claim filed thereon resolved?

❑ Have all of the decedent's necessary income tax returns been filed?

❑ If a federal estate tax return was due, has it been filed? If yes, has the PR received a closing letter from the IRS?

If the PR can answer yes to all of those questions, the estate is in a condition to be distributed and closed. To close and distribute the estate, the PR must file a **FIRST AND FINAL ACCOUNT AND REPORT AND PETITION TO DISTRIBUTE ESTATE (FINAL ACCOUNT)**. (see form 37, p.231.) (There is a sample, filled-in form in Appendix A.)

The following are hints for completing the **FINAL ACCOUNT**.

✪ The first step in closing an estate is to review the court file for the estate for **REQUESTS FOR SPECIAL NOTICES** or **CREDITORS' CLAIMS** that have been filed but not presented to the PR. They must be resolved if it is a **CREDITOR'S CLAIM**, or abided by if it is a **REQUEST FOR SPECIAL NOTICE**.

✪ Before preparing the **FINAL ACCOUNT**, the PR must obtain an Estate Income Tax Certificate from the Franchise Tax Board if the gross value of the estate (including nonprobate assets) exceeded $1,000,000, and more than $250,000 passes to a nonresident of California.

✪ To obtain the certificate, the PR must file a completed **REQUEST FOR ESTATE INCOME TAX CERTIFICATE**. (see form 36, p.331.) (A filled-in sample is in Appendix A.) The Estate Income Tax Certificate must be on file with the court at least thirty days before the hearing on the **FINAL ACCOUNT**.

✪ The PR's preparation of the **FINAL ACCOUNT** is not easy. (see form 37, p.231.) The bold text in this sample is to alert the PR that his or her fact situation will be different and to change his or her wording accordingly.

✪ The **FINAL ACCOUNT** must be on recycled paper, in a legal format. The title of the court begins on line 8. The title of the **FINAL ACCOUNT** must be modified to meet the particular requests of the PR. The title of the **FINAL ACCOUNT** must be on the bottom line of each page of the **FINAL ACCOUNT**.

Example 1:

If there is a will, all beneficiaries entitled to a residual share of the estate have signed waivers of accounting, the PR waives all statutory fees, and there are no creditors paid without claims for which court approval is sought. The title might read *First and Final Report (Account Waived) of Personal Representative; and Petition for Distribution of Testate Estate.*

Example 2:

Assume there is no will, the accounting has not been waived by all beneficiaries entitled to a residual share of the estate, and the PR is seeking statutory fees and approval of creditors paid without creditor's claims being filed. The title might read *First and Final Account and Report of Personal Representative; Petition for Approval of Debts Paid Without Claims; Statutory Fees to Personal Representative and for Distribution of Intestate Estate.*

The introductory paragraph simply tells the court what the PR is filing and recites the title of his or her Final Account.

✪ *Summary of account.* Paragraph I on the sample **FINAL ACCOUNT** is a summary of the accounting.

- If all affected beneficiaries waive the accounting—that is, receive a percentage or portion of the estate (e.g., 15% of the estate) instead of a specific bequest (e.g., a cash bequest of $500)—and there is enough in the estate to pay the specific devise, the PR can omit the summary of account paragraph.

- If there is an accounting, then the summary of account paragraph must state the account period. It should begin with the decedent's date of death, and conclude at the end of a month shortly before the accounting was prepared.

- A probate accounting must have the estate charges equal to the estate credits. The *charges* represent the sum of the **INVENTORY AND APPRAISALS**, the income receipts, principal receipts, and gains on sale. In essence the *charges* represent the assets the PR is charged with receiving. The *credits* represent the sum of the disbursements, losses on sale, and assets on hand at the end of the account period.

  Gains, losses on sales, or disposition (e.g., payoff of a municipal bond) occur when an estate asset is sold or disposed of at a value higher than (a gain) or lower than (a loss) the **INVENTORY AND APPRAISAL** value of that asset. All gains are listed under *Gains on Sale* and all losses are listed on *Losses on Sale*. If the PR is a few dollars short of balancing, most courts will permit an adjustment, as shown in the sample **FIRST ACCOUNT** in Appendix A, to balance the credit and charges.

Example 1:

The **INVENTORY AND APPRAISAL** values one share of ABC Corp. stock at $10 and the PR sells one share for $12. The estate has a gain on the sale of $2.

Example 2:

Same facts as previous example, except that before the sale ABC Corp. pays a $4 dividend, of which $1 represents a capital distribution. In that case, the gain on sale would be $3, as the value of the stock had been reduced from $10 to $9 as a result of the prior capital distribution.

- Some receipts are not reported on *Principal Receipts*. For example, the PR sells one share of ABC stock for $10 and realizes no gain or loss on the sale. The proceeds from that sale are not a principal or an income receipt because the PR has simply replaced the ABC stock asset with cash.

- Transferring a bank account balance from one bank to another is not a receipt. For that same reason, the principal portion of a loan payment received is not in report in the *Principal Receipts,* but the amount of the principal payment reduces the carry value of the remaining balance of the loan.

Example:

The PR receives a loan payment of $800 on a $20,000 note owed to the estate. Six hundred dollars of the payment is interest on the note and $200 of the payment is principal on the note. The $600 of interest would be reported as an *Income Receipt* and the $200 of principal would not be reported on the accounting. However, the carry value of the note would be reduced by the $200 of principal received, and thus, would be carried at $19,800 on the *Assets on Hand* schedule of the accounting.

✪ ***Appointment of personal representative.*** Paragraph II, entitled *Appointment of Executor* on the sample **FINAL ACCOUNT**, is relatively straightforward. The *minute order* referred to on line 12 is always entered on the date of the hearing. A minute order is the court's internal order used by the court clerk when checking orders submitted by attorneys or petitioners acting in pro per.

✪ ***Notice of death.*** Paragraph III, *Notice of Death,* is also relatively straightforward. This paragraph is simply advising the court that publication of the original Notice of Death and of Petition to Administer Estate (published before the hearing date on the **PETITION FOR PROBATE**) did occur, that proof of its publication was filed with the court (by the newspaper), and that the time for creditors' claims generally expired four months after **LETTERS** were issued to the PR.

✪ ***Creditors' claims.*** Paragraph IV, *Creditor's Claims and Debts Paid Without Claims Filed*, on the sample **FINAL ACCOUNT** is one of the more difficult paragraphs to complete.

- If the accounting is waived, there is no need to discuss debts paid without a claim being filed. If the accounting is not waived, then debts paid without a creditor's claim being filed need to be itemized and it must be stated that each said claim was paid before the expiration of the claim period, that the estate is solvent, and that each claim was in the correct amount owed to the creditor be the decedent.

- The mailing of a **NOTICE OF ADMINISTRATION** to creditors is strongly recommended, and the date of the mailing as well as the expiration date of filing claims under the **NOTICE OF ADMINISTRATION** should be stated. (see form 27, p.311.)

- Language like that found on page 5, lines 1–5 on the **FINAL ACCOUNT**, concerning suspected or known creditors and the PR's efforts to determine creditors needs to be stated.

- State the resolution of all creditors' claims. The sample **FINAL ACCOUNT** shows only claims that were allowed. Rejected claims should show the date of rejection and statement that the claims were resolved without a lawsuit, that no lawsuit was timely filed by the creditor, or that a lawsuit filed by the creditor was resolved.

✪ ***Inventory and appraisal.*** Paragraph V, *Inventory and Appraisal*, is relatively straightforward. The PR must note the total of each of the **INVENTORY AND APPRAISALS** filed as well as the cumulative total.

○ ***Beneficiaries and heirs.*** If the decedent left a will, then Paragraph VI is titled *Devisees and Legatees*. If the decedent left no will, then Paragraph VI is titled *Heirs at Law*.

- The name, age, and address of each beneficiary or heir is listed.

- If the decedent left a will, the provisions of the will that dispose of the decedent's estate are stated verbatim, and any necessary explanation is given as to survivorship requirements or the identity of beneficiaries.

- If the decedent died *intestate* (without a will), state the decedent's marital status, the names of all heirs, and the intestacy statute they inherit under. (Cal. Prob. Code, Secs. 6400–6414.)

○ ***Changes in the estate.*** Paragraph VII, *Changes in Estate*, is designed to inform the court what assets in the **INVENTORY AND APPRAISALS** have been disposed of, the details of their disposition (whether sold with court confirmation or not, whether the sale or disposition resulted in a gain or loss to the estate, etc.), and what assets have been acquired in the estate during the estate administration period.

○ ***Inheritance and estate taxes.*** Paragraph VIII is *Inheritance and Estate Taxes*. There are no inheritance taxes, unless the decedent died before July 1982. If no federal estate tax return was due because the gross value of the estate was under the applicable limit in the year of the decedent's death, then a statement to that effect is all that is necessary.

- If a federal estate tax return was due and federal estate taxes were paid, the paragraph becomes more complicated because of the proration of the taxes among the estate beneficiaries. If the decedent's will states that the federal estate tax is to be paid from the estate *residue* (the portion of the estate left after payment of all specific bequests, all debts payable by the estate, and all estate administration expenses), and the estate residue is sufficient to pay the federal estate tax, there is no proration issue. Nor is there any issue for charitable or spousal bequests, as they are free from federal estate taxes.

- If there is no will, or if the will is silent as to the payment of the federal estate taxes, the law prorates the taxes among the persons who receive assets from the decedent.

- The PR has the right to obtain the pro rata share of federal estate taxes from any nonprobate recipient of property from the decedent (e.g., the beneficiary of life insurance proceeds).

✪ ***Substantiating distribution.*** Paragraph IX, *Status of Estate Substantiating Distribution,* contains required statements. The only portions of this paragraph that could vary relate to the payment of federal estate taxes and the status of the decedent's property as separate, community, or both. There cannot be community property in the estate unless the decedent was married at the time of his or her death.

✪ ***Advertising, bond, and fees.*** Paragraph X, *Legal Advertising, Bond Premiums and Referee's Fees,* is a required paragraph to assure the court that the PR has paid the expenses of the estate administration. Legal advertising represents the costs of publishing notices in newspapers. Bond premiums are not applicable if there is no bond. Referee fees are the fees paid to the probate referee.

✪ ***Request for special notice, Notice to Medi-Cal, and Notice to Department of Corrections.*** Paragraph XI, *Request for Special Notice, Notice to Medi-Cal, and Notice to Department of Corrections*, is relatively straightforward. Any **REQUESTS FOR SPECIAL NOTICE** should be listed by name and date the request was filed.

- If the decedent or if the decedent's predeceased spouse was not a recipient of Medi-Cal, that fact should be stated and no notice to the Director of Health Care Services is required. Otherwise, notice must be given, and state the date of the notice and expiration for the filing of a claim by the Director of Health Care Services must be stated.

- If no heir or beneficiary was in a California jail or prison at the time of the decedent's death, then no notice to the Director of California Department of Corrections is required. If notice is given, however, the date of the notice and the date of the expiration for the Director to file a claim must be stated.

- State the resolution of any claim filed by Medi-Cal or the Department of Corrections.

- If a notice should be sent to the Director of Health Care Services or Director of California Department of Corrections, but is not sent due to the PR's incorrect belief that no notice is required, then the Director of the Health Care Services or the Director of California Department of Corrections can later bring an action against the PR personally for any claim amount due.

✪ *Statutory fees.* Paragraph XII, *Statutory Executor's Commissions or Waiver of Executor's Statutory Commission*s, advises the court whether or not the PR wishes to accept the statutory fee for services rendered in administering the estate. If the statutory fee is requested, the paragraph must show, as in the sample **FINAL ACCOUNT**, the computation of the statutory fee. The statutory fee for any portion of the estate over $1,000,000 is 1%.

✪ *Balance of estate.* Paragraph XIII, *Balance of the Estate*, advises the court what assets are on hand for distribution. List cash accounts as actual cash balance, name of financial institution, and account number. Noncash items are listed using their **INVENTORY AND APPRAISAL** descriptions and values. State the dollar total of the assets on hand.

✪ *Code Sections 1063 and 1064 statements.* Paragraph XIV, *Probate Code Sections 1063 and 1064 Statements*, advises the court:

- whether the estate has any debts outstanding, such as mortgages on real property;

- whether or not the PR or his or her attorney have received any fees without a court order;

- whether the PR has paid any money for services rendered to a family member or affiliate (e.g., business partner, etc.); and,

- the actual—not inventory—value of the estate assets on hand as listed on a separate schedule attached to the **Final Account**.

✪ ***Distribution of estate.*** Paragraph XV, *Distribution of Estate*, is the most important paragraph in the **Final Account**—it determines distribution of the estate. If the decedent left a will, the distribution is as directed in the will, and Paragraph XV will set forth that distribution, including both specific bequests and the residuary shares. (The sample **Final Account** describes only an equal distribution of the estate residue.) If the decedent died intestate, Paragraph XV will recite the applicable intestate succession statute.

✪ ***Graduated filing fee information.*** The court wants to know if the PR paid the proper filing fee based upon the size of the estate. Accordingly, the **Final Account** must include a calculation in the format shown on Schedule H of form 37. If there is a refund, the PR must make a claim thereon with the county clerk. If there is a further amount due, it must paid before the **Final Account** is filed and a copy of the clerk's receipt for the additional filing fee should be attached to the **Final Account**.

✪ ***Prayer.*** The *prayer* asks the court to make an order based upon the statements made in the **Final Account**.

The prayer must:

- ask the court to approve the **Final Account**;

- recite the value of the assets on hand from Paragraph XIII and what portion of those assets are cash;

- request approval of any fees to the PR;

- request the court to make a decree for distribution to the persons entitled (Paragraph XV) and should describe the assets on hand with their **INVENTORY AND APPRAISAL** values, less fees requested to the PR, less any income tax liability, plus any post-account period receipts and any subsequently discovered assets;

- request the discharge of the PR (and any bond) up on distribution of assets; and,

- request *all other proper relief* to give the court jurisdiction to make any other appropriate orders.

○ *The accounting.* The accounting details all of the financial transactions of the estate.

- Schedule A, in the sample **FINAL ACCOUNT**, is the *Income Receipts* schedule. Receipts are normally entered by asset and then sequentially by date.

  For example, if the PR receives differing amounts per month of bank interest, then normally each bank interest amount is listed separately under a subheading of that account. However, when the interest paid is nominal, some courts will permit the PR to simply list the interest by calendar year. The amounts of any accrued interest or dividends described on the **INVENTORY AND APPRAISAL** are not listed in *Income Receipts*.

- Schedule B, in the sample **FINAL ACCOUNT**, is the *Principal Receipts* schedule. If there are no principal receipts, omit this schedule. Generally, each principal receipt is individually described and explains the reason for the payment.

- Schedule C, in the sample **FINAL ACCOUNT**, is the *Gain on Sale* schedule. If there were no gains on any sales or dispositions of any estate property, this schedule would be omitted. Each gain on sale is listed in the single Gain on Sale schedule.

- Schedule D, in the sample **FINAL ACCOUNT**, is the *Disbursement* schedule. Disbursements are generally itemized, and the purpose of the payment is inserted if not otherwise obvious.

- Schedule E, in the sample **FINAL ACCOUNT**, is the *Loss on Sale* schedule. If there were no losses on any sales or dispositions of any estate property, this schedule would be omitted. Each loss on sale is listed in the single *Loss on Sale* schedule.

- Schedule F, in the sample **FINAL ACCOUNT**, is the *Assets on Hand* schedule. This schedule will itemize, segregated into cash and noncash categories, each of the assets on hand in the estate. Noncash assets will be valued at the **INVENTORY AND APPRAISAL** values.

✪ *Verification.* The final account must be verified, under penalty of perjury, by the PR as shown in the sample **FINAL ACCOUNT**.

✪ *Filing and notice.* The **FINAL ACCOUNT** needs to be filed with the clerk of the court who will set it for a hearing in court. The PR, at the time of filing, should have a second copy of the **FINAL ACCOUNT** date stamped showing the hearing date, department, and time of the hearing. Normally, the clerk will set the hearing date approximately forty days from filing.

NOTICE OF THE HEARING

The PR is responsible for mailing a **NOTICE OF HEARING** (form 34) to all beneficiaries or heirs of the estate and all persons who have filed a **REQUEST FOR SPECIAL NOTICE**. Preparation of the **NOTICE OF HEARING** is described in Chapter 4. On page two of the **NOTICE OF HEARING** is a separate document called a **PROOF OF SERVICE**. (see form 34, p.327.) The **PROOF OF SERVICE** is completed to prove that the **NOTICE OF HEARING** was mailed.

THE HEARING

Unless the matter is continued before the hearing date or is recommended for approval, the petitioner needs to appear. When the judge approves the **FINAL ACCOUNT**, he or she will make a statement such as "the account, report, and petition are approved as filed," which means that the PR was granted everything requested. Sometimes, however, the judge will modify the PR's request. Those modifications must be reflected in the **ORDER**.

ORDER SETTLING FINAL ACCOUNT

A sample **ORDER APPROVING FIRST AND FINAL ACCOUNT AND REPORT OF EXECUTOR; APPROVAL OF DEBTS PAID WITHOUT CLAIMS; APPROVAL OF STATUTORY FEES TO EXECUTOR AND DECREE FOR DISTRIBUTION OF TESTATE ESTATE (ORDER ON FINAL ACCOUNT)** can be found in Appendix A as form 40. Obviously, the exact title of the **ORDER ON FINAL ACCOUNT** should follow the title of the **FINAL ACCOUNT**, modified to include the word *Order* and to use the words *approval* or *decree* instead of *petition*.

The introductory paragraph is straightforward. Even if the matter is approved without an appearance of the PR, the statement at lines 26 and 27, *Petitioner appeared IN PRO PER*, still appears.

The first paragraph on page two of the sample **ORDER ON FINAL ACCOUNT** is modified to reflect any changes in the prayer of the **FINAL ACCOUNT** that the judge may make. For example, the following might be added at the end of that paragraph:

> ...except that the Executor's fees are to be $5,190 instead of $5,290 as prayed for.

Note that the portion *Ordered, Adjudged, and Decreed* basically follows the *prayer* section in the **FINAL ACCOUNT**.

When filing the **ORDER ON FINAL ACCOUNT**, pay for as many certified copies as there are counties where the estate has real property, plus two.

FINAL DISTRIBUTION

Record a certified copy of the **ORDER ON FINAL ACCOUNT** in each county where real property described in the **ORDER ON FINAL ACCOUNT**.

Unless the beneficiaries otherwise agree, each is entitled to whatever portion of the estate they are bequeathed. For example, if Mary Smith was left 20% of the estate, she receives 20% of each piece of property. In that event, she receives 20% of the cash on hand, 20% of each real property, and 20% of each security.

Receipts

Before distributing all of the estate assets, the PR should obtain a signed **RECEIPTS** from each beneficiary or heir at the time the beneficiary receives his or her assets from the estate. It is important that the **RECEIPTS**, when read together, distribute all of the estate.

For example, if five people were left the estate, each 20%, then each of their **RECEIPTS** should indicate they have received their 20%. That way the court can tell, by reviewing all five **RECEIPTS**, that 100% of the estate has been distributed. A filled-in, sample form **RECEIPT** is in Appendix A.

Affidavit for Discharge

After filing all **RECEIPTS**, the PR can file his or her **DECLARATION AND ORDER OF FINAL DISCHARGE**. (see form 42, p.333.) The form in Appendix B is not a statewide form. Counties may accept that form or may require their own local form. It is wise to ask the court clerk before preparing the **DECLARATION AND ORDER OF FINAL DISCHARGE**.

Once the judge signs the **DECLARATION AND ORDER OF FINAL DISCHARGE**, the PR is officially discharged as the PR and the estate is closed. If a bond was filed by the PR, a copy of the **DECLARATION AND ORDER OF FINAL DISCHARGE** should be forwarded to the bond company to release the bond. In addition, the PR may still have to file a final estate income tax return, as the estate final tax year did not end until the estate assets were distributed.

Glossary

A

administrator. A personal representative who is not named in the decedent's will. In earlier times, a female administrator was called an administratrix.

affidavit. A statement that is sworn to in the presence of a notary.

assessor's parcel number (APN). A unique number assigned to each recognized parcel of land. The number is used to identify property in property tax bills, preliminary change of ownership forms, and deeds.

B

beneficiary. The named recipient in a will of an asset belonging to a decedent, as distinguished from an heir.

C

California Probate Code. A body of written law passed by the legislature that governs the law and procedures for probates in California.

codicil. An amendment to a will.

community property. Property acquired during marriage from the efforts of one or both of the spouses, or property agreed between spouses to be community (such an agreement must be in writing if made after 1985).

D

declaration. A statement that is declared, under penalty of perjury, to be true and correct. Declarations can generally be used in lieu of an affidavit.

deed. A document where real property is conveyed from one to another.

deed of trust. A document, usually recorded, where a mortgage borrower, as the trustor, gives a security interest in his or her real property to the lender (beneficiary). Deeds of trust are used in California in lieu of recorded mortgages against property.

E

executor. A personal representative who is named in the decedent's will. In earlier times, a female executor was called an executrix.

exempt property. Property in a probate estate that, by statute, can be given to a surviving spouse or minor children of a decedent regardless of the rights of creditors, provisions in a will, or the laws of intestate succession.

F

family allowance. A cash allowance given by the court to a surviving spouse, minor children, incapacitated adult children, or parents of a decedent from the probate estate of the decedent.

filing with the court. The delivery of documents to the court clerk to be placed into the court file.

H

hearing. An open court resolution of a matter.

heir. The relative entitled to an asset belonging to a decedent when no person is named in the decedent's will (or where there is no will) as the beneficiary.

I

Independent Administration of Estates Act (IAEA). A statutory act permitting personal representatives who have been granted the IAEA powers to take certain actions with the estate without prior court permission, although many of the acts do require consent or waiver from the persons interested in the estate.

intestate. When a person dies without a will. (A person who dies with a will is said to have died *testate*.)

intestate succession. The distribution of a decedent's property subject to probate when there is either no will or the will fails to dispose of the property to the decedent's heirs. If the decedent leaves a surviving spouse, the community property interest of the decedent passes to the surviving spouse. If there is a surviving spouse and no children or other lineal descendants of the decedent, one-half of the decedent's separate property passes to the surviving spouse and one-half of the decedent's separate property passes to the decedent's family. If there is a surviving spouse and one child, one-half of the separate property passes to the surviving spouse and one-half to the child. If there is a surviving spouse and more than one child, one-third of the separate property passes to the surviving spouse and the remaining separate property passes to the children equally (if any child is deceased but leaves children of his or her own who survive the decedent, the deceased child's children take their deceased parent's share). If there is no surviving spouse but there are surviving children of the decedent, they take all of the decedent's separate property in equal shares. If there is no surviving spouse nor issue (children, grandchildren, etc.) who survive the decedent, the decedent's separate property goes to his or her parents in equal shares or all to the surviving parent. If there are no surviving parents, the decedent's separate property passes to the lineal descendants of the decedent's parents (i.e., the siblings of the decedent).

issue. Legal term to describe the lineal descendants of a person. Your issue would be your children, your grandchildren, your great-grandchildren, etc.

J

joint tenancy. A written title naming one or more persons as joint tenants, which means they have equal ownership and, in the event the death of a joint tenant, the remaining joint tenants take the share of the deceased joint tenant "by right of survivorship" regardless of contrary provisions in a will.

Judicial Council Forms (JCF). Documents prepared in a fill in the blank or check format, which have been created by the courts for use in many routine probate matters.

L

letters testamentary/letters of administration. Letters testamentary and letters of administration are documents issued by the court showing who the personal representative of a probate estate is. The letters are *testamentary* if the personal representative was named in the decedent's will as the executor. Letters are *of administration* if the personal representative was not named in the decedent's will as the executor or if the decedent had no will.

living trust. A trust created during lifetime (instead of created at someone's death via their will). Generally the trust is for the benefit of the person who creates the trust but becomes irrevocable upon the death of the person who creates it. It is a popular way to avoid probate as the assets are not held in the name of the decedent but rather in the name of the trust.

local forms. Forms created by counties for in-county use or by particular judges for their courtrooms.

N

notice. In probate matters, the personal representative must usually give a written notice of actions to be taken by the personal representative for hearings. Usually the notice must be mailed at least fifteen days before the action is taken or before the court hearing date.

O

order. The generic term used to describe the decision of the court on the subject matter brought up in the petition. Orders of the court carry the force of law and must be followed.

P

personal property. Anything that is not real property. For example: cash, securities, partnership interests, rights in a lawsuit, household furniture and furnishings, personal effects, and inventory.

personal representative. The generic term for the court appointed person or corporation who manages a decedent's probate estate.

petition. The generic term used to describe the document filed by a personal representative or other person interested in a probate estate wherein they are asking the court to make an order approving a request. Petitions, upon being filed with the court, are set for a hearing.

probate. The court supervision of the changing of title to assets from a decedent's name to the name of the beneficiaries under the decedent's will or the decedent's heirs if the decedent died with no will.

probate homestead. The right, given by the court in its discretion, to a surviving spouse or minor children of a decedent, to live in a home owned by the decedent which is part of the decedent's probate estate.

probate referee. A person appointed, county by county, by the State Controller of California who is legally responsible for the appraisal of probate assets.

proof of service. A Judicial Council Form declaration, usually filed with the court, that a written notice of a hearing or a copy of a document has been given to persons mentioned in the proof of service.

publication. As used in this book, a legal notice published in a newspaper.

Q

quasi-community property. Property acquired outside of California that would have been community property had it been acquired in California.

R

real property. Land, buildings on land, long-term leases, mineral rights, condominiums, and co-op buildings (condos where the ownership is indicated by a certificate rather than a deed).

S

separate property. Property acquired before marriage, the income during marriage of property acquired before marriage, gifts or inheritances received during marriage, and property agreed upon by the spouses to be separate property (agreement must be in writing if made after 1985).

statutory fees/commissions. Fees permitted by law to the lawyer and the personal representative for the administration of an estate. The attorney and personal representative are each entitled to 4% on the first $15,000 of the estate value, 3% on the next $85,000 of the estate value, 2% on the next $900,000 of the estate value, and 1% on the remainder of the estate value. Extraordinary fees may also be permitted to an attorney or the personal representative of the estate for sales, tax work, or litigation.

T

testate. When a person dies with a will. (A person who dies without a will is said to have died *intestate.*)

V

verification. Mandatory statement at the end of a petition where the petitioner declares, under penalty of perjury, that all factual allegations are true and correct based upon the personal knowledge of the petitioner, except those allegations that the petitioner expressly states are *on information and belief* of which the petitioner believes to be true.

W

will. A will is document that, at someone's death, directs the distribution of assets subject to the will of the deceased. A will generally cannot affect the distribution of assets held in joint tenancy, distributed pursuant to a contract (life insurance, pensions, retirement plans, annuities, etc.), or property subject to a payable on death or transfer on death designation.

Sample, Filled-in Forms

The instructions for a particular form may be found by looking up the form number in the index. Make photocopies to use for both practice worksheets and the forms you will file with the court. (Some forms have backsides that are blank.)

Recording Requested by and
When Recorded Mail to:

ROY HERE
115 Maple Dr.
Los Angeles, CA 90040

AFFIDAVIT - DEATH OF JOINT TENANT

STATE OF CALIFORNIA   )
)   ss.
COUNTY OF LOS ANGELES)

The undersigned, ROY HERE, of legal age, being first duly sworn, deposes and says:

The decedent, JANE DOE named in the attached certified copy of Certificate of Death is the same person as JANE DOE named as one of the parties in that certain Grant Deed executed on January 31, 2007, recorded on February 5, 2007, in the Orange County recorder's office as instrument no. 07-123372. This Affidavit-Death of Joint Tenant is executed to establish that the surviving joint tenant is ROY HERE. The subject real property is located at 1121 Oak St., Santa Ana, Orange County, CA and more accurately described as:

"Lot 2 of Tract 168648, in the City of Santa Ana, County of Orange, State of California, as shown by Map on file in Book 124, Pages 94 and 95 of Maps, Records of Orange County, California"
APN: 600-0240-050

Roy Here
ROY HERE

Subscribed to and sworn before me on _____2/6/07_____

Nancy Haley
Notary Public in and for
said County and State

This page intentionally left blank.

BOE-502-A (FRONT) REV. 8 (10-05)

PRELIMINARY CHANGE OF OWNERSHIP REPORT

	FOR RECORDER'S USE ONLY

[To be completed by transferee (buyer) prior to transfer of subject property in accordance with section 480.3 of the Revenue and Taxation Code.] A Preliminary Change of Ownership Report must be filed with each conveyance in the County Recorder's office for the county where the property is located; this particular form may be used in all 58 counties of California.

THIS REPORT IS NOT A PUBLIC DOCUMENT

SELLER/TRANSFEROR: Jane Smith, a.k.a. Jane Doe Smith

BUYER/TRANSFEREE: Jimmy Smith, Executor

ASSESSOR'S PARCEL NUMBER(S) 123-456-78

PROPERTY ADDRESS OR LOCATION: 1111 Main Street, Santa Ana, CA 92701

MAIL TAX INFORMATION TO: Name   Jimmy Smith, Executor

Address 2222 Swift St., Los Angeles, CA 90189

Phone Number (8 a.m.-5 p.m.) (555- 555-5555

NOTICE: A lien for property taxes applies to your property on January 1 of each year for the taxes owing in the following fiscal year, July 1 through June 30. One-half of these taxes is due November 1, and one-half is due February 1. The first installment becomes delinquent on December 10, and the second installment becomes delinquent on April 10. One tax bill is mailed before November 1 to the owner of record. **You may be responsible for the current or upcoming property taxes even if you do not receive the tax bill.**

The property which you acquired may be subject to a supplemental assessment in an amount to be determined by the **Orange** Assessor. For further information on your supplemental roll obligation, please call the **Orange** Assessor at _____.

PART I: TRANSFER INFORMATION (please answer all questions)

YES	NO	
☐	☒	A. Is this transfer solely between husband and wife (addition of a spouse, death of a spouse, divorce settlement, etc.)?
☐	☒	B. Is this transaction only a correction of the name(s) of the person(s) holding title to the property (for example, a name change upon marriage)? Please explain _____
☐	☒	C. Is this document recorded to create, terminate, or reconvey a lender's interest in the property?
☐	☒	D. Is this transaction recorded only as a requirement for financing purposes or to create, terminate, or reconvey a security interest (e.g., cosigner)? Please explain _____
☐	☒	E. Is this document recorded to substitute a trustee of a trust, mortgage, or other similar document?
☐	☒	F. Did this transfer result in the creation of a joint tenancy in which the seller (transferor) remains as one of the joint tenants?
☐	☒	G. Does this transfer return property to the person who created the joint tenancy (original transferor)?
		H. Is this a transfer of property:
☐	☒	1. to a revocable trust that may be revoked by the transferor and is for the benefit of the ☐ transferor ☐ transferor's spouse?
☐	☒	2. to a trust that may be revoked by the Creator/Grantor who is also a joint tenant, and which names the other joint tenant(s) as beneficiaries when the Creator/Grantor dies?
☐	☒	3. to an irrevocable trust for the benefit of the ☐ Creator/Grantor and/or ☐ Grantor's spouse?
☐	☒	4. to an irrevocable trust from which the property reverts to the Creator/Grantor within 12 years?
☐	☒	I. If this property is subject to a lease, is the remaining lease term 35 years or more including written options?
☐	☒	*J. Is this a transfer between ☐ parent(s) and child(ren)? ☐ or from grandparent(s) to grandchild(ren)?
☐	☒	*K. Is this transaction to replace a principal residence by a person 55 years of age or older? Within the same county? ☐ Yes ☐ No
☐	☒	*L. Is this transaction to replace a principal residence by a person who is severely disabled as defined by Revenue and Taxation Code section 69.5? Within the same county? ☐ Yes ☐ No
☐	☒	M. Is this transfer solely between domestic partners currently registered with the California Secretary of State?

*If you checked yes to J, K or L, you may qualify for a property tax reassessment exclusion, which may result in lower taxes on your property. **If you do not file a claim, your property will be reassessed.**

Please provide any other information that will help the Assessor to understand the nature of the transfer.

If the conveying document constitutes an exclusion from a change in ownership as defined in section 62 of the Revenue and Taxation Code for any reason other than those listed above, set forth the specific exclusions claimed: _____.

Please answer all questions in each section. If a question does not apply, indicate with "N/A." Sign and date at bottom of second page.

PART II: OTHER TRANSFER INFORMATION

A. Date of transfer if other than recording date 02/01/07

B. Type of transfer (please check appropriate box):
☐ Purchase ☐ Foreclosure ☐ Gift ☐ Trade or Exchange ☐ Merger, Stock, or Partnership Acquisition
☐ Contract of Sale – Date of Contract _____
☒ Inheritance – Date of Death 02/01/07 ☐ Other (please explain): _____
☐ Creation of Lease ☐ Assignment of a Lease ☐ Termination of a Lease ☐ Sale/Leaseback
☐ Date lease began _____
☐ Original term in years (including written options) _____
☐ Remaining term in years (including written options) _____
Monthly Payment _____ Remaining Term _____

C. Was only a partial interest in the property transferred? ☐ Yes ☒ No
If **yes**, indicate the percentage transferred _____%.

BOE-502-A (BACK) REV. 8 (10-05)

Please answer, to the best of your knowledge, all applicable questions, then sign and date. If a question does not apply, indicate with "N/A."

PART III: PURCHASE PRICE AND TERMS OF SALE

A. CASH DOWN PAYMENT OR value of trade or exchange *(excluding closing costs)*   Amount $ _____

B. FIRST DEED OF TRUST @ _____ % interest for _____ years. Pymts./Mo. = $ _____ (Prin. & Int. only)   Amount $ _____
- ☐ FHA(_____ Discount Points)
- ☐ Conventional
- ☐ VA (_____ Discount Points)
- ☐ Cal-Vet
- Balloon payment   ☐ Yes
- ☐ Fixed rate
- ☐ Variable rate
- ☐ All inclusive D.T. ($ _____ Wrapped)
- ☐ Loan carried by seller
- ☐ No   Due Date _____
- ☐ New loan
- ☐ Assumed existing loan balance
- ☐ Bank or savings & loan
- ☐ Finance company
- Amount $ _____

C. SECOND DEED OF TRUST @ _____ % interest for _____ years. Pymts./Mo. = $ _____ (Prin. & Int. only)   Amount $ _____
- ☐ Bank or savings & loan
- ☐ Loan carried by seller
- Balloon payment   ☐ Yes
- ☐ Fixed rate
- ☐ Variable rate
- ☐ No   Due Date _____
- ☐ New loan
- ☐ Assumed existing loan balance
- Amount $ _____

D. OTHER FINANCING: Is other financing involved not covered in (b) or (c) above?   ☐ Yes   ☐ No   Amount $ _____

Type _____ @ _____ % interest for _____ years. Pymts./Mo. = $ _____ (Prin. & Int. only)
- ☐ Bank or savings & loan
- ☐ Loan carried by seller
- Balloon payment   ☐ Yes
- ☐ Fixed rate
- ☐ Variable rate
- ☐ No   Due Date _____
- ☐ New loan
- ☐ Assumed existing loan balance
- Amount $ _____

E. WAS AN IMPROVEMENT BOND ASSUMED BY THE BUYER?   ☐ Yes   ☐ No   Outstanding Balance: Amount $ _____

F. TOTAL PURCHASE PRICE *(or acquisition price, if traded or exchanged, include real estate commission if paid)*

TOTAL ITEMS A THROUGH E $ _____

G. PROPERTY PURCHASED   ☐ Through a broker   ☐ Direct from seller   ☐ From a family member   ☐ Other *(please explain):* _____.

If purchased through a broker, provide broker's name and phone number: _____

Please explain any special terms, seller concessions, or financing and any other information that would help the Assessor understand the purchase price and terms of sale: _____

PART IV: PROPERTY INFORMATION

A. TYPE OF PROPERTY TRANSFERRED:
- ☒ Single-family residence
- ☐ Multiple-family residence (no. of units: _____)
- ☐ Commercial/Industrial
- ☐ Other (Description: i.e., timber, mineral, water rights, etc. _____)
- ☐ Agricultural
- ☐ Co-op/Own-your-own
- ☐ Condominium
- ☐ Timeshare
- ☐ Manufactured home
- ☐ Unimproved lot

B. IS THIS PROPERTY INTENDED AS YOUR PRINCIPAL RESIDENCE?   ☐ Yes   ☒ No

If **yes**, enter date of occupancy _____ / _____ , 20 _____ or intended occupancy _____ / _____ , 20 _____ .
    (month)   *(day)*   *(year)*   *(month)*   *(day)*   *(year)*

C. IS PERSONAL PROPERTY INCLUDED IN PURCHASE PRICE (i.e., furniture, farm equipment, machinery, etc.)
(other than a manufactured home subject to local property tax)?   ☐ Yes   ☒ No
If **yes**, enter the value of the personal property included in the purchase price $ _____ *(Attach itemized list of personal property.)*

D. IS A MANUFACTURED HOME INCLUDED IN PURCHASE PRICE?   ☐ Yes   ☒ No
If **yes**, how much of the purchase price is allocated to the manufactured home? $ _____
Is the manufactured home subject to local property tax?   ☐ Yes   ☐ No   What is the decal number? _____

E. DOES THE PROPERTY PRODUCE INCOME?   ☐ Yes   ☐ No   If **yes**, is the income from:
- ☐ Lease/Rent
- ☐ Contract
- ☐ Mineral rights
- ☒ Other *(please explain):* _____

F. WHAT WAS THE CONDITION OF THE PROPERTY AT THE TIME OF SALE?
- ☐ Good   ☒ Average   ☐ Fair   ☐ Poor

Please explain the physical condition of the property and provide any other information (such as restrictions, etc.) that would assist the Assessor in determining the value of the property:

CERTIFICATION

OWNERSHIP TYPE (☐)
- Proprietorship ☐
- Partnership ☐
- Corporation ☐
- Other _____ ☒

I certify that the foregoing is true, correct and complete to the best of my knowledge and belief.
This declaration is binding on each and every co-owner and/or partner.

NAME OF NEW OWNER/CORPORATE OFFICER	TITLE
Jimmy Smith	Executor
SIGNATURE OF NEW OWNER/CORPORATE OFFICER	DATE
Jimmy Smith	03/01/07
NAME OF ENTITY *(typed or printed)*	FEDERAL EMPLOYER ID NUMBER

ADDRESS *(typed or printed)*	E-MAIL ADDRESS *(optional)*	DATE
2222 Swift St, Los Angeles, CA 90189	jimmysmith@email.com	

(NOTE: The Assessor may contact you for additional information.)
If a document evidencing a change of ownership is presented to the recorder for recordation without the concurrent filing of a preliminary change of ownership report, the recorder may charge an additional recording fee of twenty dollars ($20).

BOE-58-AH (FRONT) REV. 9 (8-03)

CLAIM FOR REASSESSMENT EXCLUSION FOR TRANSFER BETWEEN PARENT AND CHILD

(Section 63.1 of the Revenue and Taxation Code)

OFFICE OF THE ASSESSOR-RECORDER, COUNTY OF MARIN
JOAN C. THAYER, ASSESSOR-RECORDER
P.O. Box C, Civic Center Branch
San Rafael, CA 94913

California law provides, with certain limitations, that a "change in ownership" does not include the purchase or transfer of:

- The principal residence between parents and children, and/or
- The first $1,000,000 of other real property between parents and children.

IMPORTANT: In order to qualify for this exclusion, a claim form must be completed and signed by the transferors and a transferee and filed with the Assessor. A claim form is timely filed if it is filed within three years after the date of purchase or transfer, or prior to the transfer of the real property to a third party, whichever is earlier. If a claim form has not been filed by the date specified in the preceding sentence, it will be timely if filed within six months after the date of mailing of a notice of supplemental or escape assessment for this property. If a claim is not timely filed, the exclusion will be granted beginning with the calendar year in which you file your claim. Complete all of Sections A, B, and C and answer each question or your claim may be denied. Proof of eligibility, including a copy of the transfer document, trust, or will, may be required.

Please note:

a. This exclusion only applies to transfers that occur on or after November 6, 1986.

b. In order to qualify, the real property must be transferred from parents to their children or children to their parents.

c. If you do not complete and return this form, it may result in this property being reassessed.

A. PROPERTY

ASSESSOR'S PARCEL NUMBER
123-456-78

PROPERTY ADDRESS	CITY
1111 Main Street	**Santa Ana**

RECORDER'S DOCUMENT NUMBER	DATE OF PURCHASE OR TRANSFER
2006-5678	**02/01/07**

PROBATE NUMBER *(if applicable)*	DATE OF DEATH *(if applicable)*	DATE OF DECREE OF DISTRIBUTION *(if applicable)*
OC A00001	**02/01/07**	

The disclosure of social security numbers is mandatory as required by Revenue and Taxation Code section 63.1. [See Title 42 United States Code, section 405(c)(2)(C)(i) which authorizes the use of social security numbers for identification purposes in the administration of any tax.] A foreign national who cannot obtain a social security number may provide a tax identification number issued by the Internal Revenue Service. The numbers are used by the Assessor and the state to monitor the exclusion limit. This claim form is not subject to public inspection.

B. TRANSFEROR(S)/SELLER(S) *(additional transferors please complete "B" on the reverse)*

1. Print full name(s) of transferor(s) **Jane Smith**
2. Social security number(s) **111-22-3333**
3. Family relationship(s) to transferee(s) **Mother**

   If adopted, age at time of adoption _____

4. Was this property the transferor's principal residence? ☒ Yes ☐ No

   If **yes**, please check which one of the following exemptions was granted on this property in the transferor's name:

   Homeowners' Exemption _____ Disabled Veterans' Exemption _____

5. Is this a transfer of real property other than the principal residence of the transferor (the exclusion for other real property is limited to the first one million dollars of value)? ☐ Yes ☒ No

   If **yes**, please attach a list of all previous transfers that qualify for this exclusion. [This list should include for each property: the County, Assessor's parcel number, address, date of transfer, names of all the transferees/buyers, and family relationship. Transferor's principal residence must be identified.]

6. Was only a partial interest in the property transferred? ☐ Yes ☒ No If **yes**, percentage transferred _____ %
7. Was this property owned in joint tenancy? ☐ Yes ☒ No
8. If the transfer was through the medium of a trust, please attach a copy of the trust.

CERTIFICATION

I certify (or declare) under penalty of perjury under the laws of the State of California that the foregoing and all information hereon, including any accompanying statements or documents, is true and correct to the best of my knowledge and that I am the parent or child of the transferees listed in Section C. I knowingly am granting this exclusion and will not file a claim to transfer the base year value of my principal residence under Revenue and Taxation Code section 69.5.

SIGNATURE OF TRANSFEROR OR LEGAL REPRESENTATIVE	DATE
Jane Smith	**03/01/07**

SIGNATURE OF TRANSFEROR OR LEGAL REPRESENTATIVE	DATE

MAILING ADDRESS	DAYTIME PHONE NUMBER
2222 Swift St., Los Angeles, CA 90189	**(555) 555-5555**

(Please complete applicable information on reverse side.) If you need help completing this form, or have questions on its content, please call the Marin County Assessor's Office at (415) 499-7360.

[125-593 (121404)]

C. TRANSFEREE(S)/BUYER(S) *(additional transferees please complete "C" below)*

1. Print full name(s) of transferee(s) _____ Jimmy Smith _____   _____ Jenny Smith _____
2. Family relationship(s) to transferor(s) _____ Son _____   _____ Daughter _____

If adopted, age at time of adoption _____

If step-parent/step-child relationship is involved, was parent still married to step-parent on the date of purchase or transfer?
☐ Yes   ☐ No

If **no**, was the marriage terminated by: ☐ Death   ☐ Divorce

If terminated by death, had the surviving step-parent remarried as of the date of purchase or transfer?   ☐ Yes   ☐ No

If in-law relationship is involved, was the son-in-law or daughter-in-law still married to the daughter or son on the date of purchase or transfer? ☐ Yes   ☐ No

If **no**, was the marriage terminated by: ☐ Death   ☐ Divorce

If terminated by death, had the surviving son-in-law or daughter-in-law remarried as of the date of purchase or transfer?
☐ Yes   ☐ No

3. ALLOCATION OF EXCLUSION (If the full cash value of the real property transferred exceeds the one million dollar value exclusion, the transferee must specify on an attachment to this claim the amount and allocation of the exclusion that is being sought.)

CERTIFICATION

I certify (or declare) under penalty of perjury under the laws of the State of California that the foregoing and all information hereon, including any accompanying statements or documents, is true and correct to the best of my knowledge and that I am the parent or child of the transferors listed in Section B; and that all of the transferees are eligible transferees within the meaning of section 63.1 of the Revenue and Taxation Code.

SIGNATURE OF TRANSFEREE OR LEGAL REPRESENTATIVE	DATE
Jimmy Smith	03/01/07

MAILING ADDRESS	DAYTIME PHONE NUMBER
2222 Swift St, Los Angeles, CA 90189 03/01/07	( )

NOTE: The Assessor may contact you for additional information.

B. ADDITIONAL TRANSFEROR(S)/SELLER(S) *(continued)*

NAME	SOCIAL SECURITY NUMBER	SIGNATURE	RELATIONSHIP

C. ADDITIONAL TRANSFEREE(S)/BUYER(S) *(continued)*

NAME	RELATIONSHIP

<u>Recording Requested by</u>:
MICHAEL HOY
<u>When recorded return to</u>:
MICHAEL HOY
17777 Boston Circle
Los Angeles, CA 90041
<u>Mail tax statements to</u>:
Same

APN: 600-212-011

<u>AFFIDAVIT—DEATH OF SPOUSE OR DOMESTIC PARTNER</u>

STATE OF CALIFORNIA   )
)   ss.
COUNTY OF LOS ANGELES)

The undersigned, MICHAEL HOY, of legal age, being first duly sworn, deposes and says:

The decedent, PATRICIA SMITH HOY, named in the attached certified copy of Certificate of Death is the same person as PATRICIA S. HOY named as one of the parties in that certain Deed executed in favor of MICHAEL HOY and PATRICIA S. HOY on November 10, 1995 and recorded on December 22, 1995 in the Riverside County recorder's office as Instrument No. 1995-7707 wherein title was taken as "community property." This Affidavit-Death of Spouse is executed to establish that the surviving spouse is MICHAEL HOY. The subject real property covered by the Deed recorded as Instrument No. 1995-77707 is located at 758 Golden Circle, Palm Desert, Riverside County, CA and more accurately described on Exhibit "A" attached hereto and made a part hereof.

This Affidavit is filed under California Probate Code Sections 13500 and 13530(b) in order to confirm the above-named real property is community property passing to MICHAEL HOY, the surviving spouse of PATRICIA SMITH HOY, and no administration is necessary. The decedent died intestate.

Michael Hoy
_____
MICHAEL HOY

Subscribed to and sworn before me on _____

_____
Notary Public in and for
said County and State

EXHIBIT "A"

Lot 126 of Tract No. 5732, in the County of Riverside, State of California, as shown on a map recorded in Book 319, Pages 24 to 30 inclusive of Maps in the office of the Riverside County Recorder"

APN: 600-212-011

Commonly known as: 758 Golden Circle, Palm Desert

DE-221

ATTORNEY OR PARTY WITHOUT ATTORNEY *(Name, State Bar number, and address):*	FOR COURT USE ONLY

John Smith, In Pro Per
1111 Main Street
Santa Ana, CA 92701
TELEPHONE NO.: **555-555-5555**   FAX NO. *(Optional):*
E-MAIL ADDRESS *(Optional):* **johnsmith@email.com**
ATTORNEY FOR *(Name):*

SUPERIOR COURT OF CALIFORNIA, COUNTY OF ORANGE
STREET ADDRESS: **341 The City Drive South**
MAILING ADDRESS:
CITY AND ZIP CODE: **Orange, CA 92668**
BRANCH NAME: **Probate**

ESTATE OF *(Name):* **Jane Smith, a.k.a. Jane Doe Smith**
DECEDENT

CASE NUMBER:
A00001

HEARING DATE:
04/15/07

[X] SPOUSAL ☐ DOMESTIC PARTNER PROPERTY PETITION	DEPT.: **L73**	TIME: **9:00 AM**

1. **Petitioner** *(name):*   John Smith   **requests**
   a. [X] determination of property passing to the surviving spouse or surviving registered domestic partner without administration (Fam. Code, § 297.5, Prob. Code, § 13500).
   b. ☐ confirmation of property belonging to the surviving spouse or surviving registered domestic partner (Fam. Code, § 297.5, Prob. Code, §§ 100, 101).
   c. ☐ immediate appointment of a probate referee.

2. Petitioner is
   a. [X] surviving spouse of the decedent.
   b. ☐ personal representative of *(name):*   , surviving spouse.
   c. ☐ guardian or conservator of the estate of *(name):*   , surviving spouse.
   d. ☐ surviving registered domestic partner of the decedent.
   e. ☐ personal representative of *(name):*   , surviving registered domestic partner.
   f. ☐ conservator of the estate of *(name):*   , surviving registered domestic partner.

3. Decedent died on *(date):* 02/01/07

4. Decedent was
   a. [X] a resident of the California county named above.
   b. ☐ a nonresident of California and left an estate in the county named above.
   c. ☐ intestate [X] testate and a copy of the will and any codicil is affixed as Attachment 4c.
      (Attach copies of will and any codicil, a typewritten copy of any handwritten document, and an English translation of any foreign-language document.)

5. a. *(Complete in all cases)* The decedent is survived by
      (1) ☐ no child. [X] child as follows: [X] natural or adopted ☐ natural, adopted by a third party.
      (2) [X] no issue of a predeceased child. ☐ issue of a predeceased child.
   b. Decedent ☐ is [X] is not survived by a stepchild or foster child or children who would have been adopted by decedent but for a legal barrier. *(See Prob. Code, § 6454.)*

6. *(Complete only if no issue survived the decedent. Check **only** the **first** box that applies.)*
   a. ☐ The decedent is survived by a parent or parents who are listed in item 9.
   b. [X] The decedent is survived by a brother, sister, or issue of a deceased brother or sister, all of whom are listed in item 9.

7. Administration of all or part of the estate is not necessary for the reason that all or a part of the estate is property passing to the surviving spouse or surviving registered domestic partner. The facts upon which petitioner bases the allegation that the property described in Attachments 7a and 7b is property that should pass or be confirmed to the surviving spouse or surviving registered domestic partner are stated in Attachment 7.
   a. [X] Attachment 7a[1] contains the legal description *(if real property add Assessor's Parcel Number)* of the deceased spouse's or registered domestic partner's property that petitioner requests to be determined as having passed to the surviving spouse or partner from the deceased spouse or partner. This includes any interest in a trade or business name of any unincorporated business or an interest in any unincorporated business that the deceased spouse or partner was operating or managing at the time of death, subject to any written agreement between the deceased spouse or partner and the surviving spouse or partner providing for a non pro rata division of the aggregate value of the community property assets or quasi-community assets, or both.

[1] See Prob. Code, § 13658 for required filing of a list of known creditors of a business and other information in certain instances. If required, include in Attachment 7a.

Page 1 of 2

Form Adopted for Mandatory Use
Judicial Council of California DE-221
[Rev. January 1, 2005]

SPOUSAL OR DOMESTIC PARTNER PROPERTY PETITION
(Probate—Decedents Estates)

Family Code, § 297.5;
Probate Code, § 13650

ESTATE OF (Name):	CASE NUMBER:
Jane Smith, a.k.a. Jane Doe Smith DECEDENT	A00001

7. b. ☐ Attachment 7b contains the legal description *(if real property add Assessor's Parcel Number)* of the community or quasi-community property petitioner requests to be determined as having belonged under Probate Code sections 100 and 101 and Family Code section 297.5 to the surviving spouse or surviving registered domestic partner upon the deceased spouse's or partner's death, subject to any written agreement between the deceased spouse or partner and the surviving spouse or partner providing for a non pro rata division of the aggregate value of the community property assets or quasi-community assets, or both.

8. There ☐ exists ☒ does not exist   a written agreement between the deceased spouse or deceased registered domestic partner and the surviving spouse or surviving registered domestic partner providing for a non pro rata division of the aggregate value of the community property assets or quasi-community assets, or both. *(If petitioner bases the description of the property of the deceased spouse or partner passing to the surviving spouse or partner or the property to be confirmed to the surviving spouse or partner, or both, on a written agreement, a copy of the agreement must be attached to this petition as Attachment 8.)*

9. The names, relationships, ages, and residence or mailing addresses so far as known to or reasonably ascertainable by petitioner of (1) all persons named in decedent's will and codicils, whether living or deceased, and (2) all persons checked in items 5 and 6

    ☒ are listed below   ☐ are listed in Attachment 9.

Name and relationship	Age	Residence or mailing address
John Smith, Husband	Adult	1111 Main St., Santa Ana, CA 92701
Jimmy Smith, Son	Adult	2222 Swift St., Los Angeles, CA 90189
Jenny Smith, Daughter	Adult	3333 Bay Ct., Newport Beach, CA 90189
Jack Jones, Brother	Adult	4444 Mesa Dr., Las Vegas, NV 89191
Jill Jones, Sister	Adult	5555 Camden Pl., Chicago, IL 60605

10. The names and addresses of all persons named as executors in the decedent's will and any codicil or appointed as personal representatives of the decedent's estate ☒ are listed below ☐ are listed in Attachment 10 ☐ none

John Smith, Husband	Adult	1111 Main St., Santa Ana, CA 92701
Jimmy Smith, Son	Adult	2222 Swift St., Los Angeles, CA 90189
Jenny Smith, Daughter	Adult	3333 Bay Ct., Newport Beach, CA 90189
Jack Jones, Brother	Adult	4444 Mesa Dr., Las Vegas, NV 89191
Jill Jones, Sister	Adult	5555 Camden Pl., Chicago, IL 60605

11. ☐ The petitioner is the trustee of a trust that is a devisee under decedent's will. The names and addresses of all persons interested in the trust who are entitled to notice under Probate Code section 13655(b)(2) are listed in Attachment 11.

12. A petition for probate or for administration of the decedent's estate

   a. ☐ is being filed with this petition.

   b. ☐ was filed on *(date):*

   c. ☒ has not been filed and is not being filed with this petition.

13. Number of pages attached: ___1___

Date:

_____   ▶   _____
(TYPE OR PRINT NAME)   (SIGNATURE OF ATTORNEY)

I declare under penalty of perjury under the laws of the State of California that the foregoing is true and correct.

Date: 03/01/07

_____   ▶ *John Smith*
     John Smith   _____
(TYPE OR PRINT NAME)   (SIGNATURE OF PETITIONER)

SPOUSAL OR DOMESTIC PARTNER PROPERTY PETITION
(Probate—Decedents Estates)

DE-221 Spousal Property Petition
Estate of Jane Smith, a.k.a. Jane Doe Smith, Deceased

Attachment 7

The subject property, the residence of decedent and her surviving spouse, is held in the name of "JOHN SMITH and JANE SMITH, as tenants in common." The Deed was executed on January 1, 1986 (a copy of which is attached hereto).

Decedent's Will was executed January 1, 1996 (a copy of which is attached hereto). Said Will, in paragraph Thrid, leaves all of Decedent's estate to her husband, John Smith, Petitioner herein.

Attachment 7a

Improved real property (single family residence) located at 1111 Main St., Santa Ana, CA, and more accurately described as:

"Lot 1 of Tract No. 1000, in the City of Santa Ana, County of Orange, California as per map recorded in Book 100, Page(s) 10-15, Inclusive of Miscellaneous Maps in the Office of the County Recorder of said County."

APN: 123-456-78

This page intentionally left blank.

DE-226

ATTORNEY OR PARTY WITHOUT ATTORNEY (Name, State Bar number, and address):
After recording return to:

John Smith, In Pro Per
1111 Main Street
Santa Ana, CA 92701

TELEPHONE NO.: 555-555-5555
FAX NO. (Optional):
E-MAIL ADDRESS (Optional): johnsmith@email.com
ATTORNEY FOR (Name):

SUPERIOR COURT OF CALIFORNIA, COUNTY OF Orange
STREET ADDRESS: 341 The City Drive South
MAILING ADDRESS:
CITY AND ZIP CODE: Orange, CA 92668
BRANCH NAME: Probate

FOR RECORDER'S USE ONLY

ESTATE OF (Name): Jane Smith, a.k.a. Jane Doe Smith

DECEDENT

CASE NUMBER: A00001

FOR COURT USE ONLY

[X] SPOUSAL [ ] DOMESTIC PARTNER PROPERTY ORDER

1. Date of hearing: 04/15/07   Time: 9:00 AM
   Dept.: L73   Room:

THE COURT FINDS

2. All notices required by law have been given.

3. Decedent died on (date): 02/01/07
   a. [ ] a resident of the California county named above.
   b. [ ] a nonresident of California and left an estate in the county named above.
   c. [ ] intestate. [X] testate.

4. Decedent's [X] surviving spouse [ ] surviving registered domestic partner
   is (name):

THE COURT FURTHER FINDS AND ORDERS

5. a. [X] The property described in Attachment 5a is property passing to the surviving spouse or surviving registered domestic partner named in item 4, and no administration of it is necessary.
   b. [ ] See Attachment 5b for further order(s) respecting transfer of the property to the surviving spouse or surviving registered domestic partner named in item 4.

6. [ ] To protect the interests of the creditors of (business name):
   an unincorporated trade or business, a list of all its known creditors and the amount owed each is on file.
   a. [ ] Within (specify):   days from this date, the surviving spouse or surviving registered domestic partner named in item 4 shall file an undertaking in the amount of $
   b. [ ] See Attachment 6b for further order(s) protecting the interests of creditors of the business.

7. a. [ ] The property described in Attachment 7a is property that belonged to the surviving spouse or surviving registered domestic partner under Family Code section 297.5 and Probate Code sections 100 and 101, and the surviving spouse's or surviving domestic partner's ownership upon decedent's death is confirmed.
   b. [ ] See Attachment 7b for further order(s) respecting transfer of the property to the surviving spouse or surviving domestic partner.

8. [ ] All property described in the *Spousal or Domestic Partner Property Petition* that is not determined to be property passing to the surviving spouse or surviving registered domestic partner under Probate Code section 13500, or confirmed as belonging to the surviving spouse or surviving registered domestic partner under Probate Code sections 100 and 101, shall be subject to administration in the estate of decedent. [ ] All of such property is described in Attachment 8.

9. [ ] Other (specify):

[ ] Continued in Attachment 9.

10. Number of pages attached: 1

Date: _____

_____
JUDICIAL OFFICER

[ ] SIGNATURE FOLLOWS LAST ATTACHMENT   Page 1 of 1

Form Adopted for Mandatory Use
Judicial Council of California
DE-226 [Rev. January 1, 2005]

SPOUSAL OR DOMESTIC PARTNER PROPERTY ORDER
(Probate—Decedents Estates)

Family Code, § 297.5;
Probate Code, § 13656

DE-226 Spousal Property Order
Estate of Jane Smith, a.k.a. Jane Doe Smith, Deceased
Case No. A00001

Attachment 5a

Improved real property (single family residence) located at 1111 Main St., Santa Ana, CA, and more accurately described as:

"Lot 1 of Tract No. 1000, in the City of Santa Ana, County of Orange, California as per map recorded in Book 100, Page(s) 10-15, Inclusive of Miscellaneous Maps in the Office of the County Recorder of said County."

APN: 123-456-78

DECLARATION FOR TRANSFER OF PERSONAL PROPERTY OF DECEDENT UNDER CALIFORNIA PROBATE CODE SECTION 13050 TO 13104

The decedent, JAN JOHNSON (ss# 500-11-111), died on March 2, 2007, in Orange County, CA

At least 40 days have elapsed since the date of the decedent's death as shown in a certified copy of the decedent's death certificate attached to this declaration.

No proceeding is now being conducted in California for the administration of decedent's estate.

The current gross fair market value of the decedent's real and personal property in California, excluding the property described in Section 13040 of the California Probate Code does not exceed one hundred thousand dollars ($100,000).

The property of the decedent that is to be paid, transferred or delivered to the declarant is 400 shares of IBM, common stock.

The declarant is the successor of the decedent (as defined in Section 13006 of the California Probate Code) to the decedent's interest in the described property.

No other person has a superior right to the interest of the decedent in the described property.

The declarant requests that the described property be paid, delivered, or transferred to the declarant.

The declarant herein declares under penalty of perjury under the laws of the State of California that the foregoing is true and correct.

Dated: 6/6/07

Les More
LES MORE

This page intentionally left blank.

DE-305

ATTORNEY OR PARTY WITHOUT ATTORNEY *(Name, state bar number, and address):*	
After recording return to: **John Smith, In Pro Per**	

TELEPHONE NO.: **555 555-5555**
FAX NO. *(Optional):* **555 555-5556**
E-MAIL ADDRESS *(Optional):* **smith@email.com**
ATTORNEY FOR *(Name):* **Joseph Law**

SUPERIOR COURT OF CALIFORNIA, COUNTY OF **Orange**
STREET ADDRESS: **341 The City Drive South**
MAILING ADDRESS:
CITY AND ZIP CODE: **Orange, CA 92668**
BRANCH NAME: **Probate**

MATTER OF *(Name):*

Jane Doe, a.k.a. Jane Doe Buck
                                                    DECEDENT

FOR RECORDER'S USE ONLY

AFFIDAVIT RE REAL PROPERTY OF SMALL VALUE
($20,000 or Less)

CASE NUMBER:
A-00001

FOR COURT USE ONLY

1. Decedent *(name):* **Jane Doe, a.k.a. Jane Doe Buck**
   died on *(date):* **01/01/07**
2. Decedent died at *(city, state):* **Los Angeles, Ca**
3. At least **six months** have elapsed since the date of death of decedent as shown in the certified copy of decedent's death certificate attached to this affidavit. *(Attach a certified copy of decedent's death certificate.)*
4. a. ☑ Decedent was domiciled in this county at the time of death.
   b. ☐ Decedent was **not** domiciled in California at the time of death. Decedent died owning real property in this county.
5. a. The following is a **legal description** of decedent's real property claimed by the declarants *(copy description from deed or other legal instrument):*
   ☐ described in an attachment labeled Attachment 5a.

   Lot 1 of Tract 100 in the County of Orange, as per map recorded in Book 12 Page 15 Orange County Records.
   APN: 545-49-2212

   Commonly known as 122 Iris, Santa Ana, Ca

   b. Decedent's interest in this real property is as follows *(specify):*
   100%

6. Each declarant is a successor of decedent (as defined in Probate Code section 13006) and a successor to decedent's interest in the real property described in item 5a, and no other person has a superior right, because each declarant is
   a. ☑ **(will)** a beneficiary who succeeded to the property under decedent's will. *(Attach a copy of the will.)*
   b. ☐ **(no will)** a person who succeeded to the property under Probate Code sections 6401 and 6402.
7. Names and addresses of each guardian or conservator of decedent's estate at date of death
   ☐ none   ☐ are as follows* *(specify):*

8. The **gross value** of all real property in decedent's estate located in California as shown by the *Inventory and Appraisal*, excluding the real property described in Probate Code section 13050 (joint tenancy, property passing to decedent's spouse, etc.), does not exceed $20,000.

9. An *Inventory and Appraisal* of decedent's **real property** in California is attached. The *Inventory and Appraisal* was made by a probate referee appointed for the county in which the property is located. *(You may use Judicial Council form DE-160.)*
10. No proceeding is now being or has been conducted in California for administration of decedent's estate.

* You must have a copy of this affidavit with attachments personally served or mailed to each person named in item 7.

Page 1 of 2

Form Approved for Mandatory Use
Judicial Council of California
DE-305 [Rev. January 1, 2003]

AFFIDAVIT RE REAL PROPERTY OF SMALL VALUE
(Probate)

Probate Code, § 13200

MATTER OF *(Name):*		CASE NUMBER:
Jane Doe, a.k.a. Jane Doe Buck	DECEDENT	A-00001

11. Funeral expenses, expenses of last illness, and all known unsecured debts of the decedent have been paid. *[NOTE: You may be personally liable for decedent's unsecured debts up to the fair market value of the real property and any income you receive from it.]*

I declare under penalty of perjury under the laws of the State of California that the foregoing is true and correct.

Date: 07/01/07

John Smith

(TYPE OR PRINT NAME)

▶ *John Smith*

(SIGNATURE OF DECLARANT)

Date:

(TYPE OR PRINT NAME)

▶

(SIGNATURE OF DECLARANT)

☐ SIGNATURE OF ADDITIONAL DECLARANTS ATTACHED

NOTARY ACKNOWLEDGMENTS *(NOTE: No notary acknowledgment may be affixed as a rider (small strip) to this page. If additional notary acknowledgments are required, they must be attached as 8-1/2- by 11-inch pages.)*

STATE OF CALIFORNIA, COUNTY OF *(specify):* Orange

On *(date):* 07/01/07 , before me *(name and title):* Nancy Haley, Notary Public
personally appeared *(name):*

personally known to me (or proved to me on the basis of satisfactory evidence) to be the person whose name is subscribed to the within instrument and acknowledged to me that he or she executed the instrument in his or her authorized capacity, and that by his or her signature on the instrument the person, or the entity upon behalf of which the person acted, executed the instrument.
WITNESS my hand and official seal.

(NOTARY SEAL)

(SIGNATURE OF NOTARY PUBLIC)

STATE OF CALIFORNIA, COUNTY OF *(specify):*
On *(date):* , before me *(name and title):*
personally appeared *(names):*

personally known to me (or proved to me on the basis of satisfactory evidence) to be the persons whose names are subscribed to the within instrument and acknowledged to me that they executed the instrument in their authorized capacities, and that by their signatures on the instrument the persons, or the entity or entities upon behalf of which the persons acted, executed the instrument.
WITNESS my hand and official seal.

(NOTARY SEAL)

(SIGNATURE OF NOTARY PUBLIC)

(SEAL)

CLERK'S CERTIFICATE

I certify that the foregoing, including any attached notary acknowledgments and any attached legal description of the property (but excluding other attachments), is a true and correct copy of the original affidavit on file in my office. *(Certified copies of this affidavit do not include the (1) death certificate, (2) will, or (3) inventory and appraisal. See Probate Code section 13202.)*

Date: Clerk, by _____ , Deputy

AFFIDAVIT RE REAL PROPERTY OF SMALL VALUE
(Probate)

DE-310

ATTORNEY OR PARTY WITHOUT ATTORNEY (Name, state bar number, and address):	TELEPHONE AND FAX NOS.:	FOR COURT USE ONLY

ATTORNEY OR PARTY WITHOUT ATTORNEY (Name, state bar number, and address):   TELEPHONE AND FAX NOS.:
555-431-1234

John Slow, In Pro Per
111 Maple St.
Los Angeles, CA 90940

ATTORNEY FOR (Name):

SUPERIOR COURT OF CALIFORNIA, COUNTY OF ORANGE
STREET ADDRESS: 341 The City Drive South
MAILING ADDRESS:
CITY AND ZIP CODE: Orange, CA 92668
BRANCH NAME: Probate

MATTER OF (Name): Jan Quick

                                                                                    DECEDENT

PETITION TO DETERMINE SUCCESSION TO REAL PROPERTY (Estates $100,000 or Less) ☐ And Personal Property	CASE NUMBER: A-00001
	HEARING DATE:
	DEPT.: TIME:

1. **Petitioner** (name of each person claiming an interest): John Slow

   requests a determination that the real property ☐ and personal property described in item 11 is property passing to petitioner and that no administration of decedent's estate is necessary.

2. Decedent (name): Jan Quick
   a. Date of death: 1/1/07
   b. Place of death (city, state): Los Angeles, Ca.

3. At least 40 days have elapsed since the date of decedent's death.

4. a. [X] Decedent was a resident of this county at the time of death.
   b. ☐ Decedent was **not** a resident of California at the time of death. Decedent died owning property in this county.

5. Decedent died ☐ intestate [X] testate and a copy of the will and any codicil is affixed as Attachment 5 or 12a.

6. a. [X] No proceeding for the administration of decedent's estate is being conducted or has been conducted in California.
   b. ☐ Decedent's personal representative's consent to use the procedure provided by Probate Code section 13150 et seq. is attached as Attachment 6b.

7. Proceedings for the administration of decedent's estate in another jurisdiction
   a. [X] have **not** been commenced.
   b. ☐ have been commenced ☐ and completed.
      (Specify state, county, court, and case number):

8. The **gross value** of all real and personal property in decedent's estate located in California as shown by the *Inventory and Appraisal* attached to this petition, excluding the property described in Probate Code section 13050 (joint tenancy, property passing to decedent's spouse, etc.), does not exceed $100,000. (Attach an Inventory and Appraisal (form DE-160) as Attachment 8.)

9. a. The decedent is survived by (check at least one box in each of items (1) - (3))
   (1) ☐ spouse [X] no spouse as follows: ☐ divorced or never married [X] spouse deceased
   (2) [X] child as follows: [X] natural or adopted ☐ natural adopted by a third party ☐ no child
   (3) ☐ issue of a predeceased child [X] no issue of a predeceased child
   b. Decedent ☐ is [X] is not survived by a stepchild or foster child or children who would have been adopted by decedent but for a legal barrier. (See Prob. Code, § 6454.)

10. (Complete if decedent was survived by (1) a spouse but no issue (only a or b apply); or (2) no spouse or issue. Check the **first** box that applies.)
    a. ☐ Decedent is survived by a parent or parents who are listed in item 14.
    b. ☐ Decedent is survived by a brother, sister, or issue of a deceased brother or sister, all of whom are listed in item 14.
    c. ☐ Decedent is survived by other heirs under Probate Code section 6400 et seq., all of whom also listed in item 14.
    d. ☐ Decedent is survived by no known next of kin.

11. Attachment 11 contains (1) the **legal description** of decedent's real property and its Assessor's Parcel Number (APN)
    ☐ and personal property in California passing to petitioner and (2) decedent's interest in the property. (Attach the legal description of the real and personal property and state decedent's interest.)

(Continued on reverse)

Form Approved by the Judicial Council of California DE-310 [Rev. January 1, 1998]	**PETITION TO DETERMINE SUCCESSION TO REAL PROPERTY** (Probate)	Probate Code, § 13151

MATTER OF *(Name)*: JAN QUICK	CASE NUMBER:
DECEDENT	A-00001

12. Each petitioner is a successor of decedent (as defined in Probate Code section 13006) and a successor to decedent's interest in the real property ☐ and personal property ☐ described in item 11 because each petitioner is

    a. ☒ **(will)** a beneficiary who succeeded to the property under decedent's will.[1]

    b. ☐ **(no will)** a person who succeeded to the property under Probate Code sections 6401 and 6402.

13. The specific property interest claimed by each petitioner in the real property ☒ and personal property ☐ described in item 11
    ☒ is stated in Attachment 13   ☐ is as follows *(specify)*:

14. The names, relationships, ages, and residence or mailing addresses so far as known to or reasonably ascertainable by petitioner of (1) all persons named or checked in items 1, 9, and 10, (2) all other heirs of decedent, and (3) all devisees of decedent (persons designated in the will to receive any property)
    ☒ are listed below ☐ are listed in Attachment 14.

Name and relationship	Age	Residence or mailing address
John Slow	Adult	2 Main Street, Old City, Ca.

15. The names and addresses of all persons named as executors in decedent's will
    ☐ are listed below ☒ are listed in Attachment 15 ☐ none named ☐ no will.

16. ☐ Petitioner is the trustee of a trust that is a devisee under decedent's will. The names and addresses of all persons interested in the trust, as determined in cases of future interests under paragraphs (1), (2), or (3) of subdivision (a) of Probate Code section 15804 are listed in Attachment 16.

17. ☐ Decedent's estate was under a ☐ guardianship ☐ conservatorship at decedent's death. The names and addresses of all persons serving as guardian or conservator ☐ are listed below ☐ are listed in Attachment 17.

18. Number of pages attached: 5

Date:

▶ _____
              (SIGNATURE OF ATTORNEY*)

* (Signature of all petitioners also required (Prob. Code, § 1020).)

I declare under penalty of perjury under the laws of the State of California that the foregoing is true and correct.

Date: 2/1/07

John Slow

....
      (TYPE OR PRINT NAME)

▶ *John Slow* _____
        (SIGNATURE OF PETITIONER[2])

▶ _____
        (SIGNATURE OF PETITIONER[2])

....
      (TYPE OR PRINT NAME)

[1] See Probate Code section 13152(c) for the requirement that a copy of the will be attached in certain instances. If required, include as Attachment 5 or 12a.
[2] Each person named in item 1 must sign.

DE-310 [Rev. January 1, 1998]

PETITION TO DETERMINE SUCCESSION TO REAL PROPERTY
(Probate)

Page two

Last Will and Testament

OF

JAN QUICK

I, JAN QUICK, a resident of Orange County, California, do make, publish and declare this to be my Last Will and Testament, and I hereby expressly revoke all other wills, codicils and testamentary writings heretofore made by me.

FIRST: I declare that I am a widow. I have two children, JOHN SLOW and LILA JONES, both adults. I have no deceased children.

SECOND: I direct that all my just debts (excluding debts barred by the statute of limitations) and funeral expenses be paid as soon as practicable after my death.

THIRD: I devise to my son, JOHN SLOW, all of my estate, real, personal and mixed, or whatsoever kind or character and wheresoever situated, of which I die possessed, or to which I may in any manner be entitled.

FOURTH: I have intentionally and with full knowledge omitted to provide for my ancestors, relatives and heirs living at the time of my demise, except for such provisions as are made specifically herein.

If any person who is or claims under or through a beneficiary of this Will, or if any person who would be entitled to share in my estate if I died intestate, should in any manner whatsoever directly or indirectly attack, contest or oppose this Will, seek to impair or invalidate any provision hereof, or conspire or cooperate with anyone attempting to do any of the actions or things aforesaid, then I hereby specifically disinherit each such person and any bequest, devise, share or interest in my estate otherwise given to each such person under this Will, or to which each such person might be entitled by law, is hereby revoked and shall pass and be distributed as though

Estate of Jan Quick
Attachment 5

each such person had predeceased me leaving no issue or heirs whatsoever.

FIFTH: I nominate and appoint my son, JOHN SLOW, as Executor of this my Last Will and Testament. If he should refuse or by reason of death, disability or other incapacity be unable to act, then I nominate and appoint ALICE QUICK as Executor.

I authorize my Executor(s) to sell, at either public or private sale, encumber or lease any property belonging to my estate, either with or without notice, subject to such confirmation as may be required by law, and to hold, manage and operate any such property.

IN WITNESS WHEREOF, I have hereunto set my hand this 1st day of December, 1998, at Fullerton, California.

Jan Quick
_____
JAN QUICK

The foregoing instrument, consisting of two (2) pages, including the page on which this attestation clause is completed and signed, was at the date hereof by JAN QUICK signed as and declared to be her Will, in the presence of us who, at her request and in her presence, and in the presence of each other, have subscribed our names as witnesses thereto. Each of us observed the signing of this Will by JAN QUICK and by each other subscribing witnesses and knows that each signature is the true signature of the person whose name was signed.

Each of us is now an adult and a competent witness and resides at the address set forth after his or her name.

We are acquainted with JAN QUICK. At this time, she is over the age of eighteen (18) years, and to the best of our knowledge, she is of sound mind and is not acting under duress, menace, fraud, misrepresentation, or undue influence.

We declare under penalty of perjury that the foregoing is true and correct.

Executed on December 1, 1998, at Fullerton, California.

*Sam Sawit*_____ Residing at 123 Elm St._____

Santa Ana, CA 92804_____

*Betty Dunit*_____ Residing at _____

_____

Estate of Jan Quick
Attachment 5

1 | Estate of Jack Quick, deceased
Case No. A-00001
2 | Petition to Determine Succession to Real Property

3

4 | Attachment 11

5 | Improved real property (single family residence) located at 4
Carrotwood, Irvine, CA, and more accurately described as:
6

    "Lot 1 of Tract 1 as per Map recorded in Book 1, Page 1 of
7 | Maps in the office of the County Recorder of the County of Orange,
State of California."
8

APN: 4848-011-0001
9

10 | Decedent's interest is 100%

11

12 | Attachment 12

13 | Petitioner John Slow is claiming a 100% interest.

14

15 | Attachment 15

16 | Alice Quick
222 Alder Rd.
17 | Fountain Valley, CA 92728

18

19

20

21

22

23

24

25

26

27

28

This page intentionally left blank.

DE-315

ATTORNEY OR PARTY WITHOUT ATTORNEY *(Name, state bar number, and address):*

After recording return to:

John Slow, In Pro Per

111 Maple St. Los Angeles, Ca 90940

TELEPHONE NO.: 555 555-5555
FAX NO. *(Optional)*:

E-MAIL ADDRESS *(Optional)*:

ATTORNEY FOR *(Name)*:

SUPERIOR COURT OF CALIFORNIA, COUNTY OF Orange

STREET ADDRESS: 341 The City Drive South

MAILING ADDRESS:

CITY AND ZIP CODE: Orange, CA 92668

BRANCH NAME: Probate

MATTER OF *(Name)*:

Jan Quick

DECEDENT

FOR RECORDER'S USE ONLY

CASE NUMBER: A-00001

ORDER DETERMINING SUCCESSION TO REAL PROPERTY
(Estates $100,000 or Less)

☐ **And Personal Property**

FOR COURT USE ONLY

1. Date of hearing: 01/01/07   Time: 9:00 AM
   Dept./Room: 73   Judge: Jonnie Bench

THE COURT FINDS

2. All notices required by law have been given.
3. Decedent died on *(date)*: 01/01/07
   a. ☑ a resident of the California county named above.
   b. ☐ a nonresident of California and left an estate in the county named above.
   c. ☐ intestate ☑ testate.
4. At least 40 days have elapsed since the date of decedent's death.
5. a. ☑ No proceeding for the administration of decedent's estate is being conducted
      or has been conducted in California.
   b. ☐ Decedent's personal representative has filed a consent to use the procedure
      provided in Probate Code section 13150 et seq.
6. The gross value of decedent's real and personal property in California, excluding
   property described in Probate Code section 13050, does not exceed $100,000.
7. Each petitioner is a successor of decedent (as defined in Probate Code section 13006) and a successor to decedent's interest in
   the real ☐ and personal property described in item 9a because each petitioner is
   a. ☑ **(will)** a beneficiary who succeeded to the property under decedent's will.
   b. ☐ **(no will)** a person who succeeded to the property under Probate Code sections 6401 and 6402.

THE COURT FURTHER FINDS AND ORDERS

8. No administration of decedent's estate is necessary in California.
9. a. The following described real ☐ and personal property is property of decedent passing to each petitioner *(give legal
      description of real property)*: ☐ described in Attachment 9a.
   Improved Real property (single family residence) located at 4 carrotwood, Irvine,
   Ca., and more accurately described as:
   "Lot 1 of Tract 1 as per map recorded in Book 1 Page 1 on Maps in the office of the
   County Recorder of the County of Orange, state of California. APN: 4848-011-0001
   b. Each petitioner's **name** and specific property interest ☐ is stated in Attachment 9b ☑ is as follows *(specify)*:

   John Slow - 100%

10. ☐ Other *(specify)*:

Date:

_____
JUDGE OF THE SUPERIOR COURT

11. Number of pages attached: _0_

☐ SIGNATURE FOLLOWS LAST ATTACHMENT

Page 1 of 1

Form Adopted for Mandatory Use
Judicial Council of California
DE-315 [Rev. January 1, 2003]

ORDER DETERMINING SUCCESSION
TO REAL PROPERTY
(Probate)

Probate Code, § 13154

This page intentionally left blank.

DE-111

ATTORNEY OR PARTY WITHOUT ATTORNEY *(Name, State Bar number, and address)*:	FOR COURT USE ONLY
John Smith , In Pro Per 1111 Main Sreet Santa Ana, CA 92701 TELEPHONE NO.: (555) 555-5555 FAX NO. *(Optional)* E-MAIL ADDRESS *(Optional)*: johnsmith@email.com ATTORNEY FOR *(Name)*:	

SUPERIOR COURT OF CALIFORNIA, COUNTY OF Orange
STREET ADDRESS: 341 The City Drive South
MAILING ADDRESS:
CITY AND ZIP CODE: Orange, CA 92668
BRANCH NAME: Probate

ESTATE OF *(Name)*:   Jane Smith, a.k.a. Jane Doe Smith

DECEDENT

PETITION FOR [ ] Probate of Will and for Letters Testamentary [ ] Probate of Will and for Letters of Administration with Will Annexed [ ] Letters of Administration [ ] Letters of Special Administration [ ] with general powers [X] Authorization to Administer Under the Independent Administration of Estates Act [ ] with limited authority	CASE NUMBER: A-00001
	HEARING DATE: 04/15/07
	DEPT.: L73 — TIME: 9:00 AM

1. Publication will be in *(specify name of newspaper)*: Local Times Newspaper
   a. [X] Publication requested.
   b. [ ] Publication to be arranged.
2. **Petitioner** *(name each)*: John Smith   **requests that**
   a. [X] decedent's will and codicils, if any, be admitted to probate.
   b. [X] *(name)*:   John Smith
      be appointed
      (1) [X] executor
      (2) [ ] administrator with will annexed
      (3) [ ] administrator
      (4) [ ] special administrator [ ] with general powers
      and Letters issue upon qualification.
   c. [X] full [ ] limited authority   be granted to administer under the Independent Administration of Estates Act.
   d. (1) [ ] bond not be required for the reasons stated in item 4d.
      (2) [X] $ 200,000.00   bond be fixed. The bond will be furnished by an admitted surety insurer or as otherwise provided by law. *(Specify reasons in Attachment 2 if the amount is different from the maximum required by Prob. Code, § 8482.)*
      (3) [ ] $ in deposits in a blocked account be allowed. Receipts will be filed.
      (Specify institution and location):

3. a. **Estimated value of the estate for filing fee purposes** *(Complete in all cases. The estimated value of the estate is the fair market value of the real and personal property of the estate at the date of the decedent's death, without reduction for encumbrances. See Gov. Code, § 26827.)*:
   (1) [ ] Less than $250,000
   (2) [X] At least $250,000 and less than $500,000
   (3) [ ] At least $500,000 and less than $750,000
   (4) [ ] At least $750,000 and less than $1 million
   (5) [ ] At least $1 million and less than $1.5 million
   (6) [ ] At least $1.5 million and less than $2 million
   (7) [ ] At least $2 million and less than $2.5 million
   (8) [ ] At least $2.5 million and less than $3.5 million
   (9) [ ] $ *
   * *(For estates of $3.5 million or more, specify total estimated value of estate.)*
   b. [ ] This petition is not the first petition for appointment of a personal representative with general powers filed in this proceeding. The first petition was filed on *(date)*:

Form Adopted for MandatoryUse
Judicial Council of California
DE-111 [Rev. January 1, 2005]

PETITION FOR PROBATE
(Probate—Decedents Estates)

Probate Code, §§ 8002, 10450,
Government Code, § 26827

ESTATE OF *(Name):* Jane Smith, a.k.a. Jane Doe Smith	CASE NUMBER:
DECEDENT	A-00001

4. a. Decedent died on *(date):* 02/01/07 at *(place):* St. James Hospital

    (1) [X] a resident of the county named above. 100 Medical Center Way Santa Ana, CA 92705

    (2) [ ] a nonresident of California and left an estate in the county named above located at *(specify location permitting publication in the newspaper named in item 1):*

  b. Street address, city, and county of decedent's residence at time of death *(specify):*

  c. **Character and estimated value of the property of the estate** *(complete in all cases):*

    (1) Personal property: $ 40,000.00

    (2) Annual gross income from

        (a) real property: $ 8,000.00

        (b) personal property: $ 2,000.00

    (3) **Subtotal** *(add (1) and (2)):* $ 50,000.00

    (4) Gross fair market value of real property: $ 200,000.00

    (5) (Less) Encumbrances: $(0.00)

    (6) Net value of real property: $ 200,000.00

    (7) **Total** *(add (3) and (6)):* $ 250,000.00

  d. (1) [ ] Will waives bond. [ ] Special administrator is the named executor, and the will waives bond.

    (2) [ ] All beneficiaries are adults and have waived bond, and the will does not require a bond. *(Affix waiver as Attachment 4d(2).)*

    (3) [ ] All heirs at law are adults and have waived bond. *(Affix waiver as Attachment 4d(3).)*

    (4) [ ] Sole personal representative is a corporate fiduciary or an exempt government agency.

  e. (1) [ ] Decedent died intestate.

    (2) [X] Copy of decedent's will dated: [ ] codicil dated *(specify for each):*

         are affixed as Attachment 4e(2).

    (Include typed copies of handwritten documents and English translations of foreign-language documents.)

    [X] The will and all codicils are self-proving (Prob. Code, § 8220).

  f. **Appointment of personal representative** *(check all applicable boxes):*

    (1) Appointment of executor or administrator with will annexed:

        (a) [X] Proposed executor is named as executor in the will and consents to act.

        (b) [ ] No executor is named in the will.

        (c) [ ] Proposed personal representative is a nominee of a person entitled to Letters. *(Affix nomination as Attachment 4f(1)(c).)*

        (d) [ ] Other named executors will not act because of [ ] death [ ] declination [ ] other reasons *(specify):*

        [ ] Continued in Attachment 4f(1)(d).

    (2) Appointment of administrator:

        (a) [ ] Petitioner is a person entitled to Letters. *(If necessary, explain priority in Attachment 4f(2)(a).)*

        (b) [ ] Petitioner is a nominee of a person entitled to Letters. *(Affix nomination as Attachment 4f(2)(b).)*

        (c) [ ] Petitioner is related to the decedent as *(specify):*

    (3) [ ] Appointment of special administrator requested. *(Specify grounds and requested powers in Attachment 4f(3).)*

PETITION FOR PROBATE
(Probate—Decedents Estates)

ESTATE OF (Name): Jane Smith, a.k.a. Jane Doe Smith	CASE NUMBER:
DECEDENT	A-00001

4. g. Proposed personal representative is a
   - [X] resident of California.
   - [ ] nonresident of California (specify permanent address):

   - [X] resident of the United States.
   - [ ] nonresident of the United States.

5. [X] Decedent's will does not preclude administration of this estate under the Independent Administration of Estates Act.

6. a. Decedent is survived by (check items (1) or (2), and (3) or (4), and (5) or (6), and (7) or (8))
   - (1) [ ] spouse.
   - (2) [ ] no spouse as follows:
     - (a) [X] divorced or never married.
     - (b) [ ] spouse deceased.
   - (3) [ ] registered domestic partner.
   - (4) [X] no registered domestic partner.
     - (See Fam. Code, § 297.5(c); Prob. Code, §§ 37(b), 6401(c), and 6402.)
   - (5) [X] child as follows:
     - (a) [X] natural or adopted.
     - (b) [ ] natural adopted by a third party.
   - (6) [ ] no child.
   - (7) [ ] issue of a predeceased child.
   - (8) [X] no issue of a predeceased child.

   b. Decedent [ ] is [X] is not survived by a stepchild or foster child or children who would have been adopted by decedent but for a legal barrier. (See Prob. Code, § 6454.)

7. (Complete if decedent is survived by (1) a spouse or registered domestic partner but no issue (only a or b apply), or (2) no spouse, registered domestic partner, or issue. (Check the **first** box that applies):
   - a. [ ] Decedent is survived by a parent or parents who are listed in item 9.
   - b. [ ] Decedent is survived by issue of deceased parents, all of whom are listed in item 9.
   - c. [ ] Decedent is survived by a grandparent or grandparents who are listed in item 9.
   - d. [ ] Decedent is survived by issue of grandparents, all of whom are listed in item 9.
   - e. [ ] Decedent is survived by issue of a predeceased spouse, all of whom are listed in item 9.
   - f. [ ] Decedent is survived by next of kin, all of whom are listed in item 9.
   - g. [ ] Decedent is survived by parents of a predeceased spouse or issue of those parents, if both are predeceased, all of whom are listed in item 9.
   - h. [ ] Decedent is survived by no known next of kin.

8. (Complete only if no spouse or issue survived decedent.)
   - a. [ ] Decedent had no predeceased spouse.
   - b. [ ] Decedent had a predeceased spouse who
     - (1) [ ] died not more than 15 years before decedent and who owned an interest in **real property** that passed to decedent,
     - (2) [ ] died not more than five years before decedent and who owned **personal property** valued at $10,000 or more that passed to decedent,
       (If you checked (1) or (2), check only the **first** box that applies):
       - (a) [ ] Decedent is survived by issue of a predeceased spouse, all of whom are listed in item 9.
       - (b) [ ] Decedent is survived by a parent or parents of the predeceased spouse who are listed in item 9.
       - (c) [ ] Decedent is survived by issue of a parent of the predeceased spouse, all of whom are listed in item 9.
       - (d) [ ] Decedent is survived by next of kin of the decedent, all of whom are listed in item 9.
       - (e) [ ] Decedent is survived by next of kin of the predeceased spouse, all of whom are listed in item 9.
     - (3) [ ] neither (1) nor (2) apply.

PETITION FOR PROBATE
(Probate—Decedents Estates)

ESTATE OF *(Name):*		CASE NUMBER:
	DECEDENT	

9. Listed below are the names, relationships to decedent, ages, and addresses, so far as known to or reasonably ascertainable by petitioner, of (1) all persons mentioned in decedent's will or any codicil, whether living or deceased; (2) all persons named or checked in items 2, 6, 7, and 8; and (3) all beneficiaries of a trust named in decedent's will or any codicil in which the trustee and personal representative are the same person.

Name and relationship to decedent	Age	Address
John Smith, Husband	Adult	1111 Main St., Santa Ana, CA 92701
Jimmy Smith, Son	Adult	2222 Swift St., Los Angeles, CA 90189
Jenny Smith, Daughter	Adult	3333 Bay Ct., Newport Beach, CA92660
Jack Jones, Brother	Adult	4444 Mesa Dr., Las Vegas, NV 89191
Jill Jones, Sister	Adult	5555 Camden Pl., Chicago, IL 60605

☐ Continued on Attachment 9.

10. Number of pages attached: _____

Date: 3

_____
(TYPE OR PRINT NAME OF ATTORNEY)

▶ _____
(SIGNATURE OF ATTORNEY)*

* (Signatures of all petitioners are also required. All petitioners must sign, but the petition may be verified by any one of them (Prob. Code, §§ 1020, 1021; Cal Rules of Court, rule 7.103).)

I declare under penalty of perjury under the laws of the State of California that the foregoing is true and correct.

Date: 03/01/07

_John Smith_____
(TYPE OR PRINT NAME OF PETITIONER)

▶ *John Smith*_____
(SIGNATURE OF PETITIONER)

_____
(TYPE OR PRINT NAME OF PETITIONER)

▶ _____
(SIGNATURE OF PETITIONER)

☐ Signatures of additional petitioners follow last attachment.

DE-111 [Rev January 1, 2005]

PETITION FOR PROBATE
(Probate—Decedents Estates)

Page 4 of 4

Last Will and Testament

OF
JANE SMITH

I, JANE SMITH, a resident of Orange County, California, being of sound and disposing mind and memory, and not acting under duress, menace, fraud, or undue influence of any person whomsoever, do make, publish, and declare this to be my Last Will and Testament; and I hereby revoke all other wills, codicils, and testamentary writings heretofore made by me.

FIRST: I declare that I am a married woman and that my spouse's name is JOHN SMITH. We have two children, JIMMY SMITH and JENNY SMITH, both adults. I have no other children living or deceased.

SECOND: I direct that all my just debts (excluding debts barred by the statute of limitations or any other provision of law) and funeral expenses be paid as soon as practicable after my death.

THIRD: I devise to my spouse, JOHN SMITH, provided my spouse survives me by two (2) months, all of my property and estate, real, personal and mixed, of whatsoever kind or character and wheresoever situated of which I die possessed, or to which I may in any manner be entitled.

If my spouse, JOHN SMITH, should predecease me or fail to survive me by two (2) months, I devise all of my personal effects, watches, jewelry, books, pictures, furniture and furnishings and all other articles of personal or household use or ornament to my children who survive me, in equal shares.

If my spouse, JOHN SMITH, should predecease me or fail to survive me by two (2) months, I devise all the rest, residue and remainder to the Trustees under that Declaration of Trust, known as the JOHN AND JANE SMITH TRUST dated January 1, 1996 in which my spouse and I are the original Trustors and the original Trustees, to be added to and commingled with the trust property of that trust and held, managed and distributed as a part of said trust according to the terms of that Declaration of Trust and not as a separate testamentary trust.

If, for any reason, the foregoing disposition to the aforesaid JOHN AND JANE SMITH TRUST should be inoperative or invalid, then all the rest, residue and remainder of my estate as aforesaid, shall go to the Trustees of the aforesaid JOHN AND JANE SMITH TRUST, in trust, to have and to hold upon the uses, trusts, purposes and conditions as provided in the aforesaid JOHN AND JANE SMITH TRUST which provisions are hereby incorporated by reference.

FOURTH: I have intentionally and with full knowledge omitted to provide for my issue, relatives, and heirs living at the time of my demise, except for such provisions as are made specifically herein.

If any person who is or claims under or through a beneficiary of this Will, or if any person who would be entitled to share in my estate if I died intestate, should in any manner whatsoever directly or indirectly attack, contest or oppose this Will, seek to impair or invalidate any provision hereof, or conspire or cooperate with anyone attempting to do any of the actions or things aforesaid, then I hereby specifically disinherit each such person; any devise, share, or interest in my estate otherwise given to each such person under this Will, or to which each such person might be entitled by law, is hereby revoked and shall pass and be distributed as though each such person had predeceased me leaving no issue or heirs whatsoever.

FIFTH: I nominate and appoint my spouse, JOHN SMITH, as Executor of this my Last Will and Testament, to serve without bond. If he should decline, or by reason of death, disability, or other incapacity be unable to act, then I nominate and appoint JIMMY SMITH, as Executor hereunder to serve without bond. If he should be ineligible, decline or, by reason of death, disability or other incapacity, be unable to act, then I nominate and appoint JENNY SMITH as Executor hereunder.

I authorize my Executor to sell, at either public or private sale, encumber, or lease any property belonging to my estate, either with or without notice, subject to such confirmation as may be required by law, and to hold, manage, and operate any such property.

SIXTH: In the event that any provision or provisions of this Will are, or are adjudged to be, for any reason, invalid or unenforceable, I direct that, disregarding such, the remaining provisions hereof shall subsist and be carried into effect.

IN WITNESS WHEREOF, I have hereunto set my hand this 1st day of January, 1996.

Jane Smith
JANE SMITH

The foregoing instrument, consisting of three (3) pages, including the page on which this attestation clause is completed and signed, was at the date hereof by JANE SMITH signed as and declared to be her Will, in the presence of us who, at her request and in her presence, and in the presence of each other, have subscribed our names as witnesses thereto. Each of us observed the signing of this Will by JANE SMITH, and by each other subscribing witnesses and knows that each signature is the true signature of the person whose name was signed.

Each of us is now an adult and a competent witness and resides at the address set forth after his or her name.

We are acquainted with JANE SMITH. At this time, she is over the age of eighteen (18) years, and to the best of our knowledge, she is of sound mind and is not acting under duress, menace, fraud, misrepresentation, or undue influence.

We declare under penalty of perjury that the foregoing is true and correct.

Executed on January 1, 1996 at Santa Ana, California.

Saul Sawit   Residing at   888 Beech Ct.

Fullerton, CA 92541

Betty Duit   Residing at   977 Cherry Dr.

Cherbourg, CA 94301

This page intentionally left blank.

1 John Smith, In Pro Per
   112 Maple St.
2 Los Angeles, CA 90040
   (213) 555-5555
3

4

5

6

7

8   SUPERIOR COURT OF THE STATE OF CALIFORNIA

9 FOR THE COUNTY OF ORANGE, LAMOREAUX JUSTICE CENTER

10

11 The Estate of   )   CASE NO. **A100001**
)
12   **JANE DOE, a.k.a.**   )   SUPPLEMENT TO PETITION
        JANE DOE BUCK,   )   FOR PROBATE
13   )
              Deceased   )   Hearing Date: 04/07/07
14 _____)   Dept: A   Time: 9:00 a.m.

15   Petitioner, **JOHN SMITH**, renders his first supplement to his

16 PETITION FOR PROBATE **OF WILL AND FOR LETTERS TESTAMENTARY (WITH**

17 **FULL AUTHORITY)** as follows:

18   1. The petition is supplemented to add another "also known

19 as" (aka) to the estate name caption, to wit: "JANE DOE BUCK."

20

21   WHEREFORE, Petitioner prays that his Petition for Probate

22 and **for Letters Testamentary with Full Authority** be approved as

23 supplemented hereby and for all other proper relief.

24 Dated **March 3 , 2007.**

25   *John Smith*
                      _____
26   JOHN SMITH

27

28

1

SUPPLEMENT TO PETITION FOR PROBATE

<u>VERIFICATION</u>

STATE OF CALIFORNIA   )
) ss.
COUNTY OF **ORANGE**   )

    I am the petitioner in the above-entitled matter; I have read the foregoing FIRST SUPPLEMENT PETITION FOR PROBATE OF WILL and know the contents thereof; and I certify that the same is true of my own knowledge, except as to those matters which are therein stated upon my information or belief, and as to those matters, I believe it to be true.

    I certify (or declare) under penalty of perjury, under the laws of the State of California, that the foregoing is true and correct.

    Executed at **Laguna Hills, CA, on March** 3 2007

John Smith
JOHN SMITH

DE-121

ATTORNEY OR PARTY WITHOUT ATTORNEY *(Name, State Bar number, and address):*	FOR COURT USE ONLY
John Smith , In Pro Per 1111 Main Sreet Santa Ana, CA 92701 TELEPHONE NO.: (555) 555-5555 FAX NO. *(Optional):* E-MAIL ADDRESS *(Optional):* johnsmith@email.com ATTORNEY FOR *(Name):*	

SUPERIOR COURT OF CALIFORNIA, COUNTY OF Orange
STREET ADDRESS: 341 The City Drive South
MAILING ADDRESS:
CITY AND ZIP CODE: Orange, CA 92668
BRANCH NAME: Probate

ESTATE OF *(Name):* Jane Smith, a.k.a. Jane Doe Smith DECEDENT	
NOTICE OF PETITION TO ADMINISTER ESTATE OF *(Name):* Jane Smith, a.k.a. Jane Doe Smith	CASE NUMBER:

1. To all heirs, beneficiaries, creditors, contingent creditors, and persons who may otherwise be interested in the will or estate, or both, of *(specify all names by which the decedent was known):*

   Jane Smith, a.k.a. Jane Doe Smith

2. A **Petition for Probate** has been filed by *(name of petitioner):* John Smith
   in the Superior Court of California, County of *(specify):* Orange

3. The Petition for Probate requests that *(name):* John Smith
   be appointed as personal representative to administer the estate of the decedent.

4. [X] The petition requests the decedent's will and codicils, if any, be admitted to probate. The will and any codicils are available for examination in the file kept by the court.

5. [X] The petition requests authority to administer the estate under the Independent Administration of Estates Act. (This authority will allow the personal representative to take many actions without obtaining court approval. Before taking certain very important actions, however, the personal representative will be required to give notice to interested persons unless they have waived notice or consented to the proposed action.) The independent administration authority will be granted unless an interested person files an objection to the petition and shows good cause why the court should not grant the authority.

6. **A hearing on the petition will be held in this court as follows:**

   a. Date: 04/15/07   Time: 9:00 AM   Dept.: L73   Room:

   b. Address of court: [X] same as noted above   [ ] other *(specify):*

7. **If you object** to the granting of the petition, you should appear at the hearing and state your objections or file written objections with the court before the hearing. Your appearance may be in person or by your attorney.

8. **If you are a creditor or a contingent creditor of the decedent,** you must file your claim with the court and mail a copy to the personal representative appointed by the court within four months from the date of first issuance of letters as provided in Probate Code section 9100. The time for filing claims will not expire before four months from the hearing date noticed above.

9. **You may examine the file kept by the court.** If you are a person interested in the estate, you may file with the court a *Request for Special Notice* (form DE-154) of the filing of an inventory and appraisal of estate assets or of any petition or account as provided in Probate Code section 1250. A *Request for Special Notice* form is available from the court clerk.

10. [X] Petitioner   [ ] Attorney for petitioner *(name):*

    (Address): 1111 Main Sreet
    Santa Ana, CA 92701

    (Telephone): (555) 555-5555

NOTE: If this notice is published, print the caption, beginning with the words NOTICE OF PETITION TO ADMINISTER ESTATE, and do not print the information from the form above the caption. The caption and the decedent's name must be printed in at least 8-point type and the text in at least 7-point type. Print the case number as part of the caption. Print items preceded by a box only if the box is checked. Do not print the italicized instructions in parentheses, the paragraph numbers, the mailing information, or the material on page 2.

Page 1 of 2

NOTICE OF PETITION TO ADMINISTER ESTATE
(Probate—Decedents' Estates)

DE-121

ESTATE OF *(Name):*	CASE NUMBER
Jane Smith, a.k.a. Jane Doe Smith DECEDENT	A00001

PROOF OF SERVICE BY MAIL

1. I am over the age of 18 and not a party to this cause. I am a resident of or employed in the county where the mailing occurred.

2. My residence or business address is *(specify):* **Willie Witness**
   6666 Wilson Ave.
   Santa Ana, CA 92701

3. I served the foregoing *Notice of Petition to Administer Estate* on each person named below by enclosing a copy in an envelope addressed as shown below **AND**

   a. [X] **depositing** the sealed envelope with the United States Postal Service on the date and at the place shown in item 4, with the postage fully prepaid.

   b. [ ] **placing** the envelope for collection and mailing on the date and at the place shown in item 4 following our ordinary business practices. I am readily familiar with this business's practice for collecting and processing correspondence for mailing. On the same day that correspondence is placed for collection and mailing, it is deposited in the ordinary course of business with the United States Postal Service, in a sealed envelope with postage fully prepaid.

4. a. Date mailed: **03/01/07**   b. Place mailed *(city, state):* **Santa Ana, CA**

5. [ ] I served, with the *Notice of Petition to Administer Estate,* a copy of the petition or other document referred to in the notice.

I declare under penalty of perjury under the laws of the State of California that the foregoing is true and correct.

Date: **03/01/07**

Willie Witness	▶ *Willie Witness*
(TYPE OR PRINT NAME OF PERSON COMPLETING THIS FORM)	(SIGNATURE OF PERSON COMPLETING THIS FORM)

NAME AND ADDRESS OF EACH PERSON TO WHOM NOTICE WAS MAILED

	Name of person served	Address *(number, street, city, state, and zip code)*
1.	John Smith, Husband	1111 Main St., Santa Ana, CA 92701
2.	Jimmy Smith, Son	2222 Swift St., Los Angeles, CA 90189
3.	Jenny Smith, Daughter	3333 Bay Ct., Newport Beach, CA92660
4.	Jack Jones, Brother	4444 Mesa Dr., Las Vegas, NV 89191
5.	Jill Jones, Sister	5555 Camden Pl., Chicago, IL 60605
6.		

[ ] Continued on an attachment. *(You may use form DE-121(MA) to show additional persons served.)*

Assistive listening systems, computer-assisted real-time captioning, or sign language interpreter services are available upon request if at least 5 days notice is provided. Contact the clerk's office for *Request for Accommodations by Persons With Disabilities and Order* (form MC-410). (Civil Code section 54.8.)

DE-147

ATTORNEY OR PARTY WITHOUT ATTORNEY *(Name, state bar number, and address):*	FOR COURT USE ONLY
John Smith, In Pro Per 1111 First St., Los Angeles, Ca 90941 TELEPHONE NO.: 555 555-5555 FAX NO. *(Optional):* E–MAIL ADDRESS *(Optional):* ATTORNEY FOR *(Name):*	

SUPERIOR COURT OF CALIFORNIA, COUNTY OF Orange
STREET ADDRESS: 341 The City Drive South
MAILING ADDRESS:
CITY AND ZIP CODE: Orange, CA 92668
BRANCH NAME: Probate

ESTATE OF *(Name):*
　　Jane Doe, a.k.a. Jane Doe Buck　　　　DECEDENT

DUTIES AND LIABILITIES OF PERSONAL REPRESENTATIVE and Acknowledgment of Receipt	CASE NUMBER: A-00001

DUTIES AND LIABILITIES OF PERSONAL REPRESENTATIVE

When the court appoints you as personal representative of an estate, you become an officer of the court and assume certain duties and obligations. An attorney is best qualified to advise you about these matters. You should understand the following:

1. MANAGING THE ESTATE'S ASSETS

a. Prudent investments
You must manage the estate assets with the care of a prudent person dealing with someone else's property. This means that you must be cautious and may not make any speculative investments.

b. Keep estate assets separate
You must keep the money and property in this estate separate from anyone else's, including your own. When you open a bank account for the estate, the account name must indicate that it is an estate account and not your personal account. Never deposit estate funds in your personal account or otherwise mix them with your or anyone else's property. Securities in the estate must also be held in a name that shows they are estate property and not your personal property.

c. Interest-bearing accounts and other investments
Except for checking accounts intended for ordinary administration expenses, estate accounts must earn interest. You may deposit estate funds in insured accounts in financial institutions, but you should consult with an attorney before making other kinds of investments.

d. Other restrictions
There are many other restrictions on your authority to deal with estate property. You should not spend any of the estate's money unless you have received permission from the court or have been advised to do so by an attorney. You may reimburse yourself for official court costs paid by you to the county clerk and for the premium on your bond. Without prior order of the court, you may not pay fees to yourself or to your attorney, if you have one. If you do not obtain the court's permission when it is required, you may be removed as personal representative or you may be required to reimburse the estate from your own personal funds, or both. You should consult with an attorney concerning the legal requirements affecting sales, leases, mortgages, and investments of estate property.

2. INVENTORY OF ESTATE PROPERTY

a. Locate the estate's property
You must attempt to locate and take possession of all the decedent's property to be administered in the estate.

b. Determine the value of the property
You must arrange to have a court-appointed referee determine the value of the property unless the appointment is waived by the court. You, rather than the referee, must determine the value of certain "cash items." An attorney can advise you about how to do this.

c. File an inventory and appraisal
Within four months after Letters are first issued to you as personal representative, you must file with the court an inventory and appraisal of all the assets in the estate.

Page 1 of 2

Form Adopted for Mandatory Use
Judicial Council of California
DE-147 [Rev. January 1, 2002]

DUTIES AND LIABILITIES OF PERSONAL REPRESENTATIVE
(Probate)

Probate Code, § 8404

ESTATE OF *(Name)*:		CASE NUMBER:
Jane Doe, a.k.a. Jane Doe Buck	DECEDENT	A-00001

d. File a change of ownership

At the time you file the inventory and appraisal, you must also file a change of ownership statement with the county recorder or assessor in each county where the decedent owned real property at the time of death, as provided in section 480 of the California Revenue and Taxation Code.

3. NOTICE TO CREDITORS

You must mail a notice of administration to each known creditor of the decedent within four months after your appointment as personal representative. If the decedent received Medi-Cal assistance, you must notify the State Director of Health Services within 90 days after appointment.

4. INSURANCE

You should determine that there is appropriate and adequate insurance covering the assets and risks of the estate. Maintain the insurance in force during the entire period of the administration.

5. RECORD KEEPING

a. Keep accounts

You must keep complete and accurate records of each financial transaction affecting the estate. You will have to prepare an account of all money and property you have received, what you have spent, and the date of each transaction. You must describe in detail what you have left after the payment of expenses.

b. Court review

Your account will be reviewed by the court. Save your receipts because the court may ask to review them. If you do not file your accounts as required, the court will order you to do so. You may be removed as personal representative if you fail to comply.

6. CONSULTING AN ATTORNEY

If you have an attorney, you should cooperate with the attorney at all times. You and your attorney are responsible for completing the estate administration as promptly as possible. **When in doubt, contact your attorney.**

NOTICE: **1. This statement of duties and liabilities is a summary and is not a complete statement of the law. Your conduct as a personal representative is governed by the law itself and not by this summary.**

2. If you fail to perform your duties or to meet the deadlines, the court may reduce your compensation, remove you from office, and impose other sanctions.

ACKNOWLEDGMENT OF RECEIPT

1. I have petitioned the court to be appointed as a personal representative.

2. My address and telephone number are *(specify)*:

   111 Maple St., Los Angeles, Ca 90940

3. I acknowledge that I have received a copy of this statement of the duties and liabilities of the office of personal representative.

Date: 05/16/07

John Smith	▶ *John Smith*
(TYPE OR PRINT NAME)	(SIGNATURE OF PETITIONER)

Date:

	▶
(TYPE OR PRINT NAME)	(SIGNATURE OF PETITIONER)

CONFIDENTIAL INFORMATION: If required to do so by local court rule, you must provide your date of birth and driver's license number on supplemental Form DE-147S. (Prob. Code, § 8404(b).)

DE-147 [Rev. January 1, 2002]

DUTIES AND LIABILITIES OF PERSONAL REPRESENTATIVE
(Probate)

CONFIDENTIAL

DE-147S

ESTATE OF *(Name)*:	CASE NUMBER:
Jane Doe, a.k.a. Jane Doe Buck DECEDENT	A-00001

CONFIDENTIAL STATEMENT OF BIRTH DATE
AND DRIVER'S LICENSE NUMBER

(Supplement to *Duties and Liabilities of Personal Representative* (Form DE-147))

*(NOTE: This supplement is to be used if the court by local rule requires the personal representative to provide a birth date and driver's license number. Do **not** attach this supplement to Form DE-147.)*

This separate *Confidential Statement of Birth Date and Driver's License Number* contains confidential information relating to the personal representative in the case referenced above. This supplement shall be kept separate from the *Duties and Liabilities of Personal Representative* filed in this case and shall not be a public record.

INFORMATION ON THE PERSONAL REPRESENTATIVE:

1. Name: John Smith

2. Date of birth: 01/01/1960

3. Driver's license number: 111111   State: CA

TO COURT CLERK:
THIS STATEMENT IS **CONFIDENTIAL**. DO NOT FILE
THIS CONFIDENTIAL STATEMENT IN A PUBLIC COURT FILE.

Form Adopted for Mandatory Use
Judicial Council of California
DE-147S [New January 1, 2001]

**CONFIDENTIAL SUPPLEMENT TO DUTIES AND
LIABILITIES OF PERSONAL REPRESENTATIVE**
(Probate)

Probate Code, § 8404

This page intentionally left blank.

DE-131

ATTORNEY OR PARTY WITHOUT ATTORNEY *(Name, state bar number, and address)* :	TELEPHONE AND FAX NOS.:	*FOR COURT USE ONLY*
John Smith, In Pro Per 111 Maple Street Los Angeles, CA 90940	555-431-1234	

ATTORNEY FOR *(Name)*:

SUPERIOR COURT OF CALIFORNIA, COUNTY OF Orange
STREET ADDRESS: 341 The City Drive South
MAILING ADDRESS:
CITY AND ZIP CODE: Orange, CA 92668
BRANCH NAME: Probate

ESTATE OF *(Name)*:
    Jane Doe, aka Jane Doe Buck

                                    DECEDENT

PROOF OF SUBSCRIBING WITNESS	CASE NUMBER: A-00001

1. I am one of the attesting witnesses to the instrument of which Attachment 1 is a photographic copy. I have examined Attachment 1 and my signature is on it.

   a. [X] The name of the decedent was signed in the presence of the attesting witnesses present at the same time by

      (1) [X] the decedent personally.

      (2) [ ] another person in the decedent's presence and by the decedent's direction.

   b. [ ] The decedent acknowledged in the presence of the attesting witnesses present at the same time that the decedent's name was signed by

      (1) [ ] the decedent personally.

      (2) [ ] another person in the decedent's presence and by the decedent's direction.

   c. [X] The decedent acknowledged in the presence of the attesting witnesses present at the same time that the instrument signed was decedent's

      (1) [X] will.

      (2) [ ] codicil.

2. When I signed the instrument, I understood that it was decedent's [X] will [ ] codicil.

3. I have no knowledge of any facts indicating that the instrument, or any part of it, was procured by duress, menace, fraud, or undue influence.

I declare under penalty of perjury under the laws of the State of California that the foregoing is true and correct.

Date: 02-20-07

Sam Sawit
....
        (TYPE OR PRINT NAME)
123 Elm Street
..........Santa Ana, CA 92804..........
        (ADDRESS)

▶   *Sam Sawit*
                (SIGNATURE OF WITNESS)

ATTORNEY'S CERTIFICATION

(Check local court rules for requirements for certifying copies of wills and codicils)

I am an active member of The State Bar of California. I declare under penalty of perjury under the laws of the State of California that Attachment 1 is a photographic copy of every page of the [X] will [ ] codicil presented for probate.

Date:

....
        (TYPE OR PRINT NAME)

▶
                (SIGNATURE OF ATTORNEY)

Form Approved by the
Judicial Council of California
DE-131 [Rev. January 1, 1998]
Mandatory Form [1/1/2000]

PROOF OF SUBSCRIBING WITNESS
(Probate)

Probate Code, § 8220

This page intentionally left blank.

DE-135

ATTORNEY OR PARTY WITHOUT ATTORNEY *(Name, state bar number, and address)*:	TELEPHONE AND FAX NOS.: 555-431-1234	FOR COURT USE ONLY

John Smith, In Pro Per
111 Maple Street
Los Angeles, CA 90940

ATTORNEY FOR *(Name)*:

SUPERIOR COURT OF CALIFORNIA, COUNTY OF ORANGE
STREET ADDRESS: 341 The City Drive South
MAILING ADDRESS:
CITY AND ZIP CODE: Orange, CA 92668
BRANCH NAME: Probate

ESTATE OF *(Name)*: Jane Doe, aka Jane Doe Buck

DECEDENT

PROOF OF HOLOGRAPHIC INSTRUMENT	CASE NUMBER: A 123456

1. I was acquainted with the decedent for the following number of years *(specify)*:   TEN YEARS

2. ☐ I was related to the decedent as *(specify)*:

3. I have personal knowledge of the decedent's handwriting which I acquired as follows:
   a. ☒ I saw the decedent write.
   b. ☐ I saw a writing purporting to be in the decedent's handwriting and upon which decedent acted or was charged. It was *(specify)*:

   c. ☐ I received letters in the due course of mail purporting to be from the decedent in response to letters I addressed and mailed to the decedent.
   d. ☒ Other *(specify other means of obtaining knowledge)*:

   I was employed by decedent and throughout my 10 year employment with her I witnessed decedent's original handwriting on numerous documents

4. I have examined the attached copy of the instrument, and its handwritten provisions were written by and the instrument was signed by the hand of the decedent. *(Affix a copy of the instrument as Attachment 4.)*

I declare under penalty of perjury under the laws of the State of California that the foregoing is true and correct.

Date: 06/15/07

Mary Smith
. . . . (TYPE OR PRINT NAME) . . . .
123 Elm Street
Anytown, CA
. . . . (ADDRESS) . . . .

▶ *Mary Smith*
(SIGNATURE)

ATTORNEY'S CERTIFICATION
(Check local court rules for requirements for certifying copies of wills and codicils)

I am an active member of The State Bar of California. I declare under penalty of perjury under the laws of the State of California that Attachment 4 is a photographic copy of every page of the holographic instrument presented for probate.

Date: 03/15/07

JOHN SMITH, In Pro Per
. . . . (TYPE OR PRINT NAME) . . . .

▶ *John Smith*
(SIGNATURE OF ATTORNEY)

PROOF OF HOLOGRAPHIC INSTRUMENT
(Probate)
Probate Code, § 8222

This page intentionally left blank.

DE-140

ATTORNEY OR PARTY WITHOUT ATTORNEY *(Name, state bar number, and address)*:	TELEPHONE AND FAX NOS.: 555-431-1234	*FOR COURT USE ONLY*

John Smith, In Pro Per
111 Maple Street
Los Angeles, CA 90940

ATTORNEY FOR *(Name)*:

SUPERIOR COURT OF CALIFORNIA, COUNTY OF ORANGE
STREET ADDRESS: 341 The City Drive South
MAILING ADDRESS:
CITY AND ZIP CODE: Orange, CA 92668
BRANCH NAME: Probate

ESTATE OF *(Name)*: Jane Doe, aka Jane Doe Buck

                               DECEDENT

ORDER FOR PROBATE	CASE NUMBER:

ORDER APPOINTING
- [x] Executor
- [ ] Administrator with Will Annexed
- [ ] Administrator   [ ] Special Administrator
- [x] Order Authorizing Independent Administration of Estate
    [x] with full authority   [ ] with limited authority

CASE NUMBER: A-00001

WARNING: THIS APPOINTMENT IS NOT EFFECTIVE UNTIL LETTERS HAVE ISSUED.

1. Date of hearing: 4/1/07   Time: 9:00a.m.   Dept./Room: L73   Judge: Robert Bench

THE COURT FINDS

2. a. All notices required by law have been given.
   b. Decedent died on *(date)*: 1/1/07
      (1) [x] a resident of the California county named above.
      (2) [ ] a nonresident of California and left an estate in the county named above.
   c. Decedent died
      (1) [ ] intestate
      (2) [x] testate
   and decedent's will dated: 12/1/98   and each codicil dated:
   was admitted to probate by Minute Order on *(date)*: 4/1/07

THE COURT ORDERS

3. *(Name)*: John Smith
   is appointed **personal representative**:
   a. [x] executor of the decedent's will
   b. [ ] administrator with will annexed
   c. [ ] administrator
   d. [ ] special administrator
      (1) [ ] with general powers
      (2) [ ] with special powers as specified in Attachment 3d(2)
      (3) [ ] without notice of hearing
      (4) [ ] letters will expire on *(date)*:
   and letters shall issue on qualification.

4. a. [x] **Full Authority** is granted to administer the estate under the Independent Administration of Estates Act.
   b. [ ] **Limited authority** is granted to administer the estate under the Independent Administration of Estates Act (there is no authority, without court supervision, to (1) sell or exchange real property or (2) grant an option to purchase real property or (3) borrow money with the loan secured by an encumbrance upon real property).

5. a. [ ] Bond is not required.
   b. [x] Bond is fixed at: $ 200,000   to be furnished by an authorized surety company or as otherwise provided by law.
   c. [ ] Deposits of: $ are ordered to be placed in a blocked account at *(specify institution and location)*:
      and receipts shall be filed. No withdrawals shall be made without a court order.   [ ] Additional orders in Attachment 5c.
   d. [ ] The personal representative is not authorized to take possession of money or any other property without a specific court order.

6. [x] *(Name)*:   is appointed probate referee.

Date: 4/10/07

                           Robert Bench
                        JUDGE OF THE SUPERIOR COURT

7. Number of pages attached: 0   [ ] SIGNATURE FOLLOWS LAST ATTACHMENT

Form Approved by the
Judicial Council of California
DE-140 [Rev. January 1, 1998]

ORDER FOR PROBATE

Probate Code, §§ 8006, 8400

This page intentionally left blank.

Form SS-4

(Rev. February 2006)

Department of the Treasury
Internal Revenue Service

Application for Employer Identification Number

(For use by employers, corporations, partnerships, trusts, estates, churches, government agencies, Indian tribal entities, certain individuals, and others.)

▶ See separate instructions for each line.   ▶ Keep a copy for your records.

OMB No. 1545-0003

EIN

1 Legal name of entity (or individual) for whom the EIN is being requested	
Estate of Jane Smith, a.k.a. Jane Doe Smith	

2 Trade name of business (if different from name on line 1)	**3** Executor, administrator, trustee, "care of" name
	John Smith, Executor

4a Mailing address (room, apt., suite no. and street, or P.O. box)	**5a** Street address (if different) (Do not enter a P.O. box.)
1111 Main Street	
4b City, state, and ZIP code	**5b** City, state, and ZIP code
Santa Ana, CA 92701	

6 County and state where principal business is located
Orange, CA

7a Name of principal officer, general partner, grantor, owner, or trustor	**7b** SSN, ITIN, or EIN
Jane Smith, a.k.a. Jane Doe Smith	111-22-3333

8a Type of entity (check only one box)

☐ Sole proprietor (SSN) _____
☐ Partnership
☐ Corporation (enter form number to be filed) ▶ _____
☐ Personal service corporation
☐ Church or church-controlled organization
☐ Other nonprofit organization (specify) ▶ _____
☐ Other (specify) ▶

☒ Estate (SSN of decedent) ___111 : 22 : 3333___
☐ Plan administrator (SSN) _____
☐ Trust (SSN of grantor) _____
☐ National Guard   ☐ State/local government
☐ Farmers' cooperative   ☐ Federal government/military
☐ REMIC   ☐ Indian tribal governments/enterprises
Group Exemption Number (GEN) ▶ _____

8b If a corporation, name the state or foreign country (if applicable) where incorporated

State	Foreign country

9 Reason for applying (check only one box)

☐ Started new business (specify type) ▶ _____
☐ Hired employees (Check the box and see line 12.)
☐ Compliance with IRS withholding regulations
☒ Other (specify) ▶ Probate Estate

☐ Banking purpose (specify purpose) ▶ _____
☐ Changed type of organization (specify new type) ▶ _____
☐ Purchased going business
☐ Created a trust (specify type) ▶ _____
☐ Created a pension plan (specify type) ▶ _____

10 Date business started or acquired (month, day, year). See instructions.	**11** Closing month of accounting year
02/01/07	June

12 First date wages or annuities were paid (month, day, year). **Note.** If applicant is a withholding agent, enter date income will first be paid to nonresident alien. (month, day, year) . . . . ▶

13 Highest number of employees expected in the next 12 months (enter -0- if none).

Do you expect to have $1,000 or less in employment tax liability for the calendar year? ☐ Yes ☐ No. (If you expect to pay $4,000 or less in wages, you can mark yes.)

Agricultural	Household	Other

14 Check **one** box that best describes the principal activity of your business.

☐ Construction ☐ Rental & leasing ☐ Transportation & warehousing
☐ Real estate ☐ Manufacturing ☐ Finance & insurance

☐ Health care & social assistance ☐ Wholesale–agent/broker
☐ Accommodation & food service ☐ Wholesale–other ☐ Retail
☒ Other (specify) Probate Estate

15 Indicate principal line of merchandise sold, specific construction work done, products produced, or services provided.
Probate Estate

16a Has the applicant ever applied for an employer identification number for this or any other business? . . . . ☐ Yes ☒ No
Note. If "Yes," please complete lines 16b and 16c.

16b If you checked "Yes" on line 16a, give applicant's legal name and trade name shown on prior application if different from line 1 or 2 above.
Legal name ▶ _____   Trade name ▶ _____

16c Approximate date when, and city and state where, the application was filed. Enter previous employer identification number if known.

Approximate date when filed (mo., day, year)	City and state where filed	Previous EIN

Third Party Designee	Complete this section **only** if you want to authorize the named individual to receive the entity's EIN and answer questions about the completion of this form.	
	Designee's name	Designee's telephone number (include area code) ( )
	Address and ZIP code	Designee's fax number (include area code) ( )

Under penalties of perjury, I declare that I have examined this application, and to the best of my knowledge and belief, it is true, correct, and complete.

Name and title (type or print clearly) ▶ John Smith, Executor

Applicant's telephone number (include area code) (310) 555-5555

Signature ▶ *John Smith*, Executor   Date ▶ 02-01-07

Applicant's fax number (include area code) ( )

For Privacy Act and Paperwork Reduction Act Notice, see separate instructions.   Cat. No. 16055N   Form **SS-4** (Rev. 2-2006)

Form SS-4 (Rev. 2-2006)

Do I Need an EIN?

File Form SS-4 if the applicant entity does not already have an EIN but is required to show an EIN on any return, statement, or other document.[1] See also the separate instructions for each line on Form SS-4.

IF the applicant...	AND...	THEN...
Started a new business	Does not currently have (nor expect to have) employees	Complete lines 1, 2, 4a–8a, 8b (if applicable), and 9–16c.
Hired (or will hire) employees, including household employees	Does not already have an EIN	Complete lines 1, 2, 4a–6, 7a–b (if applicable), 8a, 8b (if applicable), and 9–16c.
Opened a bank account	Needs an EIN for banking purposes only	Complete lines 1–5b, 7a–b (if applicable), 8a, 9, and 16a–c.
Changed type of organization	Either the legal character of the organization or its ownership changed (for example, you incorporate a sole proprietorship or form a partnership)[2]	Complete lines 1–16c (as applicable).
Purchased a going business[3]	Does not already have an EIN	Complete lines 1–16c (as applicable).
Created a trust	The trust is other than a grantor trust or an IRA trust[4]	Complete lines 1–16c (as applicable).
Created a pension plan as a plan administrator[5]	Needs an EIN for reporting purposes	Complete lines 1, 3, 4a–b, 8a, 9, and 16a–c.
Is a foreign person needing an EIN to comply with IRS withholding regulations	Needs an EIN to complete a Form W-8 (other than Form W-8ECI), avoid withholding on portfolio assets, or claim tax treaty benefits[6]	Complete lines 1–5b, 7a–b (SSN or ITIN optional), 8a–9, and 16a–c.
Is administering an estate	Needs an EIN to report estate income on Form 1041	Complete lines 1, 2, 3, 4a–6, 8a, 9-11, 12-15 (if applicable), and 16a–c.
Is a withholding agent for taxes on non-wage income paid to an alien (i.e., individual, corporation, or partnership, etc.)	Is an agent, broker, fiduciary, manager, tenant, or spouse who is required to file Form 1042, Annual Withholding Tax Return for U.S. Source Income of Foreign Persons	Complete lines 1, 2, 3 (if applicable), 4a–5b, 7a–b (if applicable), 8a, 9, and 16a–c.
Is a state or local agency	Serves as a tax reporting agent for public assistance recipients under Rev. Proc. 80-4, 1980-1 C.B. 581[7]	Complete lines 1, 2, 4a–5b, 8a, 9, and 16a–c.
Is a single-member LLC	Needs an EIN to file Form 8832, Entity Classification Election, for filing employment tax returns, **or** for state reporting purposes[8]	Complete lines 1–16c (as applicable).
Is an S corporation	Needs an EIN to file Form 2553, Election by a Small Business Corporation[9]	Complete lines 1–16c (as applicable).

[1] For example, a sole proprietorship or self-employed farmer who establishes a qualified retirement plan, or is required to file excise, employment, alcohol, tobacco, or firearms returns, must have an EIN. A partnership, corporation, REMIC (real estate mortgage investment conduit), nonprofit organization (church, club, etc.), or farmers' cooperative must use an EIN for any tax-related purpose even if the entity does not have employees.

[2] However, do not apply for a new EIN if the existing entity only (a) changed its business name, (b) elected on Form 8832 to change the way it is taxed (or is covered by the default rules), or (c) terminated its partnership status because at least 50% of the total interests in partnership capital and profits were sold or exchanged within a 12-month period. The EIN of the terminated partnership should continue to be used. See Regulations section 301.6109-1(d)(2)(iii).

[3] Do not use the EIN of the prior business unless you became the "owner" of a corporation by acquiring its stock.

[4] However, grantor trusts that do not file using Optional Method 1 and IRA trusts that are required to file Form 990-T, Exempt Organization Business Income Tax Return, must have an EIN. For more information on grantor trusts, see the Instructions for Form 1041.

[5] A plan administrator is the person or group of persons specified as the administrator by the instrument under which the plan is operated.

[6] Entities applying to be a Qualified Intermediary (QI) need a QI-EIN even if they already have an EIN. See Rev. Proc. 2000-12.

[7] See also *Household employer* on page 3. **Note.** State or local agencies may need an EIN for other reasons, for example, hired employees.

[8] Most LLCs do not need to file Form 8832. See *Limited liability company (LLC)* on page 4 for details on completing Form SS-4 for an LLC.

[9] An existing corporation that is electing or revoking S corporation status should use its previously-assigned EIN.

DE-150

ATTORNEY OR PARTY WITHOUT ATTORNEY (Name, state bar number, and address):	TELEPHONE AND FAX NOS.:	FOR COURT USE ONLY

ATTORNEY OR PARTY WITHOUT ATTORNEY (Name, state bar number, and address):

TELEPHONE AND FAX NOS.:

FOR COURT USE ONLY

John Smith
555-555-5555
1111 Main Street
Santa Ana, CA 92701

ATTORNEY FOR (Name):

SUPERIOR COURT OF CALIFORNIA, COUNTY OF Orange

STREET ADDRESS: 341 The City Drive South

MAILING ADDRESS:

CITY AND ZIP CODE: Orange, CA 92668

BRANCH NAME: Probate

ESTATE OF (Name):

Jane Smith, a.k.a Jane Doe Smith

DECEDENT

LETTERS		CASE NUMBER:
[X] **TESTAMENTARY** [ ] OF ADMINISTRATION		A00001
[ ] **OF ADMINISTRATION WITH WILL ANNEXED** [ ] SPECIAL ADMINISTRATION		

LETTERS

1. [X] The last will of the decedent named above having been proved, the court appoints (name):

   a. [X] executor.
   b. [ ] administrator with will annexed.

2. [ ] The court appoints (name):

   a. [ ] administrator of the decedent's estate.
   b. [ ] special administrator of decedent's estate
      (1) [ ] with the special powers specified in the *Order for Probate*.
      (2) [ ] with the powers of a general administrator.
      (3) [ ] letters will expire on (date):

3. [X] The personal representative is authorized to administer the estate under the Independent Administration of Estates Act [X] **with full authority**
[ ] **with limited authority** (no authority, without court supervision, to (1) sell or exchange real property or (2) grant an option to purchase real property or (3) borrow money with the loan secured by an encumbrance upon real property).

4. [ ] The personal representative is not authorized to take possession of money or any other property without a specific court order.

WITNESS, clerk of the court, with seal of the court affixed.

(SEAL)	Date:
	Clerk, by
	_____ (DEPUTY)

AFFIRMATION

1. [ ] PUBLIC ADMINISTRATOR: No affirmation required (Prob. Code, § 7621(c)).

2. [X] INDIVIDUAL: **I solemnly affirm** that I will perform the duties of personal representative according to law.

3. [ ] INSTITUTIONAL FIDUCIARY (name):

I solemnly affirm that the institution will perform the duties of personal representative according to law. I make this affirmation for myself as an individual and on behalf of the institution as an officer. (Name and title):

4. Executed on (date): 03-01-07
at (place): Santa Ana , California.

▶ *John Smith*
_____
(SIGNATURE)

CERTIFICATION

I certify that this document is a correct copy of the original on file in my office and the letters issued the personal representative appointed above have not been revoked, annulled, or set aside, and are still in full force and effect.

(SEAL)	Date:
	Clerk, by
	_____ (DEPUTY)

Form Approved by the
Judicial Council of California
DE-150 [Rev. January 1, 1998]

LETTERS
(Probate)

Probate Code, §§ 1001, 8403,
8405, 8544, 8545;
Code of Civil Procedure, § 2015.6

American LegalNet, Inc. | www.USCourtForms.com

This page intentionally left blank.

DE-154, GC-035

ATTORNEY OR PARTY WITHOUT ATTORNEY *(Name, state bar number, and address)*:	TELEPHONE AND FAX NOS.:	FOR COURT USE ONLY
ARNOLD ABLE DBA ABLE PLUMBING 1234 DRAIN STREET LOS ANGELES, CA	555-431-1234	

ATTORNEY FOR *(Name)*:

SUPERIOR COURT OF CALIFORNIA, COUNTY OF ORANGE

STREET ADDRESS: 341 THE CITY DRIVE SOUTH

MAILING ADDRESS:

CITY AND ZIP CODE: ORANGE, CA 92668

BRANCH NAME: PROBATE

MATTER OF *(Name)*: JANE DOE, a.k.a. JANE DOE BUCK

[X] DECEDENT   [ ] CONSERVATEE   [ ] MINOR   [ ] TRUST

REQUEST FOR SPECIAL NOTICE	CASE NUMBER: A-00001

1. a. [X] I am a person interested in this proceeding.

   b. [ ] I am the attorney for a person interested in this proceeding *(specify name of interested person)*: ORANGE COUNTY SUPERIOR COURT

2. I REQUEST SPECIAL NOTICE of *(complete only a or b)*

   a. [X] the following matters *(check applicable boxes)*:

      (1) [X] **all the matters** for which special notice may be requested. *(Do not check boxes (2) - (8).)*

      (2) [ ] inventories and appraisals of property, including supplements

      (3) [ ] accountings by the personal representative

      (4) [ ] reports of the status of administration

      (5) [ ] objections to an appraisal

      (6) [ ] petitions for the sale of property

      (7) [ ] *Spousal Property Petition* (form DE-221) (Prob. Code, § 13650)

      (8) [ ] other petitions: [ ] all petitions [ ] the following petitions *(specify)*:

   b. [ ] the following matters *(specify)*:

3. SEND THE NOTICES to

   a. [X] the interested person at the following address *(specify)*:

      ARNOLD ABLE DBA ABLE PLUMBING
      1234 DRAIN STREET
      LOS ANGELES, CA. 90024

   b. [ ] the attorney at the following address *(specify)*:

Date: 04-30-07

ARNOLD ABLE
······· *(TYPE OR PRINT NAME)* · · · · · ·

▶ *Arnold Able*
(SIGNATURE)

[ ] Attorney for person requesting special notice *(client's name)*:

(Continued on reverse)

REQUEST FOR SPECIAL NOTICE
(Probate)

Probate Code, §§ 1250
2700(c), 17204

MATTER OF *(Name)*: JANE DOE, a.k.a. JANE DOE BUCK	CASE NUMBER:
	A-00001

> **NOTE: A formal proof of service or a written admission of service must accompany this *Request for Special Notice* when it is filed with the court.**
>
> **You must have your request served on either the personal representative, conservator, guardian, or trustee, or his or her attorney, or obtain a signed *Admission of Service (see below).***

PROOF OF SERVICE BY MAIL

1. I am over the age of 18 and not a party to this cause. I am a resident of or employed in the county where the mailing occurred.
2. My residence or business address is *(specify)*: 222 Karo St.
   Glendale, CA 92012
3. I served the foregoing *Request for Special Notice* on each person named below by enclosing a copy in an envelope addressed as shown below AND
   a. ☐ **depositing** the sealed envelope with the United States Postal Service with the postage fully prepaid.
   b. ☐ **placing** the envelope for collection and mailing on the date and at the place shown in item 4 following our ordinary business practices. I am readily familiar with this business' practice for collecting and processing correspondence for mailing. On the same day that correspondence is placed for collection and mailing, it is deposited in the ordinary course of business with the United States Postal Service in a sealed envelope with postage fully prepaid.

4. a. Date of deposit:　　　　　　　　　　　　b. Place of deposit *(city and state)*:

I declare under penalty of perjury under the laws of the State of California that the foregoing is true and correct.

Date: 04-30-07

Joan Leak . . . . 　　　▶ *Joan Leak*
(TYPE OR PRINT NAME)　　　　　　　　　　　　　　　　　(SIGNATURE OF DECLARANT)

NAME AND ADDRESS OF EACH PERSON TO WHOM NOTICE WAS MAILED

☐ List of names and addresses continued in attachment.

ADMISSION OF SERVICE

1. I am the ☒ personal representative, conservator, guardian, or trustee　　☐ the attorney

2. I ACKNOWLEDGE that I was served a copy of the foregoing *Request for Special Notice.*

Date: 5-10-07

JOHN SMITH . . . . 　　　▶ *John Smith*
(TYPE OR PRINT NAME)　　　　　　　　　　　　　　　　　(SIGNATURE)

| DE-154, GC-035 [Rev. January 1, 1998] | **REQUEST FOR SPECIAL NOTICE**
(Probate) | Page two |

From: John Smith
            123 Maple St.
            Los Angeles, CA 90041

To: Department of Heath Services
            Recovery Section/Estate Recovery Unit
            MS-4720
            P.O. Box 997425
            Sacramento, CA 95899-7425

Re: Estate of Jane Doe, a.k.a Jane Doe Buck
            Orange County Superior A 10023

Notice is hereby given that the above-named decedent died on August 6, 2006, and that Letters Testamentary were issued John Smith on July 20, 2007. Under Probate Code Section 9200, you are requested to file any claim you may have against the decedent or the estate in the manner and within the time required by law.

A copy of the above-named decedent's death certificate is attached as required by law.

On October 20, 2007, the undersigned mailed this notice in a sealed envelope with postage thereon fully prepaid and addressed as follows:

Department of Health Services

    Recovery Section/Estate Recovery Unit
    MS-4720
    P.O. Box 997425
    Sacramento, CA 95899-74225

By placing said envelope in a U.S. Mailbox.

Dated: 10-20-07

John Smith
John Smith

This page intentionally left blank.

From: John Smith
           123 Maple St.
           Los Angeles, CA 90041

To: Corrections Standards Authority
           600 Bercut Drive
           Sacramento, CA 95814

Re: Estate of Jane Doe, aka Jane Doe Buck
           Orange County Superior A 10023

Notice is hereby given that the above-named decedent died on August 6, 2006, and that Letters Testamentary were issued John Smith on July 20, 2007. Under Probate Code Section 9200, you are requested to file any claim you may have against the decedent or the estate in the manner and within the time required by law.

A copy of the above-named decedent's death certificate is attached as required by law.

On October 20, 2007, the undersigned mailed this notice ina sealed envelope with postage thereon fully prepaid and addressed as follows:

Corrections Standards Authority
600 Bercut Drive
Sacramento, CA 95814

by placing said envelope in a U.S. Mailbox.

Dated: 10-20-07

John Smith
John Smith

This page intentionally left blank.

1 John Smith, In Pro Per
   112 Maple St.
2 Los Angeles, CA 90040
   (213) 555-5555
3

4

5

6

7

8   SUPERIOR COURT OF THE STATE OF CALIFORNIA

9   FOR THE COUNTY OF ORANGE, LAMOREAUX JUSTICE CENTER

10

11 The Estate of   )   CASE NO. **A100001**
)
12   **JANE DOE, a.k.a.**   )   EXPARTE PETITION TO INCREASE
       JANE DOE BUCK,   )   BOND AND ORDER THEREON
13   )
              Deceased   )
14 _____)

15   1. Petitioner, **JOHN SMITH**, is the Executor of the above

16 entitled estate.

17

18   2. Petitioner's bond is $100,000. Recently Petitioner has

19 learned that said bond is insufficient and should be increased

20 from $100,000 to $250,000, an increase of $150,000. Said

21 additional bond is necessary due to the discovery of additional

22 assets and increase in the market value of other assets in the

23 estate.

24   WHEREFORE, Petitioner prays for an order increasing his bond

25 from $100,000 to $250,000, an increase of $150,000.

26 Dated **March 3** , 2007

27   *John Smith*
            JOHN SMITH

28

1

EXPARTE PETITION TO INCREASE BOND AND ORDER THEREON

<u>VERIFICATION</u>

STATE OF CALIFORNIA)
) ss.
COUNTY OF **ORANGE**)

    I am the petitioner in the above-entitled matter; I have read the foregoing EXPARTE PETITION TO INCREASE BOND and know the contents thereof; and I certify that the same is true of my own knowledge, except as to those matters which are therein stated upon my information or belief, and as to those matters, I believe it to be true.

    I certify (or declare) under penalty of perjury, under the laws of the State of California, that the foregoing is true and correct.

    Executed at **Laguna Hills, CA,** on June 17, 2007

John Smith
JOHN SMITH

ORDER THEREON

Good cause showing, the exparte petition of **JOHN SMITH, Executor** of the above entitled estate, is approved and the bond of **JOHN SMITH is increased from $100,000 to $250,000, an increase of $150,000.**

Dated:

_____
JUDGE, SUPERIOR COURT

2

EXPARTE PETITION TO INCREASE BOND AND ORDER THEREON

DE-160/GC-040

ATTORNEY OR PARTY WITHOUT ATTORNEY *(Name, state bar number, and address):*	FOR COURT USE ONLY
John Smith, In Pro Per 111 Maple St. Los Angeles, Ca 90940 TELEPHONE NO.: 555 555-5555 FAX NO. *(Optional):* E-MAIL ADDRESS *(Optional):* ATTORNEY FOR *(Name):*	

SUPERIOR COURT OF CALIFORNIA, COUNTY OF Orange
STREET ADDRESS: 341 The City Drive South
MAILING ADDRESS:
CITY AND ZIP CODE: Orange, CA 92668
BRANCH NAME: Probate

ESTATE OF *(Name):* Jane Doe, a.k.a. Jane Doe Buck

☐ DECEDENT   ☐ CONSERVATEE   ☐ MINOR

INVENTORY AND APPRAISAL	CASE NUMBER: A-00001
☐ **Partial No.:** ☐ **Corrected** ☑ **Final** ☐ **Reappraisal for Sale** ☐ **Supplemental** ☐ **Property Tax Certificate**	Date of Death of Decedent or of Appointment of Guardian or Conservator:

APPRAISALS

1. Total appraisal by representative, guardian, or conservator (Attachment 1): $ 30,900
2. Total appraisal by referee (Attachment 2): $
                                    TOTAL: $

DECLARATION OF REPRESENTATIVE, GUARDIAN, CONSERVATOR, OR SMALL ESTATE CLAIMANT

3. Attachments 1 and 2 together with all prior inventories filed contain a true statement of
   ☑ all   ☐ a portion   of the estate that has come to my knowledge or possession, including particularly all money and all
   just claims the estate has against me. I have truly, honestly, and impartially appraised to the best of my ability each item set forth in
   Attachment 1.
4. ☐ No probate referee is required   ☐ by order of the court dated *(specify):*
5. **Property tax certificate.** I certify that the requirements of Revenue and Taxation Code section 480
   a. ☐ are not applicable because the decedent owned no real property in California at the time of death.
   b. ☑ have been satisfied by the filing of a change of ownership statement with the county recorder or assessor of each county in
      California in which the decedent owned property at the time of death.

I declare under penalty of perjury under the laws of the State of California that the foregoing is true and correct.
Date: 06/20/07

John Smith	►	*John Smith*
(TYPE OR PRINT NAME; INCLUDE TITLE IF CORPORATE OFFICER)		(SIGNATURE)

STATEMENT ABOUT THE BOND
(Complete in all cases. Must be signed by attorney for fiduciary, or by fiduciary without an attorney.)

6. ☐ Bond is waived, or the sole fiduciary is a corporate fiduciary or an exempt government agency.
7. ☑ Bond filed in the amount of: $ 200,000   ☑ Sufficient   ☐ Insufficient
8. ☐ Receipts for: $ have been filed with the court for deposits in a blocked account at *(specify*
      institution and location):

Date: 07/15/07

John Smith	►	*John Smith*
(TYPE OR PRINT NAME)		(SIGNATURE OF ATTORNEY OR PARTY WITHOUT ATTORNEY)

Page 1 of 2

Form Adopted for Mandatory Use Judicial Council of California DE-160/GC-040 [Rev. January 1, 2003]	**INVENTORY AND APPRAISAL**	Probate Code, §§ 2610–2616, 8800–8980; Cal. Rules of Court, rule 7.501

ESTATE OF *(Name):* Jane Doe, a.k.a. Jane Doe Buck	CASE NUMBER:
☑ DECEDENT ☐ CONSERVATEE ☐ MINOR	A-00001

DECLARATION OF PROBATE REFEREE

9. I have truly, honestly, and impartially appraised to the best of my ability each item set forth in Attachment 2.
10. A true account of my commission and expenses actually and necessarily incurred pursuant to my appointment is:

Statutory commission: $

Expenses *(specify):* $

TOTAL: $

I declare under penalty of perjury under the laws of the State of California that the foregoing is true and correct.

Date:

▶

_____
(TYPE OR PRINT NAME)

_____
(SIGNATURE OF REFEREE)

INSTRUCTIONS

(See Probate Code sections 2610–2616, 8801, 8804, 8852, 8905, 8960, 8961, and 8963 for additional instructions.)

1. See Probate Code section 8850 for items to be included in the inventory.

2. If the minor or conservatee is or has been during the guardianship or conservatorship confined in a state hospital under the jurisdiction of the State Department of Mental Health or the State Department of Developmental Services, mail a copy to the director of the appropriate department in Sacramento. (Prob. Code, § 2611.)

3. The representative, guardian, conservator, or small estate claimant shall list on Attachment 1 and appraise as of the date of death of the decedent or the date of appointment of the guardian or conservator, at fair market value, moneys, currency, cash items, bank accounts and amounts on deposit with each financial institution (as defined in Probate Code section 40), and the proceeds of life and accident insurance policies and retirement plans payable upon death in lump sum amounts to the estate, except items whose fair market value is, in the opinion of the representative, an amount different from the ostensible value or specified amount.

4. The representative, guardian, conservator, or small estate claimant shall list in Attachment 2 all other assets of the estate which shall be appraised by the referee.

5. If joint tenancy and other assets are listed for appraisal purposes only and not as part of the probate estate, they must be separately listed on additional attachments and their value excluded from the total valuation of Attachments 1 and 2.

6. Each attachment should conform to the format approved by the Judicial Council. (See *Inventory and Appraisal Attachment* (form DE-161/GC-041) and Cal. Rules of Court, rule 201.)

DE-161, GC-041

ESTATE OF *(Name)*: JANE DOE, a.k.a. JANE DOE BUCK	CASE NUMBER: A-00001

INVENTORY AND APPRAISAL
ATTACHMENT NO: 1

(In decedents' estates, attachments must conform to Probate Code section 8850(c) regarding community and separate property.)

Page: 3 of: 4 total pages.
(Add pages as required.)

Item No.	Description	Appraised value
1.	Cash found in home	200
2.	Uncashed Social Security check payable to Jane Doe	700
3.	Checking Account, Bank of America Main and 1st Streets, Santa Ana, Ca. Account #132-3455-2358 Principal $29,950.00 Accrued Interest 50.00	30,000
	Total	$30,900

All of the above property is the separate property of the decedent.

Form Approved by the
Judicial Council of California
DE-161, GC-041 [Rev. January 1, 1998]

INVENTORY AND APPRAISAL ATTACHMENT

Probate Code, §§ 301,
2610-2613, 8800-8920,
10309

DE-161, GC-041

ESTATE OF *(Name)*: JANE DOE, a.k.a. JANE DOE BUCK	CASE NUMBER:
	A-00001

INVENTORY AND APPRAISAL
ATTACHMENT NO: 2_____

(In decedents' estates, attachments must conform to Probate
Code section 8850(c) regarding community and separate property.)

Page: _4_ of: _4_ total pages.
(Add pages as required.)

Item No.	Description	Appraised value
1.	1997 Oldsmobile 88 4Door Sedan	
2.	Personal effects-Household Furniture and Furnishings	
3.	100 Shares Common-XYZ Corp. NYSE	
4.	Improved Real Property located at 1121 Oak Street Santa Ana, Ca. further described as: Lot 2 of Tract 168648, in the city of Santa Ana, County of Orange , State of California, Book 124, Pages 94 and 95 of Maps, Official Records of Orange Countu, California APN: 600-0240-050.	
	Total	

All of the above property is the separate property of the decedent.

Form Approved by the
Judicial Council of California
DE-161, GC-041 [Rev. January 1, 1998]

INVENTORY AND APPRAISAL ATTACHMENT

Probate Code, §§ 301,
2610-2613, 8800-8920,
10309

FORM

C

CHANGE IN OWNERSHIP STATEMENT
(DEATH OF REAL PROPERTY OWNER)

MAILING ADDRESS (Make corrections, if necessary)	ASSESSOR'S IDENTIFICATION NUMBER		
ESTATE OF JANE DOE C/O JOHN SMITH, EXECUTOR 111 MAPLE STREET LOS ANGELES, CA 90940	MAPBOOK	PAGE	PARCEL
	123	456	78
	PROPERTY ADDRESS 123 LEMON STREET SANTA ANA, CA 92705		

Section 480 of the Revenue and Taxation Code States:

(a) Whenever any change in ownership of real property or of a mobilehome subject to local property taxation, and which is assessed by the county assessor, occurs, the transferee shall file a signed change in ownership statement in the county where the real property or mobilehome is located, as provided for in subdivision (c). In the case of a change in ownership where the transferee is not locally assessed, no change in ownership statement is required.

(b) The personal representative shall file a change in ownership statement with the county recorder or assessor in each county where the decedent owned real property at the time of death. The statement shall be filed at the time the inventory and appraisal is filed with the court clerk.

IMPORTANT NOTICE

The law requires any transferee acquiring an interest in real property or mobilehome subject to local property taxation, and which is assessed by the county assessor, to file a change in ownership statement with the county recorder or assessor. The change in ownership statement must be filed at the time of recording or, if the transfer is not recorded, within 45 days of the date of the change in ownership. The failure to file a change in ownership statement within 45 days from the date of a written request by the assessor results in a penalty of either: (1) one hundred dollars ($100), or (2) 10 percent of the taxes applicable to the new base year value reflecting the change in ownership of the real property or mobilehome, whichever is greater but not to exceed two thousand five hundred dollars ($2,500) if such failure to file was not willful. This penalty will be added to the assessment roll and shall be collected like any other delinquent property taxes, and be subject to the same penalties for nonpayment.

This notice is a written request from the Office of the Assessor for the Change in Ownership Statement. Failure to file this Statement will result in the assessment of a penalty as stated above.

The statement will remain confidential as required by § 481 of the Revenue and Taxation Code.

Passage of Decedent's Property: Probate Code §7000 et seq.

"Subject to §7001, title to a decedent's property passes on the decedent's death to the person to whom it is devised in the decedent's last will or, in the absence of such devise, to the decedent's heirs as prescribed in the laws governing intestate succession."

Date of Change in Ownership: California Code of Regulations, Title 18, Rule 462 (n)(3)

". . . (3) Inheritance (by will or intestate succession). The date of death of decedent."

Inventory and Appraisal: Probate Code §8800

"(d) Concurrent with the filing of the inventory and appraisal pursuant to this section, the personal representative shall also file a certification that the requirements of §480 of the Revenue and Taxation Code either:

(1)   Are not applicable because the decedent owned no real property in California at the time of death.

(2)   Have been satisfied by the filing of a change in ownership statement with the county recorder or assessor of each county in which the decedent owned property at the time of death."

If you request, the Office of the Assessor will date receipt your statement and return a copy to you for your records. Also, the Probate Division of the Superior Court will forward a copy of the Inventory and Appraisal to the Office of the Assessor. An extra copy should be provided to the Court for this purpose.

Instructions: Complete a separate form for each property. Answer each question. Upon completion, mail this form and a copy of the death certificate to:

1. NAME OF DECEDENT	2. DATE OF DEATH
DOE, JANE	03/15/04

3. STREET ADDRESS OF REAL PROPERTY	4. ASSESSOR'S IDENTIFICATION NUMBER		
123 LEMON STREET	a. Mapbook	b. Page	c. Parcel
SANTA ANA, CA 92705	123	456	78

5. DESCRIPTIVE INFORMATION (Check a, b or c, if applicable)

a. [ ] Attached is copy of deed by which decedent acquired title.

b. [X] Attached is copy of most recent tax bill.

c. [ ] Deed or tax bill are not available; attached is the legal description.

6. DISPOSITION OF REAL PROPERTY WILL BE BY (Check one)

a. [ ] Intestate succession.

b. [ ] PC 13650 distribution of community property to surviving spouse.

c. [ ] Affidavit of death of joint tenant.

d. [ ] Decree of distribution pursuant to will.

e. [X] Action of trustee pursuant to terms of a trust.

7. TRANSFEREE INFORMATION (Check a, b, c, or d if applicable)

a. [ ] Transfer is to decedent's spouse. (Check even if affidavit of death of joint tenant is to be recorded.) [Article XIIIA (G)]

Name of spouse _____

b. [ ] Transfer is to a trust of which the spouse is the sole beneficiary or the income beneficiary.

Name of spouse _____

c. [ ] Transfer is to decedent's child(ren) or parent(s) and is excluded from reassessment [Article XIIIA (h)]

    [ ] Property was principal residence of decedent (fully excluded).

    [ ] Property subject to $1 million limitation to this transferee.

List name(s) of child(ren) or parent(s) in #9 below. **NOTE:** A claim for exclusion must be filed. To obtain application, call (213) 974-3211

Important: A claim must be filed within three years after the date of death or transfer, or prior to the date of transfer to a third party, whichever is earlier.

d. [X] Transfer is to decedent's other beneficiaries. *(Where known, indicate names of beneficiaries and the percentage of ownership interest each is to receive.)*

JOHN SMITH, 100% OWNERSHIP INTEREST _____

_____

8. SALE PRIOR TO DISTRIBUTION

[ ] This property has been sold or will be sold prior to distribution. (Where appropriate, attach the conveyance document and/or court order.) **NOTE:** See exclusion, item 7c, above.

9. ADDITIONAL INFORMATION

[ ] Additional sheets attached. (Should you wish to explain any of the foregoing or provide additional information, please attach additional sheets.)

JOHN SMITH	EXECUTOR	555-555-5555
NAME (Please print)	TITLE (If corporate officer/partner)	TELEPHONE NO. (8 a.m. - 5 p.m.)

I declare under penalty of perjury that the foregoing is true and correct to the best of my knowledge and belief.

_____
Signature of owner or corporate officer

Signed at, LOS ANGELES _____, California, this 1ST _____ day of MAY _____, 2007

76C448 ASSR-176 BACK (REV. 3/93)

DE-157

NOTICE OF ADMINISTRATION
OF THE ESTATE OF

JANE DOE, a.k.a. JANE DOE BUCK

(NAME)

DECEDENT

NOTICE TO CREDITORS

1. *(Name)*:   John Smith
   (Address):   111 MAPLE STREET
   LOS ANGELES, CA.

   (Telephone): 555 555-5555

   is the **personal representative** of the **ESTATE OF** *(name)*: JANE DOE, a.k.a. JANE DOE BUCK , who is deceased.

2. The personal representative HAS BEGUN ADMINISTRATION of the decedent's estate in the
   a. **SUPERIOR COURT OF CALIFORNIA, COUNTY OF *(specify)*:**   ORANGE
   STREET ADDRESS: 341 THE CITY DRIVE SOUTH
   MAILING ADDRESS:
   CITY AND ZIP CODE: ORANGE, CA 90012
   BRANCH NAME: PROBATE

   b. Case number *(specify)*:   A-00001

3. You must FILE YOUR CLAIM with the court clerk (address in item 2a) AND mail or deliver a copy to the personal representative before the **later** of the following times as provided in section 9100:

   a. **four months** after *(date)*:   August 10, 2007 , the date letters (authority to act for the estate) were first issued to the personal representative, OR

   b. **sixty days** after *(date)*:   June 4, 2007 , the date this notice was mailed or personally delivered to you.

4. LATE CLAIMS: If you do not file your claim before it is due, you must file a petition with the court for permission to file a late claim as provided in Probate Code section 9103.

> **WHERE TO GET A CREDITOR'S CLAIM FORM:** If a *Creditor's Claim* (form DE-172) did not accompany this notice, you may obtain a copy from any superior court clerk or from the person who sent you this notice. A letter to the court stating your claim is *not* sufficient.
>
> **FAILURE TO FILE A CLAIM:** Failure to file a claim with the court and serve a copy of the claim on the personal representative will in most instances invalidate your claim.
>
> **IF YOU MAIL YOUR CLAIM:** If you use the mail to file your claim with the court, for your protection you should send your claim by certified mail, with return receipt requested. If you use the mail to serve a copy of your claim on the personal representative, you should also use certified mail.

> **NOTE:** To assist the creditor and the court, please send a copy of the *Creditor's Claim* form with this notice.

(Proof of Service on reverse)

Form Approved by the
Judicial Council of California
DE-157 [Rev. January 1, 1998]

NOTICE OF ADMINISTRATION TO CREDITORS
(Probate)

Probate Code, §§ 9050,
9052

[Optional]
PROOF OF SERVICE BY MAIL

1. I am over the age of 18 and not a party to this cause. I am a resident of or employed in the county where the mailing occurred.
2. My residence or business address is *(specify)*:
   RESIDENCE - 444 NORTH ASH STREET
   SANTA ANA, CA. 92074
3. I served the foregoing *Notice of Administration to Creditors* [X] and a blank *Creditor's Claim* form * on each person named below by enclosing a copy in an envelope addressed as shown below AND
   a. [X] **depositing** the sealed envelope with the United States Postal Service with the postage fully prepaid.
   b. [ ] **placing** the envelope for collection and mailing on the date and at the place shown in item 4 following our ordinary business practices. I am readily familiar with the business' practice for collecting and processing correspondence for mailing. On the same day that correspondence is placed for collection and mailing, it is deposited in the ordinary course of business with the United States Postal Service in a sealed envelope with postage fully prepaid.

4. a. Date of deposit: 06-04-07   b. Place of deposit *(city and state)*:   SANTA ANA, CA.

I declare under penalty of perjury under the laws of the State of California that the foregoing is true and correct.

Date: 06-04-07

LILA SMITH   ▶ *Lila Smith*
_____(TYPE OR PRINT NAME)_____   _____(SIGNATURE OF DECLARANT)_____

NAME AND ADDRESS OF EACH PERSON TO WHOM NOTICE WAS MAILED
ARNOLD ABLE DBA ABLE PLUMBING, 1234 DRAIN STREET, LOS ANGELES, 90035
BANK OF BAD LOANS, 123 WRITEOFF STREET, LOS ANGELES, CA. 90042

[ ] List of names and addresses continued in attachment.

NOTE: To assist the creditor and the court, please send a copy of the Creditor's Claim (form DE-172) with the notice.

DE-172

ATTORNEY OR PARTY WITHOUT ATTORNEY (Name, state bar number, and address):	TELEPHONE AND FAX NOS.:	FOR COURT USE ONLY
John Smith, In Pro Per 111 Maple Street Los Angeles, CA 90940		

ATTORNEY FOR (Name): 555-431-1234

SUPERIOR COURT OF CALIFORNIA, COUNTY OF Orange

STREET ADDRESS: 341 The City Drive South

MAILING ADDRESS:

CITY AND ZIP CODE: Orange, CA 92668

BRANCH NAME: Probate

ESTATE OF (Name):

Jane Doe, aka Jane Doe Buck

DECEDENT

CREDITOR'S CLAIM	CASE NUMBER: A-123456

You must file this claim with the court clerk at the court address above before the LATER of (a) four months after the date letters (authority to act for the estate) were first issued to the personal representative, or (b) sixty days after the date the *Notice of Administration* was given to the creditor, if notice was given as provided in Probate Code section 9051. You must also mail or deliver a copy of this claim to the personal representative and his or her attorney. A proof of service is on the reverse.

WARNING: Your claim will in most instances be invalid if you do not properly complete this form, file it on time with the court, and mail or deliver a copy to the personal representative and his or her attorney.

1. Total amount of the claim: $275.00
2. Claimant (name):
   a. ☐ an individual
   b. ☒ an individual or entity doing business under the fictitious name of (specify):

   c. ☐ a partnership. The person signing has authority to sign on behalf of the partnership.
   d. ☐ a corporation. The person signing has authority to sign on behalf of the corporation.
   e. ☐ other (specify):
3. Address of claimant (specify): 5555 First Street, Santa Ana, CA 92705

4. Claimant is ☒ the creditor ☐ a person acting on behalf of creditor (state reason):

5. ☐ Claimant is ☐ the personal representative ☐ the attorney for the personal representative.
6. I am authorized to make this claim which is just and due or may become due. All payments on or offsets to the claim have been credited. Facts supporting the claim are ☒ on reverse ☐ attached.

I declare under penalty of perjury under the laws of the State of California that the foregoing is true and correct.

Date: 01/02/07

Joe McCormick, Owner
(TYPE OR PRINT NAME AND TITLE)

▶ *Joe McCormick*
(SIGNATURE OF CLAIMANT)

INSTRUCTIONS TO CLAIMANT

A. On the reverse, itemize the claim and show the date the service was rendered or the debt incurred. Describe the item or service in detail, and indicate the amount claimed for each item. Do not include debts incurred after the date of death, except funeral claims.

B. If the claim is not due or contingent, or the amount is not yet ascertainable, state the facts supporting the claim.

C. If the claim is secured by a note or other written instrument, the original or a copy must be attached (state why original is unavailable.) If secured by mortgage, deed of trust, or other lien on property that is of record, it is sufficient to describe the security and refer to the date or volume and page, and county where recorded. (See Prob. Code, § 9152.)

D. Mail or take this original claim to the court clerk's office for filing. If mailed, use certified mail, with return receipt requested.

E. Mail or deliver a copy to the personal representative and his or her attorney. Complete the *Proof of Mailing or Personal Delivery* on the reverse.

F. The personal representative or his or her attorney will notify you when your claim is allowed or rejected.

G. Claims against the estate by the personal representative and the attorney for the personal representative must be filed within the claim period allowed in Probate Code section 9100. See the notice box above.

(Continued on reverse)

Form Approved by the Judicial Council of California DE-172 [Rev. January 1, 1998] Mandatory Form [1/1/2000]	**CREDITOR'S CLAIM** **(Probate)**	Probate Code, §§ 9000 et seq., 9153

ESTATE OF *(Name)*: Jane Doe, a.k.a. Jane Doe Buck	CASE NUMBER:
DECEDENT	A 123456

FACTS SUPPORTING THE CREDITOR'S CLAIM
☐ See attachment *(if space is insufficient)*

Date of item	Item and supporting facts	Amount claimed
5/31/06	Ambulance Services - Transport Patient to St. Mary's Hospital	275.00
	TOTAL:	$275.00

PROOF OF ☒ **MAILING** ☐ **PERSONAL DELIVERY** **TO PERSONAL REPRESENTATIVE**
(Be sure to mail or take the original to the court clerk's office for filing)

1. I am the creditor or a person acting on behalf of the creditor. At the time of mailing or delivery I was at least 18 years of age.
2. My residence or business address is *(specify)*: 5555 First Street Santa Ana, CA 92705 (Business

3. I mailed or personally delivered a copy of this *Creditor's Claim* to the personal representative as follows *(check either a or b below)*:
   a. ☒ **Mail**. I am a resident of or employed in the county where the mailing occurred.
      (1) I enclosed a copy in an envelope AND
         (a) ☒ **deposited** the sealed envelope with the United States Postal Service with the postage fully prepaid.
         (b) ☐ **placed** the envelope for collection and mailing on the date and at the place shown in items below following our ordinary business practices. I am readily familiar with this business' practice for collecting and processing correspondence for mailing. On the same day that correspondence is placed for collection and mailing, it is deposited in the ordinary course of business with the United States Postal Service in a sealed envelope with postage fully prepaid.
      (2) The envelope was addressed and mailed first-class as follows:
         (a) Name of personal representative served: John Smith
         (b) Address on envelope: 111 Maple Street
            Los Angeles, CA 90940
         (c) Date of mailing:
         (d) Place of mailing *(city and state)*: Santa Ana, California
   b. ☐ **Personal delivery**. I personally delivered a copy of the claim to the personal representative as follows:
      (1) Name of personal representative served:
      (2) Address where delivered:

      (3) Date delivered:
      (4) Time delivered:

I declare under penalty of perjury under the laws of the State of California that the foregoing is true and correct.
Date: 01/02/07

Joe McCormick   ▶   *Joe McCormick*
(TYPE OR PRINT NAME OF CLAIMANT)   (SIGNATURE OF CLAIMANT)

CREDITOR'S CLAIM
(Probate)

WEST GROUP
Official Publisher

DE-174

ATTORNEY OR PARTY WITHOUT ATTORNEY (Name, state bar number, and address):	FOR COURT USE ONLY
John Smith, In Pro Per 111 Maple Street Los Angeles, CA 90940 TELEPHONE NO.: 555-431-1234 FAX NO.: ATTORNEY FOR (Name):	

SUPERIOR COURT OF CALIFORNIA, COUNTY OF Orange
STREET ADDRESS: 341 The City Drive South
MAILING ADDRESS:
CITY AND ZIP CODE: Orange, CA 92668
BRANCH NAME: Probate

ESTATE OF (Name):
    Jane Doe, a.k.a. Jane Doe Buck
                                DECEDENT

ALLOWANCE OR REJECTION OF CREDITOR'S CLAIM	CASE NUMBER: A-123456

NOTE: Attach a copy of the creditor's claim. If allowance or rejection by the court is not required, do not include any pages attached to the creditor claim form.

PERSONAL REPRESENTATIVE'S ALLOWANCE OR REJECTION

1. Name of creditor (specify): McCormick Ambulence Services
2. The claim was filed on (date): 1/3/07
3. Date of first issuance of letters: 7/15/06
4. Date of Notice of Administration: 8/1/06
5. Date of decedent's death: 5/31/06
6. Estimated value of estate: $ 300,000.00
7. Total amount of the claim: $ 275.00
8. [X] Claim is allowed for: $ 275.00   (The court must approve certain claims before they are paid.)
9. [ ] Claim is rejected for: $ (A creditor has three months to act on a rejected claim. See box below.)
10. Notice of allowance or rejection given on (date): February 1, 2007
11. [X] The personal representative is authorized to administer the estate under the Independent Administration of Estates Act.

Date: 2/1/07

. . . . John Smith . . . . ▶   *John Smith*
          (TYPE OR PRINT NAME)   (SIGNATURE OF PERSONAL REPRESENTATIVE)

REJECTED CLAIMS: From the date notice of rejection is given, the creditor must act on the rejected claim (e.g., file a lawsuit) as follows:

    a. **Claim due:** within three months after the notice of rejection.
    b. **Claim not due:** within three months after the claim becomes due.

COURT'S APPROVAL OR REJECTION

12. [ ] Approved for: $

13. [ ] Rejected for: $

Date:

14. Number of pages attached: _____

SIGNATURE OF [ ] JUDGE [ ] COMMISSIONER
[ ] SIGNATURE FOLLOWS LAST ATTACHMENT

(Proof of Service on reverse)

Form Adopted for Mandatory Use
Judicial Council of California
DE-174 [Rev. January 1, 2000]

ALLOWANCE OR REJECTION OF CREDITOR'S CLAIM
(Probate)

Probate Code, § 9000 et seq.,
9250–9256, 9353

ESTATE OF *(Name)*: Jane Doe, a.k.a. Jane Doe Buck	CASE NUMBER:
DECEDENT	A-123456

PROOF OF [X] MAILING [ ] PERSONAL DELIVERY TO CREDITOR

1. At the time of mailing or personal delivery I was at least 18 years of age and **not a party** to this proceeding.

2. My residence or business address is *(specify)*: 111 Maple Street
   Los Angeles, CA 90940

3. I mailed or personally delivered a copy of the *Allowance or Rejection of Creditor's Claim* as follows *(complete either a or b)*:

   a. [X] **Mail.** I am a resident of or employed in the county where the mailing occurred.
      (1) I enclosed a copy in an envelope AND
         (a) [X] **deposited** the sealed envelope with the United States Postal Service with the postage fully prepaid.
         (b) [ ] **placed** the envelope for collection and mailing on the date and at the place shown in items below following our ordinary business practices. I am readily familiar with this business's practice for collecting and processing correspondence for mailing. On the same day that correspondence is placed for collection and mailing, it is deposited in the ordinary course of business with the United States Postal Service in a sealed envelope with postage fully prepaid.
      (2) The envelope was addressed and mailed first-class as follows:
         (a) Name of creditor served: McCormick Ambulence Services
         (b) Address on envelope: 5555 First Street, Santa Ana, CA 92705

         (c) Date of mailing: February 1, 2007
         (d) Place of mailing *(city and state)*: Los Angeles, California

   b. [ ] **Personal delivery.** I personally delivered a copy to the creditor as follows:
      (1) Name of creditor served:
      (2) Address where delivered:

      (3) Date delivered:
      (4) Time delivered:

I declare under penalty of perjury under the laws of the State of California that the foregoing is true and correct.

Date: 02/01/07

John Smith	▶ *John Smith*
(TYPE OR PRINT NAME OF DECLARANT)	(SIGNATURE OF DECLARANT)

ALLOWANCE OR REJECTION OF CREDITOR'S CLAIM
(Probate)

DE-165

ATTORNEY OR PARTY WITHOUT ATTORNEY *(Name, state bar number, and address)*:	TELEPHONE AND FAX NOS.: 555-431-1234	FOR COURT USE ONLY

John Smith, In Pro Per
111 Maple St.
Los Angeles, CA 90940

ATTORNEY FOR *(Name)*:

SUPERIOR COURT OF CALIFORNIA, COUNTY OF ORANGE
STREET ADDRESS: 341 THE CITY DRIVE SOUTH
MAILING ADDRESS:
CITY AND ZIP CODE: ORANGE, CA 92668
BRANCH NAME: PROBATE

ESTATE OF *(Name)*: JANE DOE, a.k.a. JANE DOE BUCK

DECEDENT

NOTICE OF PROPOSED ACTION **Independent Administration of Estates Act** ☐ Objection ☐ Consent	CASE NUMBER: A-00001

> **NOTICE:** If you do not object in writing or obtain a court order preventing the action proposed below, you will be treated as if you consented to the proposed action and you may not object after the proposed action has been taken. If you object, the personal representative may take the proposed action only under court supervision. An objection form is on the reverse. If you wish to object, you may use the form or prepare your own written objection.

1. The personal representative (executor or administrator) of the estate of the deceased is *(names)*:   John Smith

2. The personal representative has authority to administer the estate without court supervision under the Independent Administration of Estates Act (Prob. Code, § 10400 et seq.)
   a. ☒ with **full authority** under the act.
   b. ☐ with **limited authority** under the act (there is no authority, without court supervision, to (1) sell or exchange real property or (2) grant an option to purchase real property or (3) borrow money with the loan secured by an encumbrance upon real property).

3. On or after *(date)*: ☐08-15-07☐ , the personal representative will take the following action without court supervision *(describe in specific terms here or in Attachment 3)*:
   ☒ The proposed action is described in an attachment labeled Attachment 3.

4. ☒ **Real property transaction** *(Check this box and complete item 4b if the proposed action involves a sale or exchange or a grant of an option to purchase real property.)*
   a. The material terms of the transaction are specified in item 3, including any sale price and the amount of or method of calculating any commission or compensation to an agent or broker.
   b. $ 90,000   is the value of the subject property in the probate inventory.   ☐ No inventory yet.

> **NOTICE:** A sale of real property without court supervision means that the sale will NOT be presented to the court for confirmation at a hearing at which higher bids for the property may be presented and the property sold to the highest bidder.

(Continued on reverse)

Form Approved by the
Judicial Council of California
DE-165 [Rev. January 1, 1998]

NOTICE OF PROPOSED ACTION
Objection - Consent
(Probate)

Probate Code, § 10580 et seq.

ESTATE OF *(Name)*: JANE DOE, a.k.a. JANE DOE BUCK	CASE NUMBER:
DECEDENT	A-00001

5. **If you OBJECT to the proposed action**

    a. **Sign** the objection form below and deliver or mail it to the personal representative at the following address *(specify name and and address)*:

        OR

    b. **Send** your own written objection to the address in item 5a. *(Be sure to identify the proposed action and state that you object to it.)*
        OR

    c. **Apply** to the court for an order preventing the personal representative from taking the proposed action without court supervision.

    d. **NOTE:** Your written objection or the court order must be received by the personal representative before the date in the box in item 3, or before the proposed action is taken, whichever is later. If you object, the personal representative may take the proposed action only under court supervision.

6. **If you APPROVE the proposed action**, you may sign the consent form below and return it to the address in item 5a. If you do not object in writing or obtain a court order, you will be treated as if you consented to the proposed action.

7. **If you need more INFORMATION, call** *(name)*:   John Smith
                      (telephone):   (714) 555-5555

Date: 07-20-07

John Smith
        (TYPE OR PRINT NAME)

▶ *John Smith*
      (SIGNATURE OF PERSONAL REPRESENTATIVE OR ATTORNEY)

OBJECTION TO PROPOSED ACTION

☐ **I OBJECT** to the action proposed in item 3.

NOTICE:	Sign and return this form (both sides) to the address in item 5a. The form must be received before the date in the box in item 3, or before the proposed action is taken, whichever is later. *(You may want to use certified mail, with return receipt requested. Make a copy of this form for your records.)*

Date:

        (TYPE OR PRINT NAME)

▶
      (SIGNATURE OF OBJECTOR)

CONSENT TO PROPOSED ACTION

☐ **I CONSENT** to the action proposed in item 3.

NOTICE:	You may indicate your *consent* by signing and returning this form (both sides) to the address in item 5a. If you do not object in writing or obtain a court order, you will be treated as if you consented to the proposed action.

Date:

        (TYPE OR PRINT NAME)

▶
      (SIGNATURE OF CONSENTER)

NOTICE OF PROPOSED ACTION

ATTACHMENT 3

1. Property to be sold consists of a 100% interest in a single family residence located at 300 Orange Street, Santa Ana, California, legally described as:

> Lot 9 of Tract 111, in the City of Santa Ana, County of Orange, State of California, as per map thereof recorded in Book 15, page 25 of Miscellaneous Records of Orange County.

2. Seller to pay sales commission of 6% ($5,400.00) as follows:

> 3% ($2,700.00) to be paid to Anthony Haley Real Estate
>
> 3% ($2,700.00) to be paid to Tim Thomas Real Estate

3. Buyers are John Lemmon and Jeanette Lemmon, husband and wife, as joint tenants.

4. Seller to pay pest corrective work and general repairs not to exceed $10,000.00.

5. Property to be sold in "as is" condition for 300,000.00.

6. Seller and buyer to pay all "customary" escrow and other charges not enumerated above.

7. Escrow to close not later than October 10, 2007.

This page intentionally left blank.

DE-166

ATTORNEY OR PARTY WITHOUT ATTORNEY *(Name, state bar number, and address):*	TELEPHONE AND FAX NOS.:	FOR COURT USE ONLY

555-431-1234

John Smith, In Pro Per
111 Maple St.
Los Angeles, CA 90940

ATTORNEY FOR *(Name)*:

SUPERIOR COURT OF CALIFORNIA, COUNTY OF ORANGE
  STREET ADDRESS: 341 THE CITY DRIVE SOUTH
  MAILING ADDRESS:
  CITY AND ZIP CODE: ORANGE, CA 92668
  BRANCH NAME: PROBATE

ESTATE OF *(Name)*: JANE DOE, a.k.a. JANE DOE BUCK

                           DECEDENT

WAIVER OF NOTICE OF PROPOSED ACTION (Probate Code section 10583) (Revocation of Waiver)	CASE NUMBER: A-00001

WARNING
READ BEFORE YOU SIGN

A. The law requires the personal representative to give you notice of certain actions he or she proposes to take to administer the estate. If you sign this form, the personal representative will NOT have to give you notice.

B. You have the right (1) to object to a proposed action and (2) to require the court to supervise the proposed action. If you do not object before the personal representative acts, you lose your right and you cannot object later.

C. IF YOU SIGN THIS FORM, YOU GIVE UP YOUR RIGHT TO RECEIVE NOTICE. This means you give the personal representative the right to take actions concerning the estate without first giving you the notice otherwise required by law. You cannot object after the action is taken.

D. You have the right to revoke (cancel) this waiver at any time. Your revocation must be in writing and is not effective until it is actually received by the personal representative. *(A form to revoke your waiver is on the reverse. You may want to revoke this waiver later. Keep a copy of this form so you can.)*

E. If you do not understand this form, ask a lawyer to explain it to you.

WAIVER OF RIGHT TO NOTICE

1. **I understand** that the **personal representative** named here has authority to administer the estate of the decedent without court supervision under the Independent Administration of Estates Act (California Probate Code sections 10400-10592).
   a. *(name):* John Smith
   b. *(address):* 111 Maple Street, Los Angeles, Ca. 90940

(Mail or deliver notices to the personal representative at this address.)

2. **I understand** I have the right to receive notice of certain actions the personal representative may propose to take. I understand that those actions may affect my interest in the estate.

3. **I understand** that by signing this waiver form I give up my right to receive notices from the personal representative of actions he or she may decide to take.

(Continued on reverse)

WAIVER OF NOTICE OF PROPOSED ACTION
(Probate)

Probate Code, §§ 10583, 10584

ESTATE OF *(Name)*: JANE DOE, a.k.a. JANE DOE BUCK	CASE NUMBER:
DECEDENT	A-00001

4. By signing below, **I WAIVE MY RIGHT** to receive prior notice of *(CHECK ONLY ONE BOX to indicate your choice)*:

   a. [X] Any and all actions the personal representative is authorized to take under the Independent Administration of Estates Act.

   b. [ ] Any of the kinds of transactions I have listed below that the personal representative is authorized to take under the Independent Administration of Estates Act *(specify which actions you are waiving your right to receive notice of)*:

        [ ] See Attachment 4.

Date: 07-02-07

Benjamin Ficiary
....
(TYPE OR PRINT NAME)

▶ *Benjamin Ficiary*
           (SIGNATURE)

My address is *(type or print)*: 702 Oak Lane, Irvine, Ca.

(Keep a copy for your records.)

REVOCATION OF WAIVER OF NOTICE OF PROPOSED ACTION

1. I previously signed a waiver of my right to receive notices of proposed actions by the personal representative under the Independent Administration of Estates Act.

2. **I revoke** (cancel) any previous waiver of my right to receive notices of proposed actions by the personal representative of the estate of the decedent.

3. I request the personal representative to send me all notices required by law.

Date:

▶
....
(TYPE OR PRINT NAME)
           (SIGNATURE)

My address is *(type or print)*:

(Mail or deliver this revocation to the personal representative at the address in item 1 on the reverse. Keep a copy for your records.)

PROOF OF SERVICE BY MAIL

1. I mailed a copy of the [X] *Waiver of Notice of Proposed Action* [ ] *Revocation* to the personal representative by [X] depositing a copy of the revocation with the United States Postal Service, in a sealed envelope with postage fully prepaid by first-class mail or [ ] placing the envelope for collection and mailing on the date and place below following our ordinary business practices. I am readily familiar with this business' practice for collecting and processing correspondence for mailing. On the same day that correspondence is placed for collection and mailing, it is deposited in the ordinary course of business with the Untied States Postal Service in a sealed envelope with postage fully prepaid.
   I am a resident of or employed in the county where the mailing occurred.

2. The envelope was addressed and mailed as follows:
   a. Name of personal representative served: John Smith
   b. Address on envelope: 111 Maple Street, Los Angeles, CA 92625

   c. Date of mailing: 07-03-07
   d. Place of mailing *(city and state)*: Los Angeles, Ca.

I declare under penalty of perjury under the laws of the State of California that the foregoing is true and correct.
Date: 07-04-07

Benjamin Ficiary
....
(TYPE OR PRINT NAME)

▶ *Benjamin Ficiary*
           (SIGNATURE)

DE-166 [Rev. January 1, 1996]   **WAIVER OF NOTICE OF PROPOSED ACTION**   Page two
                                      (Probate)

DE-270, GC-070

ATTORNEY OR PARTY WITHOUT ATTORNEY (Name, state bar number, and address):	TELEPHONE AND FAX NOS.: 555-431-1234	FOR COURT USE ONLY

John Smith, In Pro Per
111 Maple St.
Los Angeles, CA 90940

ATTORNEY FOR (Name):

SUPERIOR COURT OF CALIFORNIA, COUNTY OF ORANGE

STREET ADDRESS: 341 THE CITY DRIVE SOUTH

MAILING ADDRESS:

CITY AND ZIP CODE: ORANGE, CA 92668

BRANCH NAME: PROBATE

ESTATE OF (Name): JANE DOE, a.k.a. JANE DOE BUCK

[X] DECEDENT [ ] CONSERVATEE [ ] MINOR

EX PARTE PETITION FOR AUTHORITY TO SELL SECURITIES AND ORDER	CASE NUMBER: A-00001

1. **Petitioner** (name of each. See footnote[1] before completing): John Smith

   is the [X] personal representative [ ] conservator [ ] guardian of the estate and requests a court order authorizing sale of estate securities.

2. a. The estate's securities described on the reverse should be sold for cash at the market price at the time of sale on an established stock or bond exchange, or, if unlisted, the sale will be made for not less than the minimum price stated on the reverse.

   b. [X] Authority is given in decedent's will to sell property; **or**

   c. [ ] The sale is necessary to raise cash to pay
      (1) [ ] debts
      (2) [ ] legacies
      (3) [ ] family allowance
      (4) [ ] expenses
      (5) [ ] support of ward
      (6) [ ] other (specify):

   d. [X] The sale is for the advantage, benefit, and best interests of the estate, and those interested in the estate.

   e. Other facts pertinent to this petition are as follows:
      (1) [ ] Special notice has not been requested.
      (2) [ ] Waivers of all special notices are presented with this petition.
      (3) [ ] No security to be sold is specifically bequeathed.
      (4) [ ] Other (specify):

Date: ▶ _____

(SIGNATURE OF ATTORNEY*)

* (Signature of all petitioners also required (Prob. Code , § 1020).)

I declare under penalty of perjury under the laws of the State of California that the foregoing is true and correct.

Date: 08-05-07

John Smith
_____
(TYPE OR PRINT NAME)

▶ *John Smith*
_____
(SIGNATURE OF PETITIONER)

_____
(TYPE OR PRINT NAME)

▶ _____
(SIGNATURE OF PETITIONER)

[1] Each personal representative, guardian, or conservator must sign the petition.

(Continued on reverse)

Form Approved by the
Judicial Council of California
DE-270, GC-070 [Rev. January 1, 1998]

EX PARTE PETITION FOR AUTHORITY TO SELL SECURITIES AND ORDER

Probate Code, §§9630, 10000, 10200, 10201, 10252, 10261

ESTATE OF *(Name)*: JANE DOE, a.k.a. JANE DOE BUCK	CASE NUMBER:
	A-00001

LIST OF SECURITIES

Number of shares or face value of bonds	Name of security	Name of exchange *(when required by local rule)*	Recent bid asked *(when required by local rule)*	Minimum selling price
100	XYZ Corp.	NYSE	$80.00/share	$75.00/share

ORDER AUTHORIZING SALE OF SECURITIES

THE COURT FINDS the sale is proper.

THE COURT ORDERS

the ☐ personal representative ☐ guardian ☐ conservator is authorized to sell the securities described above upon the terms and conditions specified. Notice of hearing on the petition is dispensed with.

Date: _____

_____
JUDGE OF THE SUPERIOR COURT

☐ SIGNATURE FOLLOWS LAST ATTACHMENT

DE-270, GC-070 [Rev. January 1, 1998]

**EX PARTE PETITION FOR AUTHORITY
TO SELL SECURITIES AND ORDER**

Page two

DE-260/GC-060

ATTORNEY OR PARTY WITHOUT ATTORNEY *(Name, State Bar number, and address)*:	FOR COURT USE ONLY

Jimmy Smith, In Pro Per
2222 Swift Street
Los Angeles, CA 90189
TELEPHONE NO.:(555) 555-5555 FAX NO. *(Optional)*:
E-MAIL ADDRESS *(Optional)*:jimmysmith@email.com
ATTORNEY FOR *(Name)*:

SUPERIOR COURT OF CALIFORNIA, COUNTY OF
STREET ADDRESS: 1111 Main Street, Santa Ana, CA 92701
MAILING ADDRESS:
CITY AND ZIP CODE: 2222 Swift St., Los Angeles, CA 90189
BRANCH NAME: Probate

[X] ESTATE   [ ] CONSERVATORSHIP   [ ] GUARDIANSHIP   OF
(Name): Jane Smith, a.k.a Jane Doe Smith
[X] DECEDENT   [ ] CONSERVATEE   [ ] MINOR

**REPORT OF SALE AND PETITION FOR ORDER
CONFIRMING SALE OF REAL PROPERTY**
[ ] **and Sale of Other Property Sold as a Unit**

CASE NUMBER: A00001

HEARING DATE AND TIME: 04/15/07, 9:00 AM   DEPT.: L73

1. **Petitioner** *(name of each)*:

    is the [X] personal representative [ ] conservator [ ] guardian   of the estate of the decedent, conservatee, or minor
    [ ] purchaser (30 days have passed since the sale) *(Attach supporting declaration (Prob. Code, § 10308(b).)*

    and **requests** a court order for *(check all that apply)*:
    a. confirmation of sale of the estate's interest in the real property described in Attachment 2e
    b. [ ] confirmation of sale of the estate's interest in other property sold as a unit as described in Attachment 2c.
    c. [X] approval of commission of *(specify)*:   % of the amount of: $ 12,000.00
    d. additional bond [ ] is fixed at: $ [X] is not required.

2. **Description of property sold**
    a. Interest sold: [X] 100% [ ] Undivided *(specify)*:   %
    b. [X] Improved [ ] Unimproved
    c. [ ] Real property sold as a unit with other property *(describe in Attachment 2c)*.
    d. Street address and location *(specify)*:

        1111 Main St., Santa Ana, CA 92701

    e. Legal description is affixed as Attachment 2e.

3. **Appraisal**
    a. Date of death of decedent or appointment of conservator or guardian *(specify)*: 02/01/07
    b. Appraised value at above date: $ 2000,000.00
    c. Reappraised value within one year before the hearing: $ [ ] Amount includes value of other property
        sold as a unit. *(If more than one year has elapsed from the date in item 3a to the date of the hearing, reappraisal is required.)*
    d. Appraisal or reappraisal by probate referee [X] has been filed [ ] will be filed
        [ ] has been waived by order dated:

4. **Manner and terms of sale**
    a. Name of purchaser and manner of vesting title *(specify)*: Bobby Buyer, an unmarried man

    b. [ ] Purchaser is the [ ] personal representative [ ] attorney for the personal representative.
    c. Sale was [X] private [ ] public   on *(date)*: 02/15/07
    d. Amount bid: $ 20,000.00   Deposit: $ 20,000.00
    e. Payment [X] Cash [ ] Credit *(specify terms on Attachment 4e)*.
    f. [X] Other terms of sale *(specify terms on Attachment 4f)*.
    g. [ ] Mode of sale specified in will. [ ] Petitioner requests relief from complying for the reasons stated in Attachment 4g.
    h. [ ] Terms comply with Probate Code section 2542 *(guardianships and conservatorships)*.

Page 1 of 2

Form Adopted for Mandatory Use
Judicial Council of California
DE-260/GC-060 [Rev. January 1, 2006]

**REPORT OF SALE AND PETITION FOR ORDER
CONFIRMING SALE OF REAL PROPERTY**
(Probate—Decedents' Estates and Guardianships and Conservatorships)

Probate Code, §§ 2540 10308
www.courtinfo.ca.gov

DE-260/GC-060

[X] ESTATE [ ] CONSERVATORSHIP [ ] GUARDIANSHIP OF	CASE NUMBER:
(Name): Jane Smith, a.k.a. Jane Doe Smith	A00001

5. **Commission**
   a. [ ] Sale without broker
   b. [X] A written [ ] exclusive [ ] nonexclusive contract for commission was entered into with *(name):*
      First Real Estate, Inc.
   c. [X] Purchaser was procured by *(name):* Billy Broker
      a licensed real estate broker who is not buying for his or her account.
   d. [X] Commission is to be divided as follows: 100% to Billy Broker

6. **Bond**
   a. Amount before sale: $ 200,000.00   [ ] none.
   b. Additional amount needed: $ [X] none.
   c. [ ] Proceeds are to be deposited in a blocked account. Receipts will be filed. *(Specify institution and location):*

7. **Notice of sale**
   a. [ ] Published [ ] Posted as permitted by Probate Code section 10301 ($5,000 or less)
   b. [X] Will authorizes sale of the property
   c. [ ] Will directs sale of the property

8. **Notice of hearing**
   a. Special devisee:
      (1) [X] None.
      (2) [ ] Consent to be filed.
      (3) [ ] Written notice will be given.
   c. Personal representative, conservator of the estate, or guardian of the estate:
      (1) [X] Petitioner (consent or notice not required).
      (2) [ ] Consent to be filed.
      (3) [ ] Written notice will be given.
   b. Special notice:
      (1) [X] None requested.
      (2) [ ] Has been or will be waived.
      (3) [ ] Required written notice will be given.

9. **Reason for sale** *(need not complete if item 7b or 7c checked)*
   a. [ ] Necessary to pay
      (1) [ ] debts
      (2) [ ] devise
      (3) [ ] family allowance
      (4) [ ] expenses of administration
      (5) [ ] taxes
   b. [X] The sale is to the advantage of the estate and in the best interest of the interested persons.

10. **Formula for overbids**
    a. Original bid: $ 200,000.00
    b. 10% of first $10,000 of original bid: $ 1,000.00
    c. 5% of (original bid minus $10,000): $ 9,500.00
    d. Minimum overbid (a + b + c): $ 210,500.00

11. **Overbid.** Required amount of first overbid *(see item 10):* $ 210,500.00

12. **Petitioner's efforts** to obtain the highest and best price reasonably attainable for the property were as follows *(specify activities taken to expose the property to the market, e.g., multiple listings, advertising, open houses, etc.):*

    Listed on Multiple Listing Service for over three months, advertised in newspaper, 500 flyers mailed by realtor, at least 10 private showings.

13. Number of pages attached: 1

Date:

▶

_____
(TYPE OR PRINT NAME OF ATTORNEY)

_____
(SIGNATURE OF ATTORNEY*)
* (Signature of all petitioners also required (Prob. Code, § 1020))

I declare under penalty of perjury under the laws of the State of California that the foregoing is true and correct.

Date: 06/10/04

Jimmy Smith
_____
(TYPE OR PRINT NAME OF PETITIONER)

▶ *Jimmy Smith*
_____
(SIGNATURE OF PETITIONER)

DE-260 GC-060 [Rev. January 1, 2006]

REPORT OF SALE AND PETITION FOR ORDER CONFIRMING SALE OF REAL PROPERTY
(Probate—Decedents' Estates and Guardianships and Conservatorships)

Page 2 of 2

DE-260 Report of Sale and Petition for Order Confirming Sale of Real Property
Estate of Jane Smith, a.k.a., Jane Doe Smith, Deceased
Case No. A00001

Attachment 2e

Improved real property (single family residence) located at 1111 Main St., Santa Ana, CA, and more accurately described as:

> "Lot 1 of Tract No. 1000, in the City of Santa Ana, County of Orange, California as per map recorded in Book 100, Page(s) 10-15, Inclusive of Miscellaneous Maps in the Office of the County Recorder of said County."

> APN: 123-456-78

Attachment 4f

1. Escrow cost to be divided ½ to Seller, ½ to Buyer.

2. Escrow to close within 30 days of Court Order Approving Sale.

3. Seller to pay customary Seller's costs, including but not limited to, county transfer tax, any city transfer tax/fee, zone disclosure reports, smoke detectors and/or water heater bracing, owner's title insurance policy, recommended work to correct conditions described in Pest Control Report as "Section 1."

4. The cost of the items described herein shall not exceed $10,000.

5. Property is sold "as is" except as to title.

This page intentionally left blank.

DE-120

ATTORNEY OR PARTY WITHOUT ATTORNEY *(Name, State Bar number, and address)*: John Smith, In Pro Per 1111 Main Street Santal Ana, CA 92701 TELEPHONE NO.: (555) 555-5555 FAX NO. *(Optional)*: E-MAIL ADDRESS *(Optional)*: johnsmith@email.com ATTORNEY FOR *(Name)*:	FOR COURT USE ONLY

SUPERIOR COURT OF CALIFORNIA, COUNTY OF Orange
  STREET ADDRESS: 341 The City Drive South
  MAILING ADDRESS:
  CITY AND ZIP CODE: Orange, CA 9268
  BRANCH NAME: Probate

[X] ESTATE OF *(Name)*: [ ] IN THE MATTER OF *(Name)*:
Jane Smith, a.k.a. Jane Doe Smith
       [x] DECEDENT [ ] TRUST [ ] OTHER

NOTICE OF HEARING—DECEDENT'S ESTATE OR TRUST	CASE NUMBER: A00001

This notice is required by law.
This notice does not require you to appear in court, but you may attend the hearing if you wish.

---

1. NOTICE is given that *(name)*:   John Smith
   (representative capacity, if any): Executor

   has filed *(specify)*:*

   Report of Sale and Petition for Order Confirming Sale of Real Property

2. You may refer to the filed documents for more information. *(Some documents filed with the court are confidential.)*

3. A HEARING on the matter will be held as follows:

   a.   Date: 04/15/07   Time: 9:00 AM Dept.:   L73   Room:

   b. Address of court [X] shown above   [ ] is *(specify)*:

Assistive listening systems, computer-assisted real-time captioning, or sign language interpreter services are available upon request if at least 5 days notice is provided. Contact the clerk's office for *Request for Accommodations by Persons With Disabilities and Order* (form MC-410). (Civil Code section 54.8.)

---

* Do **not** use this form to give notice of a petition to administer estate (see Prob. Code, § 8100 and form DE-121) or notice of a hearing in a guardianship or conservatorship (see Prob. Code, §§ 1511 and 1822 and form GC-020).

Page 1 of 2

NOTICE OF HEARING—DECEDENT'S ESTATE OR TRUST
(Probate—Decedents' Estates)

	ESTATE OF *(Name):*		IN THE MATTER OF *(Name):*	CASE NUMBER:
X				A00001

| | X DECEDENT | | TRUST | | OTHER |

CLERK'S CERTIFICATE OF POSTING

1. I certify that I am not a party to this cause.
2. A copy of the foregoing *Notice of Hearing—Decedent's Estate or Trust*
   a. was posted at *(address):*

   b. was posted on *(date):*

Date: _____   Clerk, by _____ , Deputy

PROOF OF SERVICE BY MAIL *

1. I am over the age of 18 and not a party to this cause. I am a resident of or employed in the county where the mailing occurred.
2. My residence or business address is *(specify):*

   Willie Witness
   6666 Wilson Ave.
   Santa Ana, CA 92701

3. I served the foregoing *Notice of Hearing—Decedent's Estate or Trust* on each person named below by enclosing a copy in an envelope addressed as shown below AND
   a. [X] **depositing** the sealed envelope on the date and at the place shown in item 4 with the United States Postal Service with the postage fully prepaid.
   b. [ ] **placing** the envelope for collection and mailing on the date and at the place shown in item 4 following our ordinary business practices. I am readily familiar with this business's practice for collecting and processing correspondence for mailing. On the same day that correspondence is placed for collection and mailing, it is deposited in the ordinary course of business with the United States Postal Service in a sealed envelope with postage fully prepaid.

4. a. Date mailed: 03/01/07   b. Place mailed *(city, state):* Santa Ana, CA

5. [X] I served with the *Notice of Hearing—Decedent's Estate or Trust* a copy of the petition or other document referred to in the Notice.

I declare under penalty of perjury under the laws of the State of California that the foregoing is true and correct.

Date: 03/01/07   .

_____   _____
(TYPE OR PRINT NAME OF PERSON COMPLETING THIS FORM)   (SIGNATURE OF PERSON COMPLETING THIS FORM)

NAME AND ADDRESS OF EACH PERSON TO WHOM NOTICE WAS MAILED

	Name of person served	Address *(number, street, city, state, and zip code)*
1.	John Smith, Husband	1111 Main St., Santa Ana, CA 92701
2.	Jimmy Smith, Son	2222 Swift St., Los Angeles, CA 90189
3.	Jenny Smith, Daughter	3333 Bay Ct., Newport Beach, CA 90189
4.	Jack Jones, Brother	4444 Mesa Dr., Las Vegas, NV 89191

[ ] Continued on an attachment. *(You may use* Attachment to Notice of Hearing Proof of Service by Mail, *form DE-120(MA)/GC-020(MA), for this purpose.)*

* Do not use this form for proof of personal service. You may use form DE-120(P) to prove personal service of this Notice.

NOTICE OF HEARING—DECEDENT'S ESTATE OR TRUST
(Probate—Decedents' Estates)

DE-265/GC-065

ATTORNEY OR PARTY WITHOUT ATTORNEY *(Name, State Bar number, and address):*
After recording return to:

Jimmy Smith, In Pro Per
2222 Swift Street
Los Angeles, CA 90189

TELEPHONE NO.: (555) 555-5555
FAX NO. *(Optional):*
E-MAIL ADDRESS *(Optional):*
ATTORNEY FOR *(Name):*

SUPERIOR COURT OF CALIFORNIA, COUNTY OF Orange
STREET ADDRESS: 341 The City Drive South
MAILING ADDRESS:
CITY AND ZIP CODE: Orange, CA 92668
BRANCH NAME: Probate

FOR RECORDER'S USE

[✓] ESTATE OF
[ ] CONSERVATORSHIP OF   *(Name):* Jane Doe, a.k.a. Jane Doe Buck
[ ] GUARDIANSHIP OF   [✓] DECEDENT   [ ] CONSERVATEE   [ ] MINOR

ORDER CONFIRMING SALE OF REAL PROPERTY
[ ] **and Confirming Sale of Other Property as a Unit**

CASE NUMBER:
A-00001

1. Hearing date: 4/15/07   Time: 9:00 AM Dept.: L73   Rm.:

FOR COURT USE ONLY

THE COURT FINDS

2. All notices required by law were given and, if required, proof of notice of sale was made.
3. a. [✓] Sale was authorized or directed by the will
   b. [ ] Good reason existed for the sale
   of the property commonly described as *(street address or location):*

   1111 Main St., Santa Ana, CA 92701

4. The sale was legally made and fairly conducted.
5. The confirmed sale price is not disproportionate to the value of the property.
6. [✓] Private sale: The amount bid is 90% or more of the appraised value of the property as appraised within one year of the date of the hearing.
7. An offer exceeding the amount bid by the statutory percentages [✓] cannot be obtained   [ ] was obtained in open court. The offer complies with all applicable law.
8. The [✓] personal representative [ ] conservator [ ] guardian   of the estate of the decedent, conservatee, or minor has made reasonable efforts to obtain the highest and best price reasonably attainable for the property.

THE COURT ORDERS

9. The sale of the real property legally described [✓] in item 15 on page 2 [ ] on Attachment 9
   [ ] and other property sold as a unit described [ ] in item 15 on page 2 [ ] on Attachment 9   is confirmed to *(name):*

   (manner of vesting title): an unmarried man
   for the sale price of: $ 200,000.00   on the following terms *(use item 15 on page 2 or Attachment 9 if necessary):*

   [✓] Continued in item 15 on page 2.   [ ] Continued on Attachment 9.

10. The [✓] personal representative [ ] conservator [ ] guardian   of the estate of the decedent, conservatee, or minor
    (name): Jimmy Smith
    is directed to execute and deliver a conveyance of the estate's interest in the real property described in item 9
    [ ] and other property described in item 9 sold as a unit   upon receipt of the consideration for the sale.

    Page 1 of 2

Form Adopted for Mandatory Use
Judicial Council of California
DE-265/GC-065 [Rev. January 1, 2006]

ORDER CONFIRMING SALE OF REAL PROPERTY
(Probate—Decedents' Estates and Guardianships and Conservatorships)

Probate Code, §§ 2543, 10313
www.courtinfo.ca.gov

American LegalNet, Inc.
www.USCourtForms.com

DE-265/GC-065

✓ ESTATE ☐ CONSERVATORSHIP ☐ GUARDIANSHIP OF	CASE NUMBER:
(Name): Jane Doe, a.k.a. Jane Doe Smith	A00001

11. a. ☐ No additional bond is required.
    b. ☐ Additional bond is required in the amount of: $ _____ , surety, or otherwise, as provided by law.
    c. ✓ Net sale proceeds must be deposited by escrow holder in a blocked account to be withdrawn only on court order. Receipts must be filed. *(Specify institution and location):*

   Bank of America, 7777 Oak Pkwy., Santa Ana, CA 92701

12. a. ☐ No commission is payable.
    b. ✓ A commission from the proceeds of the sale is approved in the amount of: $ 12,000.00
       to be paid as follows *(specify):* First Real Estate, Inc.

13. Other *(specify, use Attachment 13 if necessary):*

14. Number of pages attached: ___0___

Date: _____

_____
JUDICIAL OFFICER
☐ Signature follows last attachment.

15. ✓ *(Check all that apply):* ✓ **Legal description** of the ✓ real property ☐ personal property in item 9:
    ✓ Additional terms of sale from item 9:

Lot 1 of Tract No. 1000, in the City of Santa Ana, County of Orange, California as per map recorded in Book 100, Page(s) 10-15, Inclusive of Miscellaneous Maps in the Office of the County Recorder of said County. (APN: 123-456-78)

1. Escrow cost to be divided ½ to Seller, ½ to Buyer.

2. Escrow to close within 30 days of Court Order Approving Sale.

3. Seller to pay customary Seller's costs, including but not limited to, county transfer tax, any city transfer tax/fee, zone disclosure reports, smoke detectors and/or water heater bracing, owner's title insurance policy, recommended work to correct conditions described n Pest Control Report as "Section 1."

4. The Cost of the items described herein shall not exceed $10,000.00.

5. Property is sold "as is" except as to title.

[SEAL]	**CLERK'S CERTIFICATE**
	I certify that the foregoing *Order Confirming Sale of Real Property,* including any attached description of real or personal property, is a true and correct copy of the original on file in my office.
	Date: _____ CLERK, by _____, Deputy

ORDER CONFIRMING SALE OF REAL PROPERTY
(Probate—Decedents' Estates and Guardianships and Conservatorships)

STATE OF CALIFORNIA
FRANCHISE TAX BOARD
Telephone (916) 845-4210

REQUEST FOR ESTATE
INCOME TAX CLEARANCE CERTIFICATE
As required under California Revenue
and Taxation Code Section 19513

☐ **Expedite Request (see instructions)**

PLEASE READ INSTRUCTIONS ON SIDE 2 BEFORE COMPLETING THIS FORM

MAIL TO: ESTATE INCOME TAX CLEARANCE CERTIFICATE UNIT MS D-7
FRANCHISE TAX BOARD
PO BOX 1468
SACRAMENTO CA 95812-1468

FILE AT LEAST 30 DAYS PRIOR TO THE COURT HEARING ON FINAL ACCOUNT. APPROXIMATE DATE OF COURT HEARING _04/15/07_

Estate of
Jane Smith, a.k.a. Jane Doe Smith

Federal Employer Id. No.	Date of Death 02/01/06

Name of Fiduciary
John Smith

Area Code and Phone No. 555 555-5555	Decedent's Social Security No. 123-456-78

Address of Fiduciary (Number and Street)
1111 Main Street

Probate No. **A00001**

City or Town, State, and ZIP Code
Santa Ana, CA 92701

County of Probate **Orange**

Name of Attorney
John Smith, In Pro Per

Area Code and Phone No. **555-555-5555**

Address of Attorney (Number and Street)
1111 Main Street

Mail Tax Clearance Certificate to:

City or Town, State, and ZIP Code
Santa Ana, CA 92701

☐ Attorney
☒ Fiduciary

ANSWER THESE QUESTIONS AND FURNISH THE REQUIRED DOCUMENTS

1. Was decedent a resident of the State of California on the date of death? _yes_
   (If "no," furnish a copy of the California Estate Tax Return (Form ET-1) and Declaration Concerning Residence (Form IT-2) if filed with the California State Controller).

2. Have probate proceedings been instituted in any other state? _no_

3. Value of the assets of this estate on date of death. (Please attach federal Form 706.) _500,000_
   (If not exceeding $1,000,000, you do not need an Estate Income Tax Clearance Certificate. **See instructions on Side 2.**)

4. Are assets exceeding $250,000 distributable to one or more nonresident beneficiaries? _yes_
   (If "no," you do not need an Estate Income Tax Clearance Certificate. **See instructions on Side 2.**)

5. Has a preliminary distribution been made? _no_
   (If "yes," furnish a copy of the court order authorizing the distribution.)

> **You must file a return for all taxable years that have ended (even if a return is not yet due), or submit a deposit in the form of check or bond in an amount to be determined by this office. We require a Specialized Tax Service Fee for Expedited Estate Income Tax Clearance Certificate Requests. See instructions on Side 2.**

DECLARATION REGARDING CALIFORNIA RETURNS FOR DECEDENT AND FOR ESTATE
(To be completed for the four taxable years immediately preceding the date of this request.)

A. DECEDENT
California Individual Income Tax Returns (Form 540, 540A, 540 2EZ, or Long or Short Form 540NR) have been filed by or on behalf of the decedent for the following years: _03_ _04_ _05_ _06_ . If the returns were not filed for any of the above years, explain in full: _____

_____

B. ESTATE
California Fiduciary Income Tax Returns (Form 541) have been filed for the following years:
_____ _____ _____ _____ . If fiduciary returns were not filed for any of the last four years during which the estate was in existence, explain in full: _Fiscal year return not yet due._

_____

I declare, under penalties of perjury, that the information given above is true to the best of my knowledge and belief.

John Smith   Executor   03/01/0
SIGNATURE OF FIDUCIARY OR REPRESENTATIVE   TITLE   DATE

ALLOW AT LEAST 30 DAYS FOR A RESPONSE TO THIS APPLICATION

INSTRUCTIONS

A. California Revenue and Taxation Code Section 19513 Estate Income Tax Clearance Certificates

For certain estates, Section 19513 prohibits the probate court from allowing the final account of the fiduciary unless the Franchise Tax Board certifies that all taxes have been paid or secured as required by law.

The Estate Income Tax Clearance Certificate is only required if an estate meets **BOTH** of the following **TWO** requirements:
(1) Had assets with a fair market value exceeding $1,000,000 on the date of death, **AND**
(2) Is to distribute assets exceeding $250,000 to one or more nonresident beneficiaries.

In determining if the assets exceed $1,000,000, include the fair market value of all assets on date of death, wherever situated, for decedents who were California residents. Nonresident decedents should only include the value of those assets located in California.

In determining if assets exceeding $250,000 are distributable to nonresident beneficiaries, the residency of a trust which is a beneficiary of the decedent's estate is determined by the residency of the trust's fiduciaries and beneficiaries.

Before issuing the Estate Income Tax Clearance Certificate, we require payment of all accrued taxes of the decedent and the estate. We may also require a deposit by check, or bond to secure the payment of any taxes which may later become payable.

The Estate Income Tax Clearance Certificate is valid only to the end of the current taxable year. We will only issue a new Estate Income Tax Clearance Certificate extending the expiration date when a return is filed for each subsequent year and the tax for that year, if any, is paid.

The Estate Income Tax Clearance Certificate is issued to the fiduciary or representative designated on the application. THE ACTUAL FILING OF THE ESTATE INCOME TAX CLEARANCE CERTIFICATE WITH THE COURT IS THE RESPONSIBILITY OF THE FIDUCIARY OR REPRESENTATIVE.

B. Effect of the Estate Income Tax Clearance Certificate and Continuing Liability of the Fiduciary

The Estate Income Tax Clearance Certificate issued under California Revenue and Taxation Code Section 19513 does not relieve the estate of liability for any taxes due or which may become due from the decedent or the estate. Neither does the certificate relieve the fiduciary of the personal liability for taxes and other expenses as imposed by California Revenue and Taxation Code Section 19516.

C. Other Information

You do not need to submit a copy of the Final Account of the fiduciary unless we request it.

We may require fiduciaries to withhold tax on California source income distributed to nonresident beneficiaries. Income from intangible personal property such as interest and dividend income or gain from the sale of stocks or bonds is generally not taxable to a nonresident beneficiary and therefore not subject to withholding. Failure to withhold when required may make the fiduciary personally liable for the amount due. For information on determining requirements for withholding, telephone **(888)** 792-4900 (toll free) or write to: Withholding Services and Compliance Section, Franchise Tax Board, PO Box 942867, Sacramento, CA 94267-0651.

Income earned by the estate in the final year in which its assets are distributed pursuant to a decree of final distribution is taxable to the beneficiaries. The estate must file a final return and properly report the income distribution.

You should compute the return for the fractional part of the year prior to death on the basis of the method of accounting followed by the decedent. You can **not** include income and deductions for expenses, interest, taxes, and depletion accrued solely by reason of death in the return of a decedent for the period in which death occurred. Include those items in the return of the estate or beneficiary, as the case may be, upon receipt or payment.

Return filing requirements are in the applicable instructions for the:

- California Individual Income Tax Returns (Form 540, 540A, 540 2EZ, or Long or Short Form 540NR)
- California Fiduciary Income Tax Returns (Form 541)

D. Returns Required

You must file a final fiduciary return (Form 541) for the year in which the estate closes if the filing requirements are met. You should also file a return to establish any excess deductions allowed to beneficiaries in the final year.

The decedents final personal income tax return (Form 540, 540A, 540 2EZ, or Long or Short Form 540NR) must be marked "FINAL" at the top of the return in block letters.

In addition, please furnish copies of any other returns filed for the decedent or the estate within the last 12 months. Write "COPY – DO NOT PROCESS" in bold letters on the face of each copy. If you submit original returns with this application, include an additional copy of each return with the words, **"COPY – DO NOT PROCESS"** in bold letters on the face of each copy. Mail the completed Estate Income Tax Request for Clearance Certificate and required returns to:

ESTATE INCOME TAX CLEARANCE CERTIFICATE UNIT
MS D-7
FRANCHISE TAX BOARD
PO BOX 1468
SACRAMENTO CA 95812-1468

Expedited Estate Income Tax Clearance Certificate Request

We charge a non-refundable $100 specialized service fee to process an Expedited Tax Clearance Certificate request. The fee is due and payable at the time you submit the request and **must** be paid by certified funds (cashiers check or money order). (CR&TC section 19591) Submit form FTB 3571, along with all necessary documentation and payment with certified funds (marked "Specialized Tax Service Fee") via overnight private mail service to:

Franchise Tax Board
Estate Income Tax Clearance Unit MS D-7
Sacramento CA 95827

ASSISTANCE

From within the United States, call ....(800) 852-5711
From outside the United States, call (not toll-free) ....(916) 845-6500

Website at: **www.ftb.ca.gov**

Assistance for persons with disabilities: We comply with the Americans with Disabilities Act. Persons with hearing or speech impairments please call TTY/TDD (800) 822-6268.

John Smith, In Pro Per
112 Maple St.
Los Angeles, CA 90040
(213) 555-5555

SUPERIOR COURT OF THE STATE OF CALIFORNIA

FOR THE COUNTY OF **ORANGE, LAMOREAUX JUSTICE CENTER**

The Estate of	)	CASE NO. A100001
	)	
JANE DOE, a.k.a.	)	FIRST AND FINAL ACCOUNT
	)	**(omit the words "ACCOUNT**
	)	**AND", add "(ACCOUNT WAIVED)"**
	)	**if there is no accounting)**
JANE DOE BUCK,	)	AND REPORT OF EXECUTOR **(or**
	)	**Administrator or Administrator C.T.A.**
	)	**as the case may be)**
	)	AND PETITION FOR APPROVAL
	)	OF DEBTS PAID WITHOUT
Deceased	)	CLAIMS; STATUTORY FEES TO
	)	EXECUTOR **(or ADMINISTRATOR**
	)	**or ADMINISTRATOR C.T.A.**
	)	**as the case may be)** AND FOR
	)	DISTRIBUTION OF TESTATE
	)	ESTATE **(or "INTESTATE"**
_____)	**if there is no Will)**

TO THE SUPERIOR COURT OF THE STATE OF CALIFORNIA, COUNTY OF **ORANGE:**

JOHN SMITH, as **Executor (or Administrator or Administrator, CTA)** of the estate of the above-named decedent, renders to the Court his **(the following description should follow the language used in the caption above)** first and final account and report of his administration of said estate and presents herewith his petition for approval of debts paid without claims filed **(if applicable)**, statutory fees to **Executor (if applicable)** and for distribution of testate **(or "intestate")** estate follows:

FIRST AND FINAL ACCOUNT AND REPORT OF EXECUTOR, ETC.

REPORT AND PETITION

The report and petition of the Executor of the estate of said decedent respectfully represents:

I

IF THE ACCOUNTING IS "WAIVED" THE FOLLOWING PARAGRAPH IS OMITTED

Summary of Account

Petitioner is chargeable with and is entitled to the charges and credits set forth in this summary of account. The account begins with Decedent's date of death, **January 1, 2007, and ends September 30, 2007.** The attached supporting schedules are incorporated herein by this reference.

CHARGES:

Inventory and Appraisement	$ 190,000.00
Income Receipts (Schedule A)	$ 4,000.00
Principal Receipts (Schedule B)	$ 1,000.00
Gain on Sale: (Schedule C)	$ 10,000.00
TOTAL CHARGES:	**$ 205,000.00**

CREDITS:

Disbursements (Schedule D)	$ 55,000.00
Loss on Sale: (Schedule E)	$ 995.00
Adjustment:	5.00
Assets on Hand (Schedule F)	
Cash **$140,000.00**	
Other **9,000.00**	$ 149,000.00

TOTAL CREDITS:	**$ 205,000.00**

(obviously the numbers will be different and some schedules may not even be applicable. Please note that the Total Credits and Total Charges "balance." Under "Credits" or "Charges" can be a nominal "adjustment" if necessary and as shown on this accounting)

II

Appointment of **Executor**

(Or Adminstrator, Administrator C.T.A., as the case may be)

On **January 1, 2007**, the above-named decedent, a resident of the County of **Orange**, State of California, died in **Fullerton, California**. On or about **February 1, 2007**, Petitioner filed herein his Petition for Probate and for Letters **Testamentary (or Letters of Administration as the case may be)** and on **March 15, 2007**, by a minute order of the above-entitled Court duly made and entered, Petitioner

FIRST AND FINAL ACCOUNT AND REPORT OF EXECUTOR, ETC.

was appointed as **Executor** of decedent's estate. Petitioner qualified as such **Executor** and Letters **Testamentary**, with **Full Authority to Administer Under the Independent Administration of Estates Act** were issued to Petitioner, on **March 15, 2007**. Thereupon Petitioner entered upon the administration of said estate and has ever since continued to administer it.

III

Notice of Death

Notice of Death and of Petition to Administer Estate, which included a notice to creditors, was given and published as required by law, and an Affidavit of Publication was filed herein on or about **March 19, 2007**. The time for presentation of claims (not covered by a written Notice of Administration of The Estate of J**ane Doe, a.k.a., Jane Doe Buck, mailed June 4, 2007)** against said estate expired **July 15, 2007 (time for filing claims not covered by written Notice of Administration of the Estate is 4 months).**

IV

Creditors' Claims **and Debts Paid Without Claims Filed**

(if applicable. If no such debts paid, title the paragraph "Creditors' Claims" and omit following paragraph)

Petitioner herein paid decedent's funeral expense and several pre-mortem debts without the filing of formal claims. Said debts were paid by Petitioner without the filing of a formal claim within the period in which a creditor's claim could have been filed. Said debts were justly due and paid by Petitioner in good faith. The amount being paid was the true amount of such indebtedness over and above all payments or set-offs, and the estate is solvent. Said claims paid without a formal creditor's claim being filed and paid within the time for filing claims were:

Sears	**Credit Card Debt**	290.35
OC Register	**Newspaper**	2.20
Gas Co.	**Utilities**	170.75
Pac. Bell	**Utilities**	22.14
Bank of America	**Credit Card**	1,509.83
Advanta	**Funeral**	7,764.00
Total:		$ 9,759.27

On **June 4, 2007**, Petitioner caused to be mailed a written Notice of Administration of The Estate of **Jane Doe, a.k.a., Jane Doe Buck**, to **six** suspected creditors of which Petitioner had knowledge. The time for filing claims by said noticed creditors was **August 3, 2007**.

FIRST AND FINAL ACCOUNT AND REPORT OF EXECUTOR, ETC.

Petitioner is unaware of any other creditors, and thus has given no other notices pursuant to Probate Code Section 9050. Petitioner did make a reasonable search for creditors after decedent's death by monitoring decedent's mail and searching locations where decedent kept financial records.

Two creditor's claim were filed or presented in this estate:

1. Robert Sisson, M.D. was given specific written notice on June 4, 2007 as indicated above and presented his claim of $147.15 before August 3, 2007. Said claim was approved in full and has been paid in full.

2. Carol Thomas was filed her claim on May 28, 2007, in the amount of $1,200.00. Petitioner rejected said claim in full on May 28, 2007, and mailed notice to said creditor on the same date. Said rejection and proof of service of mailing rejection dated were filed herein on June 3, 2007. No action taken by creditor and more than 90 days has elapsed since rejection sent to creditor and thus said claim is barred by law.

V

Inventory and Appraisement

On or about **May 5, 2007**, Petitioner duly made and returned to this Court a Complete and Final Inventory and Appraisement of the estate of said decedent, as of the date of her death, showing such property to be of the value of **$185,000.00**. On or about **August 10, 2007**, Petitioner duly made and returned to this Court a Supplemental No. 1 Inventory and Appraisement of said estate of said decedent, as of the date of her death, showing additional property to be of the value of **$5,000.00**, resulting in a total estate value of **$190,000.00**.

THE FOLLOWING PARAGRAPH IS USED IF DECEDENT LEFT A WILL

VI

Devisees and Legatees

The following are the only devisees and legatees under the Last Will and Testament of said decedent:

Name and Relationship	Age	Address
1. Lila Jones - daughter	Adult	444 Elm St. Lompoc, CA 93444
2. John Smith - son	Adult	112 Maple St. Los Angeles, CA 90040

FIRST AND FINAL ACCOUNT AND REPORT OF EXECUTOR, ETC.

The Last Will and Testament of decedent, duly admitted to probate herein provides for disposition of said estate as follows:

"THIRD: I devise to my children, JOHN SMITH and LILA JONES, all of my estate, real, personal and mixed, or whatsoever kind or character and wheresoever situated, of which I die possessed, or to which I may in any manner be entitled, in equal shares. In the event either of said beneficiaries should predecease me leaving issue surviving me, his/her share shall go and be distributed to his/her issue who survive me, by right of representation. In the event either of my children should predecease me and leave no issue who survive me then his/her share shall lapse."

Both said beneficiaries survived the decedent.

OR, IF THE ESTATE IS WITHOUT A WILL (INTESTATE), USE THE FOLLOWING SUBSTITUTE PARAGRAPH TYPE:

Heirs at Law

Decedent was single (divorced). Decedent had three children who are the only heirs under California Probate Code Sections 6402(a), to wit:

Name and Relationship	Age	Address
1. Lila Jones - daughter	Adult	444 Elm St.
		Lompoc, CA 93444
2. John Smith - son	Adult	112 Maple St.
		Los Angeles, CA 90040

Both said heirs are now living.

VII

Changes in Estate

During the course of the administration of the estate it was determined that it would be in the best interest of the estate to **sell items 1 and 2, attachment 2, of the Complete Inventory and Appraisement, i.e., decedent's car which sold for $4,000.00; $1,000.00 under its appraised value and decedent's residence which sold for $150,000.00; $10,000.00 more than its appraised value. Accordingly, said two sales resulted in a gain of $10,000.00 and a loss of $1,000.00 respectively to the estate. Said real property was sold via a Notice of Proposed Action to which all heirs affirmatively consented and the sale and the automobile was sold without notice or confirmation under Probate Code Section 10252(c) as an asset likely to depreciate in value or incur expense to the estate by being kept.**

Item 2 of attachment 1 of the Complete Inventory and Appraisement, a pre-mortem check, was converted to cash.

FIRST AND FINAL ACCOUNT AND REPORT OF EXECUTOR, ETC.

VIII
Inheritance and Estate Taxes

No California inheritance taxes are due as the decedent died in **2007**.

A Federal Estate Tax Return will not be filed for this estate, and no estate taxes will be paid as said estate subject to Federal Estate Taxes is less than **$1,500,000.00 (the federal estate tax "exemption" amount increases to $2,000,000 in 2006 with subsequent increases thereafter until 2011 when the federal estate tax exemption is reduced to $1,000,000. If a Federal Estate Tax Return was due this paragraph is be accordingly changed and the amount of tax and confirmation of its payment would be stated. Further, if a Federal Estate Tax is paid the allocation of that tax among the estate beneficiaries/heirs should be calculated and reflected on the paragraph entitled "Distribution of Estate" and in the "prayer" for distribution as an amount to be subtracted from each beneficiary/heir's distributable share, e.g., "From each beneficiary shall be deducted his/her share of the Federal Estate Taxes").**

IX
Status of Estate Substantiating Distribution

The time for presentation of claims against said estate has expired, and all filed creditor's claims have been paid in full. No inheritance or Federal Estate taxes were due **(If Federal Estate Taxes have been paid it should be alleged and further alleged that the Federal Estate Taxes due have been paid)**. All personal property taxes due or payable by said estate have been paid. All income taxes imposed under the provisions of the Personal Income Tax Law, which have become payable, have been paid.

Funeral and burial expense, and all expenses of the administration of said estate, excepting closing expenses, have been paid and discharged.

The whole of said estate is separate **(or community or separate and community. NOTE: A single person can only have separate property)** property, and said estate is now in a condition to be finally settled and distributed.

All cash received by Petitioner not necessary for the immediate expenses of the estate has been held in interest bearing savings accounts during the entire period of this accounting.

FIRST AND FINAL ACCOUNT AND REPORT OF EXECUTOR, ETC.

X

Legal Advertising, Bond Premiums and Referee's Fees

All legal advertising, bond premiums and fees of the probate referee have been paid, and there are none outstanding.

XI

Request for Special Notice, Notice to MediCal, and Notice to Department of Corrections

No requests for special notice of these proceedings have been made or filed herein.

The decedent was not a recipient of MediCal. Accordingly, notice under Probate Code Section 9209 was not given. **(If a notice was given because the decedent was a recipient of MediCal or because the Executor isn't sure if the decedent was or was not a recipient of MediCal it should be so stated as to the date NOTICE given and whether any claim was made within the four-month statutory period. If a notice is given to the Director of the California Department of Corrections because a beneficiary or heir was in a California jail or prison at the time of the decedent's death, it should be so stated as to the date notice is given and whether any claim is filed within the four month statutory period. If a claim was made to either then the resolution, i.e., payment or rejection, of the claim must be stated).**

IF THE PERSONAL REPRESENTATIVE IS CLAIMING ALL OR PART OF HIS/HER STATUTORY FEES:

XII

Statutory **Executor's** Commissions

JOHN SMITH, Executor hereunder, has rendered services in the administration of said estate for which no compensation has as yet been paid. The statutory amount allowable for such services is the sum of **$7,140.00,** computed as follows:

Amount of Inventory & Appraisement	$ 190,000.00
Add Income Receipts	4,000.00
Add Gain on Sale	10,000.00
Subtract Loss on Sale	(1,000.00)
Amount on which compensation is based	**207,000.00**

FIRST AND FINAL ACCOUNT AND REPORT OF EXECUTOR, ETC.

$100,000.00 at 4%	$ 4,000.00
$100,000.00 at 3%	3,000.00
$7,000.00 at 2%	140.00
Total statutory compensation	**$ 7,140.00**

IF THE PERSONAL REPRESENTATIVE IS WAIVING HIS OR HER STATUTORY FEES:

Waiver of **Executor's** Statutory Commissisons

Petitioner herein waives his statutory commissions for his services rendered to this estate as **Executor**.

XIII

Balance of Estate

The balance of said estate now remaining in the hands of Petitioner as of **September 31, 2007, consists of cash in the amount of $140,000.00 ($70,000.00 is held at Bank of America, acct#123-456 and $70,000.00 is held at Corona National Bank, acct#890-321), 100 shares, common, of XYZ Corp., valued at $8,000.00 and decedent's household furniture and furnishings and personal effects valued at $1,000.00 for a total estate on hand of $149,000.00.**

As shown on Schedule G, "9/30/07 Actual Value of Assets on Hand", the actual value of the estate on hand for distribution is $142,000.00 due to a decline in value of the 100 shares, common, of XYZ Corp., which have an inventory value of $8,000.00 but a 9/30/07 actual value of $1,000.00.

XIV

PROBATE CODE SECTIONS 1063 AND 1064 STATEMENTS

There are no liabilities of the Estate under Probate Code Section 1063(g) **(if there are any liabilities you must list them by amount and payee and property secured if a secured lien)**

There has been no compensation paid from the assets subject to the estate to the fiduciary or the attorney for the fiduciary other than pursuant to a prior court order. **(describe any monies paid to yourself or your attorney - this should not be the case)**

There is no family or affiliate relationship between the fiduciary and any agent hired by the fiduciary during the administration period **EXCEPT that Petitioner hired her nephew, Barry Worker, at the rate of $10 per hour, to clean and repair Decedent's car for the purpose of sale.**

As shown on Schedule G, "9/30/07 Actual Value of Assets on Hand", the actual value of the estate on hand for distribution is $142,000.00 due to a decline in value of the 100 shares, common, of XYZ Corp., which have an inventory value of $8,000.00 but a 9/30/07 actual value of $1,000.00.

FIRST AND FINAL ACCOUNT AND REPORT OF EXECUTOR, ETC.

XV

Distribution of Estate

IF THE DECEDENT DIED WITHOUT A WILL:

As set forth in Paragraph VI of this report and petition, decedent died intestate. Decedent died leaving no surviving spouse but did leave two children, all adults. Decedent had no predeceased children who died leaving issue. Accordingly, under Probate Code §6402(a) the decedent's estate is distributable one-half (1/2) to each of decedent's two children, **JOHN SMITH and LILA JONES.**

IF THE DECEDENT DIED WITH A WILL:

As set forth in Paragraph VI of this report and petition, decedent's Will, paragraph THIRD, distributes all her estate to her two children, JOHN SMITH and LILA JONES, in equal shares. Both said children survived decedent.

WHEREFORE, Petitioner prays:

1.   That the First and Final Account **(or First and Final Report ("Account Waived") if no accounting is made)** and Report of the **Executor** showing Assets of Hand with a total value of $149,000.00 of which $140,000.00 is cash, be approved, allowed and settled;

2.   That the Court approve and allow the sum of **$5,290.00 to JOHN SMITH** as and for his statutory commission as **Executor (omit this paragraph is commissions are "waived");**

3.   That a decree be made for the distribution of said estate, to those entitled thereto as follows:

To: **JOHN SMITH: ONE-HALF (1/2)** OF THE ESTATE; and,

To: **LILA JONES: ONE-HALF (1/2)** OF THE ESTATE;

The "ESTATE" consists of **100 shares of XYZ corporation with a carry value of $8,000.00, decedent's household furniture and furnishings and personal effects with a carry value of $1,000.00 and cash in the sum of $140,000.00 less $5,290.00 statutory Executor's commission, less any fiduciary income tax liability plus all post September 31, 2007** receipts and any hereafter discovered property whether real, personal or mixed **(the "any hereafter discovered property" language should permit the recovery and distribution of same discovered after the probate is closed without reopening a probate proceeding); and,**

4.   For all other proper relief **(this "omnibus" clause permits the court, in some situation, to make orders not specifically requested)**.

Dated: _____

                              JOHN SMITH, Executor

IF AN ACCOUNTING IS PRESENTED INSTEAD OF BEING WAIVED THE FOLLOWING FORMAT SHOULD BE USED:

SCHEDULE A
INCOME RECEIPTS

2007
March

B. Johnson	Rent	$900.00
April		
B. Johnson	Rent	$900.00
May		
B. Johnson	Rent	$900.00
June		
B. Johnson	Rent	$900.00
Bank of America	Interest	$ 25.00
September		
Bank of America	Interest	$375.00

TOTAL INCOME RECEIPTS $4,000.00

SCHEDULE B
PRINCIPAL RECEIPTS

2007
March

Advance from Estate Heirs	$900.00
May	
Medicare refund	$100.00

TOTAL PRINCIPAL RECEIPTS $1,000.00

FIRST AND FINAL ACCOUNT AND REPORT OF EXECUTOR, ETC.

SCHEDULE C
GAIN ON SALE

2007
August

Sale of Residence (I&A Item 2, Attach 2)
Sales Price: 150,000.00
I&A Value: 140,000.00

TOTAL GAIN ON SALE: $10,000.00

SCHEDULE D
DISBURSEMENTS

2007
February

Home Sav.	Mortgage	413.00
Sears	Credit Card Debt	290.35
OC Register	Newspaper	2.20
Gas Co.	Utilities	170.75
Pac. Bell	Utilities	22.14
L. Jones	Reimb. Vet bill/Dc's cat	272.16
Bank of America	Credit Card	1,509.83
Advanta	Funeral	7,764.00
R. Nelson	1998 Inc. Tax Prep	120.00
Home Savings	Mortgage	413.00
OC Tax Collection	Prop. Txs	258.37

March

BSC	Probate Publication	285.00
J. Smith	Reimb. Probate filing fee	185.00
Allstate	Car ins.	300.00
Home Savings	Mort.	413.00

April

Allstate	Ins. Hse	354.25
Home Sav.	Mort.	413.00

May

V. Rossini	Probate Referee	253.40

June

Home Sav.	Mort.	413.00

August

Dr. R. Sisson	Med. bill	147.55

(Schedule D Continued on next page)

FIRST AND FINAL ACCOUNT AND REPORT OF EXECUTOR, ETC.

Costs of Sale of Real Property:

Commission	$9,000.00	
Buyer Credit	2,500.00	
Prop. Taxes	(200.00)	
Escrow Fee	700.00	
Doc. Stamps	200.00	
Termite Work	1,700.00	
Warranty	300.00	
Home Sav Mort.	26,000.00	
Title Ins.	800.00	$41,000.00

TOTAL DISBURSEMENTS $ 55,000.00

SCHEDULE E
LOSS ON SALE

2007
March
Sold 1987 Olds Auto

Sales Price:	4,000.00
I&A Value:	5,000.00
TOTAL LOSS ON SALE:	$1,000.00

SCHEDULE F
ASSETS ON HAND

CASH
1. Bank of America
   checking acct. 00000-000001 $140,000.00
OTHER
1. Household furniture and furnishings
   and personal effects   1,000.00
2. 100 shares, common, XYZ Corp.   8,000.00

     TOTAL ASSETS ON HAND   **$149,000.00**

SCHEDULE G
9/30/04 ACTUAL VALUE OF ASSETS ON HAND

CASH
1. Bank of America
   checking acct. 00000-000001 $140,000.00
OTHER
1. Household furniture and furnishings
   and personal effects   1,000.00
2. 100 shares, common, XYZ Corp.   1,000.00

     TOTAL ASSETS ON HAND   **$142,000.00**

FIRST AND FINAL ACCOUNT AND REPORT OF EXECUTOR, ETC.

SCHEDULE H

GRADUATED FILING FEE INFORMATION

A. The first-filed Petition for Probate in this proceeding was filed on or about February 1, 2007 by Petitioner herein.

B. The estimated value of the estate for filing fee purposes shown on the first-filed Petition for Probate in this proceeding is under $250,000.00.

C. The filing fee paid by or for the petitioner on the first-filed Petition for Probate in this proceeding was $185.00.

D. The following Inventories and Appraisals have been filed in this proceeding:

Type   Date Filed Appraised Value

Final (5/5/07) $185,000.00

Supplemental (8/10/07) $5,000.00

Total appraised value of estate: $190,000.00

E. Corrected Filing Fee:

Total appraised value of estate: $190,000.00

Filing fee as of the date in A above, based on

total appraised value of estate: $185.00.

Adjustment to reflect proportional reduction

of expenses of administration for insolvent

estate under CRC, rule 7.552(e): None

Corrected Filing Fee: $185.00 (for filing in year 2007).

F. Difference between estimated and corrected filing fee:

Estimated filing fee from C above: $185.00

Corrected filing fee from E above: ($185.00)

Difference: None

FIRST AND FINAL ACCOUNT AND REPORT OF EXECUTOR, ETC.

VERIFICATION

STATE OF CALIFORNIA   )
) ss.

COUNTY OF ORANGE   )

I am the petitioner in the above-entitled action; I have read the foregoing **(the following language must be as stated in the caption on page 1)** FIRST AND FINAL ACCOUNT AND REPORT OF EXECUTOR AND PETITION FOR APPROVAL OF DEBTS PAID WITHOUT CLAIMS; FOR STATUTORY COMMISSIONS TO EXECUTOR AND FOR DISTRIBUTION OF TESTATE ESTATE and know the contents thereof; and I certify that the same is true of my own knowledge, except as to those matters which are therein stated upon my information or belief, and as to those matters, I believe it to be true.

I certify (or declare) under penalty of perjury, under the laws of the State of California, that the foregoing is true and correct.

Executed at **Los Angeles**, California, on **October 10, 2007**.

John Smith
_____
JOHN SMITH

FIRST AND FINAL ACCOUNT AND REPORT OF EXECUTOR, ETC.

John Smith, In Pro Per
112 Maple St.
Los Angeles, CA   90040
(213) 555-5555

SUPERIOR COURT OF THE STATE OF CALIFORNIA

FOR THE COUNTY OF **ORANGE, LAMOREAUX JUSTICE CENTER**

The Estate of	)	CASE NO. **A100001**
	)	
JANE DOE, a.k.a.	)	WAIVER OF ACCOUNTING
JANE DOE BUCK,	)	
	)	
Deceased	)	
_____)		

The undersigned, **LORI LARSON, being a one-third residual** beneficiary of the above entitled testate Estate, hereby approves the
foregoing First and Final Report and Petition of the **Executor** of the
Estate and hereby waives any accounting by said **Executor.**

Dated: **December 10, 2007**   *Lori Larson*
                              _____
                              LORI LARSON

This page intentionally left blank.

1 | John Smith, In Pro Per
  | 112 Maple St.
2 | Los Angeles, CA 90040
  | (213) 555-5555
3
4
5
6
7
8   SUPERIOR COURT OF THE STATE OF CALIFORNIA

9   FOR THE COUNTY OF **ORANGE, LAMOREAUX JUSTICE CENTER**

10
The Estate of   )   CASE NO. **A100001**
11   )
    JANE DOE, a.k.a.   )   ORDER APPROVING FIRST AND
12   )   FINAL ACCOUNT (**omit the
)   words "ACCOUNT AND, add
13   )   the words "(ACCOUNT WAIVED)"
)   if there is no accounting**)
14   **JANE DOE BUCK,**   )   AND REPORT OF EXECUTOR
)   APPROVAL OF DEBTS PAID
15   )   WITHOUT CLAIMS; APPROVAL OF
              Deceased   )   STATUTORY FEES TO
16   )   EXECUTOR (**or ADMINISTRATOR
)   or ADMINISTRATOR C.T.A. as
17   )   the case may be**) AND DECREE
)   FOR DISTRIBUTION OF TESTATE
18   )   ESTATE (**or "INTESTATE"
)   if there is no Will**)
19   _____)
         The (**the following description should follow the language
20
used in the caption above**) First and Final Account and Report of
21
Executor (**or Administrator, etc., as the case may be**); Petition
22
for Approval of Debts Paid Without Claims; Approval of Statutory
23
Fees to Executor; and Petition for Distribution of testate Estate
24
of **JOHN SMITH, Executor**, came on regularly for hearing in
25
Department L73, on November 5, 2007, at 9:00 a.m. before the
26
Honorable **JAMES A. OTTO**, Judge Presiding.   Petitioner appeared
27
IN PRO PER.
28

1

ORDER APPROVING 1ST & FIN. ACCT. OF EX'OR; STAT. FEES TO EX'OR & DECREE FOR DIST. OF TESTATE EST.

1   After examining the Petition **(add "as supplemented" if the**
2 **petition was supplemented)** and the evidence, the Court finds that
3 Notice of the Hearing has been given as required by law, that the
4 estate is the separate **(or "community" or "separate and**
5 **community" as the case may be)** property of the decedent and that
6 the allegations of said Petition are true.

7

8   IT IS THEREFORE ORDERED, ADJUDGED AND DECREED THAT:
9   1.   That the **First and Final Account and Report of the**
10 **Executor** showing Assets of Hand with a total value of **$149,000.00**
11 **of which $140,000.00** is cash, is approved, allowed and settled;
12   2. **(this paragaph is omitted if the personal representative**
13 **is requesting no fees)** That the Court approves, allows and orders
14 paid the sum of **$5,290.00 to JOHN SMITH** as and for his statutory
15 commission as **Executor;**
16   3.   That distribution of said estate, to those entitled
17 thereto as follows:
18   To: **JOHN SMITH: ONE-HALF (1/2) OF THE ESTATE;** and,
19   To: **LILA JONES: ONE-HALF (1/2) OF THE ESTATE;**
20   The "ESTATE" consists of **100 shares of XYZ corporation with**
21 **a carry value of $8,000.00,** decedent's household furniture and
22 **furnishings and personal effects with a carry value of $1,000.00**
23 **and cash in the sum of $140,000.00 less $5,290.00 statutory**
24 **Executor's commission,** less any fiduciary income tax liability
25 plus all post **September 31, 2007** , receipts and any hereafter
26 discovered property whether real, personal or mixed; and,
27   4.   **JOHN SMITH, Executor,** may be discharged after the filing
28 of the appropriate receipts of distribution and his affidavit for

ORDER APPROVING 1ST & FIN. ACCT. OF EX'OR; STAT. FEES TO EX'OR & DECREE FOR DIST. OF TESTATE EST.

1 | discharge.

2

3 | Dated: **November** 4 , 2007

_____
JUDGE, SUPERIOR COURT

4

5

6

7

8

9

10

11

12

13

14

15

16

17

18

19

20

21

22

23

24

25

26

27

28

This page intentionally left blank.

1 John Smith, In Pro Per
   112 Maple St.
2 Los Angeles, CA 90040
   (213) 555-5555
3

4

5

6

7

8   SUPERIOR COURT OF THE STATE OF CALIFORNIA

9   FOR THE COUNTY OF ORANGE, LAMOREAUX JUSTICE CENTER

10

11 The Estate of   ) CASE NO. A100001
)
12   JANE DOE, a.k.a.   ) SUPPLEMENT TO FIRST AND
) FINAL ACCOUNT
13   ) (omit the words "ACCOUNT
) AND", add "(ACCOUNT WAIVED)"
14   ) if there is no accounting)
      JANE DOE BUCK,   ) AND REPORT OF EXECUTOR (or
15   ) Administrator or Adminis-
) trator C.T.A. as the case)
16   ) may be)
) AND PETITION FOR APPROVAL
17   ) OF DEBTS PAID WITHOUT
             Deceased   ) CLAIMS; STATUTORY FEES TO
18   ) EXECUTOR (or ADMINISTRATOR
) or ADMINISTRATOR C.T.A. as
19   ) the case may be) AND FOR
) DISTRIBUTION OF TESTATE
20   ) ESTATE (or "INTESTATE"
) if there is no Will)
21   )
) Hearing Date: 4/7/07
22 _____) Dept. A   Time: 9:00 a.m.

23   JOHN SMITH, as Executor of the estate of the above-named

24 decedent, renders to the Court his SUPPLEMENT to his first and

25 final account and report of his administration of said estate and

26 presents herewith his petition for approval of debts paid without

27 claims filed, for approval of statutory fees to Executor and for

28 distribution of testate estate, as follows:

                                    1

SUPPLEMENT TO FIRST AND FINAL ACCOUNT AND REPORT OF EXECUTOR, ETC.

1. **All California and Federal income taxes payable by the Estate have been paid.**

WHEREFORE, PETITIONER PRAYS:

1. That his account and petition, as supplemented hereby, be approved and ordered as prayed for; and,

2. For all other proper relief.

Dated: 3/20/07

John Smith
_____
JOHN SMITH, Executor

<u>VERIFICATION</u>

STATE OF CALIFORNIA   )
) ss.
COUNTY OF **ORANGE**   )

I am the petitioner in the above-entitled action; I have read the foregoing **(the following language must be as stated in the caption on page 1)** SUPPLEMENT TO FIRST AND FINAL ACCOUNT AND REPORT OF EXECUTOR AND PETITION FOR APPROVAL OF DEBTS PAID WITHOUT CLAIMS; FOR STATUTORY COMMISSIONS TO EXECUTOR AND FOR DISTRIBUTION OF TESTATE ESTATE and know the contents thereof; and I certify that the same is true of my own knowledge, except as to those matters which are therein stated upon my information or belief, and as to those matters, I believe it to be true.

I certify (or declare) under penalty of perjury, under the laws of the State of California, that the foregoing is true and correct.

Executed at **Los Angeles**, California, on 3/20/07.

John Smith
_____
JOHN SMITH

SUPPLEMENT TO FIRST AND FINAL ACCOUNT AND REPORT OF EXECUTOR, ETC.

1 John Smith, In Pro Per
   112 Maple St.
2 Los Angeles, CA 90040
   (213) 555-5555
3

4

5

6

7

8   SUPERIOR COURT OF THE STATE OF CALIFORNIA

9   FOR THE COUNTY OF ORANGE, LAMOREAUX JUSTICE CENTER

10

11   The Estate of   )   CASE NO. **A100001**
)
12   **JANE DOE, a.k.a.**   )   COMPLETE RECEIPT OF
         JANE DOE BUCK,   )   BENEFICIARY
13   )
                   Deceased   )
14   _____)

15   The undersigned, **LORI LARSON**, a one-third residual

16   beneficiary of the above entitled estate, does hereby acknowledge

17   receipt of all of her interest in said estate, being **$3,212.07**

18   **cash**, from **JOHN SMITH, Executor**.

19

20   Dated: **December** 9 , 2007   *Lori Larson*
                                       _____
21   LORI LARSON

22

23

24

25

26

27

28
                                    1
                    COMPLETE RECEIPT OF LORI LARSON

This page intentionally left blank.

NAME, ADDRESS AND TELEPHONE NUMBER OF ATTORNEY(S)

John Slow, In Pro Per
111 Maple St.
Los Angeles, CA 90940

Bar No.:
Attorney(s) for _____

SUPERIOR COURT OF CALIFORNIA, COUNTY OF _____Orange_____

IN THE MATTER OF THE ___Jan Quick estate_____

_____Deceased_____
(Deceased/Minor/Incompetent, Etc.)

CASE NUMBER
A-00001

DECLARATION FOR FINAL DISCHARGE

I, _____John Slow_____, say:

I am the ____administrator_____ of the above entitled estate; that I have, under approval, authoriza-
(Executor/Administrator/Guardian, Etc.)

tion and order of the Court, paid all sums of money due from me as such ____administrator_____
(Executor/Administrator/Guardian, Etc.)

and all required receipts and vouchers for same are on file in said estate; that distribution and delivery has been made of all the property and assets of said estate in accordance with the decree therefor made and that receipts from all the respective distributees are on file in said estate and that I have performed all acts lawfully required of me as such ____administrator_____
(Executor/Administrator/Guardian, Etc.)

I declare under penalty of perjury that the foregoing is true and correct.

Executed on ____04/09/07_____ at _____Orange_____ , California.
                 (Date)   (Place)

ORDER OF FINAL DISCHARGE

It appearing from the aforesaid declaration that the above entitled estate has been fully administered and that a final decree of discharge is in order.

It is therefore ORDERED, ADJUDGED AND DECREED that _____John Slow_____
                                                                              (Name)

as ____administrator_____ of the above entitled estate is hereby released and discharged
(Executor/Administrator/Guardian, Etc.)

and that _he_ and _his_ sureties are discharged and released from all liability to be incurred hereafter.
        (He/She)   (His/Her)

Dated: _____   _____
                                          JUDGE OF THE SUPERIOR COURT

DECLARATION AND ORDER OF FINAL DISCHARGE

LS-1327

This page intentionally left blank.

DECLARATION FOR TRANSFER OF DECEDENT'S PROPERTY TO SURVIVING SPOUSE OR DOMESTIC PARTNER UNDER CALIFORNIA PROBATE CODE SECTION 13500

The decedent, JAN JOHNSON (ss# 500-11-111), a resident of Santa Ana, CA, died on March 2, 2007, in Orange County, CA

At least 40 days have elapsed since the date of the decedent's death as shown in a certified copy of the decedent's death certificate attached to this declaration.

The property of the decedent that is to be paid, transferred or delivered to the declarant is 400 shares of IBM, common stock.

The declarant is the surviving spouse of the decedent. The declarant is entitled to the above referenced property under the decedent's will or under the laws of intestate succession.

Under California Probate Code Section 13500 said property is to be paid, delivered or transferred to declarant without probate.

No other person has a superior right to the interest of the decedent in the described property.

The declarant requests that the described property be paid, delivered, or transferred to the declarant.

The declarant herein declares under penalty of perjury under the laws of the State of California that the foregoing is true and correct.

Dated: 6/6/07

Les More
_____
LES MORE

Blank Forms

appendix b

Some forms listed in Appendix A are so involved that reproducing them in a blank format would be useless. Therefore, some form numbers are skipped in this appendix. Please refer to Appendix A when you need a filled-in sample of any of the forms, including those skipped here. All form numbers correspond to the same form in both Appendix A and Appendix B. The instructions for a particular form may be found by looking up the form number in the index. Make photocopies to use for both practice worksheets and the forms you will file with the court.

NOTE: *Forms 37–41 are so involved that they are provided only as filled-in samples in Appendix A. Please find forms 37–41 on pages 231–254.*

Recording Requested by and
When Recorded Mail to:

_____

AFFIDAVIT - DEATH OF JOINT TENANT

_____

STATE OF CALIFORNIA   )
)   ss.
COUNTY OF   )

The undersigned,_____, of legal age, being first
duly sworn, deposes and says:

The decedent, _____, named in the attached certified
copy of Certificate of Death is the same person as
_____named as one of the parties in that certain Joint
Tenancy Grant Deed executed on _____ recorded on
_____ in the _____ County recorder's office as
Instrument No. _____. This Affidavit-Death of Joint
Tenant is executed to establish that the surviving joint tenant is
_____. The subject real property is located at
_____, City of _____, County of _____,
State of California and is legally described as:

APN:

_____
Surviving Joint Tenant
        Subscribed to and sworn before me on _____

                              _____
                              Notary Public in and for
                              said County and State

This page intentionally left blank.

BOE-502-A (FRONT) REV. 8 (10-05)

PRELIMINARY CHANGE OF OWNERSHIP REPORT

[To be completed by transferee (buyer) prior to transfer of subject property in accordance with section 480.3 of the Revenue and Taxation Code.] A Preliminary Change of Ownership Report must be filed with each conveyance in the County Recorder's office for the county where the property is located; this particular form may be used in all 58 counties of California.

THIS REPORT IS NOT A PUBLIC DOCUMENT

SELLER/TRANSFEROR:

BUYER/TRANSFEREE:

ASSESSOR'S PARCEL NUMBER(S)

PROPERTY ADDRESS OR LOCATION:

MAIL TAX INFORMATION TO: Name
                            Address
                            Phone Number (8 a.m.-5 p.m.) (_____) _____

NOTICE: A lien for property taxes applies to your property on January 1 of each year for the taxes owing in the following fiscal year, July 1 through June 30. One-half of these taxes is due November 1, and one-half is due February 1. The first installment becomes delinquent on December 10, and the second installment becomes delinquent on April 10. One tax bill is mailed before November 1 to the owner of record. **You may be responsible for the current or upcoming property taxes even if you do not receive the tax bill.**

The property which you acquired may be subject to a supplemental assessment in an amount to be determined by the _____

Assessor. For further information on your supplemental roll obligation, please call the _____ Assessor

at _____ .

PART I: TRANSFER INFORMATION *(please answer all questions)*

YES	NO	
☐	☐	A. Is this transfer solely between husband and wife (addition of a spouse, death of a spouse, divorce settlement, etc.)?
☐	☐	B. Is this transaction only a correction of the name(s) of the person(s) holding title to the property (for example, a name change upon marriage)? Please explain _____
☐	☐	C. Is this document recorded to create, terminate, or reconvey a lender's interest in the property?
☐	☐	D. Is this transaction recorded only as a requirement for financing purposes or to create, terminate, or reconvey a security interest (e.g., cosigner)? Please explain _____
☐	☐	E. Is this document recorded to substitute a trustee of a trust, mortgage, or other similar document?
☐	☐	F. Did this transfer result in the creation of a joint tenancy in which the seller (transferor) remains as one of the joint tenants?
☐	☐	G. Does this transfer return property to the person who created the joint tenancy (original transferor)?
		H. Is this a transfer of property:
☐	☐	1. to a revocable trust that may be revoked by the transferor and is for the benefit of the ☐ transferor ☐ transferor's spouse?
☐	☐	2. to a trust that may be revoked by the Creator/Grantor who is also a joint tenant, and which names the other joint tenant(s) as beneficiaries when the Creator/Grantor dies?
☐	☐	3. to an irrevocable trust for the benefit of the ☐ Creator/Grantor and/or ☐ Grantor's spouse?
☐	☐	4. to an irrevocable trust from which the property reverts to the Creator/Grantor within 12 years?
☐	☐	I. If this property is subject to a lease, is the remaining lease term 35 years or more including written options?
☐	☐	*J. Is this a transfer between ☐ parent(s) and child(ren)? ☐ or from grandparent(s) to grandchild(ren)?
☐	☐	*K. Is this transaction to replace a principal residence by a person 55 years of age or older? Within the same county? ☐ Yes ☐ No
☐	☐	*L. Is this transaction to replace a principal residence by a person who is severely disabled as defined by Revenue and Taxation Code section 69.5? Within the same county? ☐ Yes ☐ No
☐	☐	M. Is this transfer solely between domestic partners currently registered with the California Secretary of State?

*If you checked yes to J, K or L, you may qualify for a property tax reassessment exclusion, which may result in lower taxes on your property. **If you do not file a claim, your property will be reassessed.**

Please provide any other information that will help the Assessor to understand the nature of the transfer.

If the conveying document constitutes an exclusion from a change in ownership as defined in section 62 of the Revenue and Taxation Code for any reason other than those listed above, set forth the specific exclusions claimed: _____ .

Please answer all questions in each section. If a question does not apply, indicate with "N/A." Sign and date at bottom of second page.

PART II: OTHER TRANSFER INFORMATION

A. Date of transfer if other than recording date _____

B. Type of transfer *(please check appropriate box)*:
  ☐ Purchase   ☐ Foreclosure   ☐ Gift   ☐ Trade or Exchange   ☐ Merger, Stock, or Partnership Acquisition
  ☐ Contract of Sale – Date of Contract _____
  ☐ Inheritance – Date of Death _____ ☐ Other *(please explain):* _____
  ☐ Creation of Lease   ☐ Assignment of a Lease   ☐ Termination of a Lease   ☐ Sale/Leaseback
  ☐ Date lease began _____
  ☐ Original term in years (including written options) _____
  ☐ Remaining term in years (including written options) _____
    Monthly Payment _____ Remaining Term _____

C. Was only a partial interest in the property transferred? ☐ Yes ☐ No
  If **yes**, indicate the percentage transferred _____ %.

PART III: PURCHASE PRICE AND TERMS OF SALE

A. CASH DOWN PAYMENT OR value of trade or exchange *(excluding closing costs)*   Amount $ _____

B. FIRST DEED OF TRUST @ _____ % interest for _____ years. Pymts./Mo. = $ _____ (Prin. & Int. only)   Amount $ _____
- ☐ FHA(_____ Discount Points)
- ☐ Conventional
- ☐ VA (_____ Discount Points)
- ☐ Cal-Vet
- Balloon payment ☐ Yes
- ☐ Fixed rate
- ☐ Variable rate
- ☐ All inclusive D.T. ($ _____ Wrapped)
- ☐ Loan carried by seller
- ☐ No
- ☐ New loan
- ☐ Assumed existing loan balance
- ☐ Bank or savings & loan
- ☐ Finance company
- Due Date _____ Amount $ _____

C. SECOND DEED OF TRUST @ _____ % interest for _____ years. Pymts./Mo. = $ _____ (Prin. & Int. only)   Amount $ _____
- ☐ Bank or savings & loan
- ☐ Loan carried by seller
- Balloon payment ☐ Yes
- ☐ Fixed rate
- ☐ Variable rate
- ☐ No
- ☐ New loan
- ☐ Assumed existing loan balance
- Due Date _____ Amount $ _____

D. OTHER FINANCING: Is other financing involved not covered in (b) or (c) above?   ☐ Yes ☐ No   Amount $ _____

Type _____ @ _____ % interest for _____ years. Pymts./Mo. = $ _____ (Prin. & Int. only)
- ☐ Bank or savings & loan
- ☐ Loan carried by seller
- Balloon payment ☐ Yes
- ☐ Fixed rate
- ☐ Variable rate
- ☐ No
- ☐ New loan
- ☐ Assumed existing loan balance
- Due Date _____ Amount $ _____

E. WAS AN IMPROVEMENT BOND ASSUMED BY THE BUYER? ☐ Yes ☐ No   Outstanding Balance: Amount $ _____

F. TOTAL PURCHASE PRICE *(or acquisition price, if traded or exchanged, include real estate commission if paid)*

TOTAL ITEMS A THROUGH E $ _____

G. PROPERTY PURCHASED ☐ Through a broker ☐ Direct from seller ☐ From a family member ☐ Other *(please explain)*: _____

If purchased through a broker, provide broker's name and phone number: _____

Please explain any special terms, seller concessions, or financing and any other information that would help the Assessor understand the purchase price and terms of sale: _____

PART IV: PROPERTY INFORMATION

A. TYPE OF PROPERTY TRANSFERRED:
- ☐ Single-family residence
- ☐ Multiple-family residence (no. of units: _____)
- ☐ Commercial/Industrial
- ☐ Other (Description: i.e., timber, mineral, water rights, etc. _____)
- ☐ Agricultural
- ☐ Co-op/Own-your-own
- ☐ Condominium
- ☐ Timeshare
- ☐ Manufactured home
- ☐ Unimproved lot

B. IS THIS PROPERTY INTENDED AS YOUR PRINCIPAL RESIDENCE? ☐ Yes ☐ No

If **yes**, enter date of occupancy _____ / _____ , 20 _____ or intended occupancy _____ / _____ , 20 _____ .
(month) (day) (year)   *(month) (day) (year)*

C. IS PERSONAL PROPERTY INCLUDED IN PURCHASE PRICE (i.e., furniture, farm equipment, machinery, etc.)
(other than a manufactured home subject to local property tax)? ☐ Yes ☐ No
If **yes**, enter the value of the personal property included in the purchase price $ _____ *(Attach itemized list of personal property.)*

D. IS A MANUFACTURED HOME INCLUDED IN PURCHASE PRICE? ☐ Yes ☐ No
If **yes**, how much of the purchase price is allocated to the manufactured home? $ _____
Is the manufactured home subject to local property tax? ☐ Yes ☐ No   What is the decal number? _____

E. DOES THE PROPERTY PRODUCE INCOME? ☐ Yes ☐ No If **yes**, is the income from:
☐ Lease/Rent   ☐ Contract   ☐ Mineral rights   ☐ Other *(please explain)*: _____

F. WHAT WAS THE CONDITION OF THE PROPERTY AT THE TIME OF SALE?
☐ Good   ☐ Average   ☐ Fair   ☐ Poor

Please explain the physical condition of the property and provide any other information (such as restrictions, etc.) that would assist the Assessor in determining the value of the property: _____

CERTIFICATION

OWNERSHIP TYPE (☐)
- Proprietorship ☐
- Partnership ☐
- Corporation ☐
- Other _____ ☐

I certify that the foregoing is true, correct and complete to the best of my knowledge and belief. This declaration is binding on each and every co-owner and/or partner.

NAME OF NEW OWNER/CORPORATE OFFICER   TITLE

SIGNATURE OF NEW OWNER/CORPORATE OFFICER   DATE

NAME OF ENTITY *(typed or printed)*   FEDERAL EMPLOYER ID NUMBER

ADDRESS *(typed or printed)*   E-MAIL ADDRESS *(optional)*   DATE

(NOTE: The Assessor may contact you for additional information.)
If a document evidencing a change of ownership is presented to the recorder for recordation without the concurrent filing of a preliminary change of ownership report, the recorder may charge an additional recording fee of twenty dollars ($20).

BOE-58-AH (FRONT) REV. 9 (8-03)

CLAIM FOR REASSESSMENT EXCLUSION FOR TRANSFER BETWEEN PARENT AND CHILD

(Section 63.1 of the Revenue and Taxation Code)

OFFICE OF THE ASSESSOR-RECORDER, COUNTY OF MARIN
JOAN C. THAYER, ASSESSOR-RECORDER
P.O. Box C, Civic Center Branch
San Rafael, CA 94913

California law provides, with certain limitations, that a "change in ownership" does not include the purchase or transfer of:

- The principal residence between parents and children, and/or
- The first $1,000,000 of other real property between parents and children.

IMPORTANT: In order to qualify for this exclusion, a claim form must be completed and signed by the transferors and a transferee and filed with the Assessor. A claim form is timely filed if it is filed within three years after the date of purchase or transfer, or prior to the transfer of the real property to a third party, whichever is earlier. If a claim form has not been filed by the date specified in the preceding sentence, it will be timely if filed within six months after the date of mailing of a notice of supplemental or escape assessment for this property. If a claim is not timely filed, the exclusion will be granted beginning with the calendar year in which you file your claim. Complete all of Sections A, B, and C and answer each question or your claim may be denied. Proof of eligibility, including a copy of the transfer document, trust, or will, may be required.

Please note:

a. This exclusion only applies to transfers that occur on or after November 6, 1986.

b. In order to qualify, the real property must be transferred from parents to their children or children to their parents.

c. If you do not complete and return this form, it may result in this property being reassessed.

A. PROPERTY

ASSESSOR'S PARCEL NUMBER

PROPERTY ADDRESS	CITY
RECORDER'S DOCUMENT NUMBER	DATE OF PURCHASE OR TRANSFER

PROBATE NUMBER *(if applicable)*	DATE OF DEATH *(if applicable)*	DATE OF DECREE OF DISTRIBUTION *(if applicable)*

The disclosure of social security numbers is mandatory as required by Revenue and Taxation Code section 63.1. [See Title 42 United States Code, section 405(c)(2)(C)(i) which authorizes the use of social security numbers for identification purposes in the administration of any tax.] A foreign national who cannot obtain a social security number may provide a tax identification number issued by the Internal Revenue Service. The numbers are used by the Assessor and the state to monitor the exclusion limit. This claim form is not subject to public inspection.

B. TRANSFEROR(S)/SELLER(S) *(additional transferors please complete "B" on the reverse)*

1. Print full name(s) of transferor(s) _____   _____

2. Social security number(s) _____   _____

3. Family relationship(s) to transferee(s) _____   _____

   If adopted, age at time of adoption _____   _____

4. Was this property the transferor's principal residence? ☐ Yes ☐ No

   If **yes**, please check which one of the following exemptions was granted on this property in the transferor's name:

   Homeowners' Exemption _____ Disabled Veterans' Exemption _____

5. Is this a transfer of real property other than the principal residence of the transferor (the exclusion for other real property is limited to the first one million dollars of value)? ☐ Yes ☐ No

   If **yes**, please attach a list of all previous transfers that qualify for this exclusion. [This list should include for each property: the County, Assessor's parcel number, address, date of transfer, names of all the transferees/buyers, and family relationship. Transferor's principal residence must be identified.]

6. Was only a partial interest in the property transferred? ☐ Yes ☐ No If **yes**, percentage transferred _____ %

7. Was this property owned in joint tenancy? ☐ Yes ☐ No

8. If the transfer was through the medium of a trust, please attach a copy of the trust.

CERTIFICATION

I certify (or declare) under penalty of perjury under the laws of the State of California that the foregoing and all information hereon, including any accompanying statements or documents, is true and correct to the best of my knowledge and that I am the parent or child of the transferees listed in Section C. I knowingly am granting this exclusion and will not file a claim to transfer the base year value of my principal residence under Revenue and Taxation Code section 69.5.

SIGNATURE OF TRANSFEROR OR LEGAL REPRESENTATIVE	DATE
SIGNATURE OF TRANSFEROR OR LEGAL REPRESENTATIVE	DATE
MAILING ADDRESS	DAYTIME PHONE NUMBER ( )

(Please complete applicable information on reverse side.) If you need help completing this form, or have questions on its content, please call the Marin County Assessor's Office at (415) 499-7360.

[125-593 (121404)]

BOE-58-AH (BACK) REV. 9 (8-03)

C. TRANSFEREE(S)/BUYER(S) *(additional transferees please complete "C" below)*

1. Print full name(s) of transferee(s) _____ _____

2. Family relationship(s) to transferor(s) _____ _____

   If adopted, age at time of adoption _____

   If step-parent/step-child relationship is involved, was parent still married to step-parent on the date of purchase or transfer?
   ☐ Yes ☐ No

   If **no**, was the marriage terminated by: ☐ Death ☐ Divorce

   If terminated by death, had the surviving step-parent remarried as of the date of purchase or transfer? ☐ Yes ☐ No

   If in-law relationship is involved, was the son-in-law or daughter-in-law still married to the daughter or son on the date of purchase or transfer? ☐ Yes ☐ No

   If **no**, was the marriage terminated by: ☐ Death ☐ Divorce

   If terminated by death, had the surviving son-in-law or daughter-in-law remarried as of the date of purchase or transfer?
   ☐ Yes ☐ No

3. ALLOCATION OF EXCLUSION (If the full cash value of the real property transferred exceeds the one million dollar value exclusion, the transferee must specify on an attachment to this claim the amount and allocation of the exclusion that is being sought.)

CERTIFICATION

I certify (or declare) under penalty of perjury under the laws of the State of California that the foregoing and all information hereon, including any accompanying statements or documents, is true and correct to the best of my knowledge and that I am the parent or child of the transferors listed in Section B; and that all of the transferees are eligible transferees within the meaning of section 63.1 of the Revenue and Taxation Code.

SIGNATURE OF TRANSFEREE OR LEGAL REPRESENTATIVE	DATE
MAILING ADDRESS	DAYTIME PHONE NUMBER ( )

NOTE: The Assessor may contact you for additional information.

B. ADDITIONAL TRANSFEROR(S)/SELLER(S) *(continued)*

NAME	SOCIAL SECURITY NUMBER	SIGNATURE	RELATIONSHIP

C. ADDITIONAL TRANSFEREE(S)/BUYER(S) *(continued)*

NAME	RELATIONSHIP

Recording Requested by:

When recorded return to:

Mail tax statements to:
Same

_____
APN:
AFFIDAVIT—DEATH OF SPOUSE OR DOMESTIC PARTNER
STATE OF CALIFORNIA   )
)   ss.
COUNTY OF   )
    The undersigned, _____, of legal age, being first duly sworn, deposes and says:

The decedent,_____, named in the attached certified copy of Certificate of Death is the same person as _____ named as one of the parties in that certain Deed executed in favor of_____ on _____ and recorded on _____ in the _____ County recorder's office as Instrument No._____wherein title was taken as "_____" This Affidavit-Death of Spouse is executed to establish that the surviving spouse is _____. The subject real property covered by the Deed recorded as Instrument No. _____ is located at _____County, CA and more accurately described on Exhibit "A" attached hereto and made a part hereof.

    This Affidavit is filed under California Probate Code Sections 13500 and 13530(b) in order to confirm the above-named real property is community property passing to _____ ,the surviving spouse of _____and no administration is necessary. The decedent died ___testate.

_____
             -Affiant
Subscribed to and sworn before me on _____

                    _____
                    Notary Public in and for
                    said County and State

This page intentionally left blank.

DE-221

ATTORNEY OR PARTY WITHOUT ATTORNEY *(Name, State Bar number, and address):*	*FOR COURT USE ONLY*
TELEPHONE NO.: FAX NO. *(Optional):*	
E-MAIL ADDRESS *(Optional):*	
ATTORNEY FOR *(Name):*	

SUPERIOR COURT OF CALIFORNIA, COUNTY OF
STREET ADDRESS:
MAILING ADDRESS:
CITY AND ZIP CODE:
BRANCH NAME:

ESTATE OF *(Name):*	CASE NUMBER:
DECEDENT	HEARING DATE:

☐ **SPOUSAL** ☐ **DOMESTIC PARTNER** **PROPERTY PETITION**	DEPT.:	TIME:

1. **Petitioner** *(name):*   **requests**
   a. ☐ determination of property passing to the surviving spouse or surviving registered domestic partner without administration (Fam. Code, § 297.5, Prob. Code, § 13500).
   b. ☐ confirmation of property belonging to the surviving spouse or surviving registered domestic partner (Fam. Code, § 297.5, Prob. Code, §§ 100, 101).
   c. ☐ immediate appointment of a probate referee.

2. Petitioner is
   a. ☐ surviving spouse of the decedent.
   b. ☐ personal representative of *(name):*   , surviving spouse.
   c. ☐ guardian or conservator of the estate of *(name):*   , surviving spouse.
   d. ☐ surviving registered domestic partner of the decedent.
   e. ☐ personal representative of *(name):*   , surviving registered domestic partner.
   f. ☐ conservator of the estate of *(name):*   , surviving registered domestic partner.

3. Decedent died on *(date):*

4. Decedent was
   a. ☐ a resident of the California county named above.
   b. ☐ a nonresident of California and left an estate in the county named above.
   c. ☐ intestate ☐ testate and a copy of the will and any codicil is affixed as Attachment 4c.
       (Attach copies of will and any codicil, a typewritten copy of any handwritten document, and an English translation of any foreign-language document.)

5. a. *(Complete in all cases)* The decedent is survived by
   (1) ☐ no child. ☐ child as follows: ☐ natural or adopted ☐ natural, adopted by a third party.
   (2) ☐ no issue of a predeceased child. ☐ issue of a predeceased child.
   b. Decedent ☐ is ☐ is not survived by a stepchild or foster child or children who would have been adopted by decedent but for a legal barrier. *(See Prob. Code, § 6454.)*

6. *(Complete only if no issue survived the decedent. Check **only** the **first** box that applies.)*
   a. ☐ The decedent is survived by a parent or parents who are listed in item 9.
   b. ☐ The decedent is survived by a brother, sister, or issue of a deceased brother or sister, all of whom are listed in item 9.

7. Administration of all or part of the estate is not necessary for the reason that all or a part of the estate is property passing to the surviving spouse or surviving registered domestic partner. The facts upon which petitioner bases the allegation that the property described in Attachments 7a and 7b is property that should pass or be confirmed to the surviving spouse or surviving registered domestic partner are stated in Attachment 7.
   a. ☐ Attachment 7a[1] contains the legal description *(if real property add Assessor's Parcel Number)* of the deceased spouse's or registered domestic partner's property that petitioner requests to be determined as having passed to the surviving spouse or partner from the deceased spouse or partner. This includes any interest in a trade or business name of any unincorporated business or an interest in any unincorporated business that the deceased spouse or partner was operating or managing at the time of death, subject to any written agreement between the deceased spouse or partner and the surviving spouse or partner providing for a non pro rata division of the aggregate value of the community property assets or quasi-community assets, or both.

[1] See Prob. Code, § 13658 for required filing of a list of known creditors of a business and other information in certain instances. If required, include in Attachment 7a.

Page 1 of 2

Form Adopted for Mandatory Use Judicial Council of California DE-221 [Rev. January 1, 2005]	**SPOUSAL OR DOMESTIC PARTNER PROPERTY PETITION** **(Probate—Decedents Estates)**	Family Code, § 297.5; Probate Code, § 13650

ESTATE OF *(Name):*	CASE NUMBER:
DECEDENT	

7. b. ☐ Attachment 7b contains the legal description *(if real property add Assessor's Parcel Number)* of the community or quasi-community property petitioner requests to be determined as having belonged under Probate Code sections 100 and 101 and Family Code section 297.5 to the surviving spouse or surviving registered domestic partner upon the deceased spouse's or partner's death, subject to any written agreement between the deceased spouse or partner and the surviving spouse or partner providing for a non pro rata division of the aggregate value of the community property assets or quasi-community assets, or both.

8. There ☐ exists ☐ does not exist a written agreement between the deceased spouse or deceased registered domestic partner and the surviving spouse or surviving registered domestic partner providing for a non pro rata division of the aggregate value of the community property assets or quasi-community assets, or both. *(If petitioner bases the description of the property of the deceased spouse or partner passing to the surviving spouse or partner or the property to be confirmed to the surviving spouse or partner, or both, on a written agreement, a copy of the agreement must be attached to this petition as Attachment 8.)*

9. The names, relationships, ages, and residence or mailing addresses so far as known to or reasonably ascertainable by petitioner of (1) all persons named in decedent's will and codicils, whether living or deceased, and (2) all persons checked in items 5 and 6

☐ are listed below ☐ are listed in Attachment 9.

Name and relationship	Age	Residence or mailing address

10. The names and addresses of all persons named as executors in the decedent's will and any codicil or appointed as personal representatives of the decedent's estate ☐ are listed below ☐ are listed in Attachment 10 ☐ none

11. ☐ The petitioner is the trustee of a trust that is a devisee under decedent's will. The names and addresses of all persons interested in the trust who are entitled to notice under Probate Code section 13655(b)(2) are listed in Attachment 11.

12. A petition for probate or for administration of the decedent's estate
   a. ☐ is being filed with this petition.
   b. ☐ was filed on *(date):*
   c. ☐ has not been filed and is not being filed with this petition.

13. Number of pages attached: _____

Date:

_____ ▶ _____
(TYPE OR PRINT NAME)   (SIGNATURE OF ATTORNEY)

I declare under penalty of perjury under the laws of the State of California that the foregoing is true and correct.

Date:

_____ ▶ _____
(TYPE OR PRINT NAME)   (SIGNATURE OF PETITIONER)

SPOUSAL OR DOMESTIC PARTNER PROPERTY PETITION
(Probate—Decedents Estates)

DE-226

ATTORNEY OR PARTY WITHOUT ATTORNEY *(Name, State Bar number, and address)* After recording return to:	
TELEPHONE NO.: FAX NO. *(Optional)*: E-MAIL ADDRESS *(Optional)*: ATTORNEY FOR *(Name)*:	

SUPERIOR COURT OF CALIFORNIA, COUNTY OF

STREET ADDRESS:

MAILING ADDRESS:

CITY AND ZIP CODE:

BRANCH NAME:

FOR RECORDER'S USE ONLY

ESTATE OF *(Name)*:	CASE NUMBER:
DECEDENT	

☐ **SPOUSAL** ☐ **DOMESTIC PARTNER** **PROPERTY ORDER**	*FOR COURT USE ONLY*

1. Date of hearing: Time:

   Dept.:   Room:

THE COURT FINDS

2. All notices required by law have been given.

3. Decedent died on *(date)*:

   a. ☐ a resident of the California county named above.

   b. ☐ a nonresident of California and left an estate in the county named above.

   c. ☐ intestate. ☐ testate.

4. Decedent's ☐ surviving spouse ☐ surviving registered domestic partner
   is *(name)*:

THE COURT FURTHER FINDS AND ORDERS

5. a. ☐ The property described in Attachment 5a is property passing to the surviving spouse or surviving registered domestic partner named in item 4, and no administration of it is necessary.

   b. ☐ See Attachment 5b for further order(s) respecting transfer of the property to the surviving spouse or surviving registered domestic partner named in item 4.

6. ☐ To protect the interests of the creditors of *(business name)*:
   an unincorporated trade or business, a list of all its known creditors and the amount owed each is on file.

   a. ☐ Within *(specify)*:   days from this date, the surviving spouse or surviving registered domestic partner named in item 4 shall file an undertaking in the amount of $

   b. ☐ See Attachment 6b for further order(s) protecting the interests of creditors of the business.

7. a. ☐ The property described in Attachment 7a is property that belonged to the surviving spouse or surviving registered domestic partner under Family Code section 297.5 and Probate Code sections 100 and 101, and the surviving spouse's or surviving domestic partner's ownership upon decedent's death is confirmed.

   b. ☐ See Attachment 7b for further order(s) respecting transfer of the property to the surviving spouse or surviving domestic partner.

8. ☐ All property described in the *Spousal or Domestic Partner Property Petition* that is not determined to be property passing to the surviving spouse or surviving registered domestic partner under Probate Code section 13500, or confirmed as belonging to the surviving spouse or surviving registered domestic partner under Probate Code sections 100 and 101, shall be subject to administration in the estate of decedent. ☐ All of such property is described in Attachment 8.

9. ☐ Other *(specify)*:

   ☐ Continued in Attachment 9.

10. Number of pages attached: _____

Date:

JUDICIAL OFFICER

☐ SIGNATURE FOLLOWS LAST ATTACHMENT

Page 1 of 1

Form Adopted for Mandatory Use
Judicial Council of California
DE-226 [Rev. January 1, 2005]

SPOUSAL OR DOMESTIC PARTNER PROPERTY ORDER
(Probate—Decedents Estates)

Family Code, § 297.5;
Probate Code, § 13656

This page intentionally left blank.

DECLARATION FOR TRANSFER OF PERSONAL PROPERTY OF DECEDENT UNDER CALIFORNIA PROBATE CODE SECTION 13050 TO 13104

The decedent, _____ (ss# _____), died on _____ 20__, in _____ County, CA

At least 40 days have elapsed since the date of the decedent's death as shown in a certified copy of the decedent's death certificate attached to this declaration.

No proceeding is now being conducted in California for the administration of decedent's estate.

The current gross fair market value of the decedent's real and personal property in California, excluding the property described in Section 13040 of the California Probate Code does not exceed one hundred thousand dollars ($100,000).

The property of the decedent that is to be paid, transferred or delivered to the declarant(s) is _____.

The declarant(s) is/are the successor of the decedent (as defined in Section 13006 of the California Probate Code) to the decedent's interest in the described property.

No other person has a superior right to the interest of the decedent in the described property.

The declarant(s) request(s) that the described property be paid, delivered, or transferred to the declarant(s).

The declarant(s) herein declare(s) under penalty of perjury under the laws of the State of California that the foregoing is true and correct.

Dated:

_____
Declarant

This page intentionally left blank.

DE-305

ATTORNEY OR PARTY WITHOUT ATTORNEY *(Name, state bar number, and address):*
After recording return to:

TELEPHONE NO.:
FAX NO. *(Optional):*
E-MAIL ADDRESS *(Optional):*
ATTORNEY FOR *(Name):*

SUPERIOR COURT OF CALIFORNIA, COUNTY OF
STREET ADDRESS:
MAILING ADDRESS:
CITY AND ZIP CODE:
BRANCH NAME:

MATTER OF *(Name):*

DECEDENT

FOR RECORDER'S USE ONLY

CASE NUMBER:

FOR COURT USE ONLY

AFFIDAVIT RE REAL PROPERTY OF SMALL VALUE
($20,000 or Less)

1. Decedent *(name):*
   died on *(date):*

2. Decedent died at *(city, state):*

3. At least **six months** have elapsed since the date of death of decedent as shown in the certified copy of decedent's death certificate attached to this affidavit. *(Attach a certified copy of decedent's death certificate.)*

4. a. ☐ Decedent was domiciled in this county at the time of death.
   b. ☐ Decedent was **not** domiciled in California at the time of death. Decedent died owning real property in this county.

5. a. The following is a **legal description** of decedent's real property claimed by the declarants *(copy description from deed or other legal instrument):*
   ☐ described in an attachment labeled Attachment 5a.

   b. Decedent's interest in this real property is as follows *(specify):*

6. Each declarant is a successor of decedent (as defined in Probate Code section 13006) and a successor to decedent's interest in the real property described in item 5a, and no other person has a superior right, because each declarant is
   a. ☐ **(will)** a beneficiary who succeeded to the property under decedent's will. *(Attach a copy of the will.)*
   b. ☐ **(no will)** a person who succeeded to the property under Probate Code sections 6401 and 6402.

7. Names and addresses of each guardian or conservator of decedent's estate at date of death
   ☐ none   ☐ are as follows* *(specify):*

8. The **gross value** of all real property in decedent's estate located in California as shown by the *Inventory and Appraisal,* excluding the real property described in Probate Code section 13050 (joint tenancy, property passing to decedent's spouse, etc.), does not exceed $20,000.

9. An *Inventory and Appraisal* of decedent's **real property** in California is attached. The *Inventory and Appraisal* was made by a probate referee appointed for the county in which the property is located. *(You may use Judicial Council form DE-160.)*

10. No proceeding is now being or has been conducted in California for administration of decedent's estate.

* You must have a copy of this affidavit with attachments personally served or mailed to each person named in item 7.

Page 1 of 2

Form Approved for Mandatory Use
Judicial Council of California
DE-305 [Rev. January 1, 2003]

AFFIDAVIT RE REAL PROPERTY OF SMALL VALUE
(Probate)

Probate Code, § 13200

MATTER OF *(Name):*	CASE NUMBER:
DECEDENT	

11. Funeral expenses, expenses of last illness, and all known unsecured debts of the decedent have been paid. *[NOTE: You may be personally liable for decedent's unsecured debts up to the fair market value of the real property and any income you receive from it.]*

I declare under penalty of perjury under the laws of the State of California that the foregoing is true and correct.

Date:

_____ ▶ _____
(TYPE OR PRINT NAME)   (SIGNATURE OF DECLARANT)

Date:

_____ ▶ _____
(TYPE OR PRINT NAME)   (SIGNATURE OF DECLARANT)

☐ SIGNATURE OF ADDITIONAL DECLARANTS ATTACHED

NOTARY ACKNOWLEDGMENTS   *(NOTE: No notary acknowledgment may be affixed as a rider (small strip) to this page. If additional notary acknowledgments are required, they must be attached as 8-1/2- by 11-inch pages.)*

STATE OF CALIFORNIA, COUNTY OF *(specify):*

On *(date):*   , before me *(name and title):*

personally appeared *(name):*

personally known to me (or proved to me on the basis of satisfactory evidence) to be the person whose name is subscribed to the within instrument and acknowledged to me that he or she executed the instrument in his or her authorized capacity, and that by his or her signature on the instrument the person, or the entity upon behalf of which the person acted, executed the instrument. WITNESS my hand and official seal.

(NOTARY SEAL)

_____
(SIGNATURE OF NOTARY PUBLIC)

STATE OF CALIFORNIA, COUNTY OF *(specify):*

On *(date):*   , before me *(name and title):*

personally appeared *(names):*

personally known to me (or proved to me on the basis of satisfactory evidence) to be the persons whose names are subscribed to the within instrument and acknowledged to me that they executed the instrument in their authorized capacities, and that by their signatures on the instrument the persons, or the entity or entities upon behalf of which the persons acted, executed the instrument. WITNESS my hand and official seal.

(NOTARY SEAL)

_____
(SIGNATURE OF NOTARY PUBLIC)

(SEAL)	**CLERK'S CERTIFICATE**
	I certify that the foregoing, including any attached notary acknowledgments and any attached legal description of the property (but excluding other attachments), is a true and correct copy of the original affidavit on file in my office. *(Certified copies of this affidavit do not include the (1) death certificate, (2) will, or (3) inventory and appraisal. See Probate Code section 13202.)*
	Date: Clerk, by _____, Deputy

DE-305 [Rev. January 1, 2003]

AFFIDAVIT RE REAL PROPERTY OF SMALL VALUE
(Probate)

Page 2 of 2

DE-310

ATTORNEY OR PARTY WITHOUT ATTORNEY *(Name, state bar number, and address):*	TELEPHONE AND FAX NOS.:	*FOR COURT USE ONLY*

ATTORNEY FOR *(Name):*

SUPERIOR COURT OF CALIFORNIA, COUNTY OF
STREET ADDRESS:
MAILING ADDRESS:
CITY AND ZIP CODE:
BRANCH NAME:

MATTER OF *(Name):*

DECEDENT

PETITION TO DETERMINE SUCCESSION TO REAL PROPERTY (Estates $100,000 or Less) ☐ And Personal Property	CASE NUMBER:
	HEARING DATE:
	DEPT.: TIME:

1. Petitioner *(name of each person claiming an interest):*

   requests a determination that the real property ☐ and personal property   described in item 11 is property passing to petitioner and that no administration of decedent's estate is necessary.

2. Decedent *(name):*
   a. Date of death:
   b. Place of death *(city, state):*
3. At least 40 days have elapsed since the date of decedent's death.
4. a. ☐ Decedent was a resident of this county at the time of death.
   b. ☐ Decedent was **not** a resident of California at the time of death. Decedent died owning property in this county.
5. Decedent died ☐ intestate ☐ testate and a copy of the will and any codicil is affixed as Attachment 5 or 12a.
6. a. ☐ No proceeding for the administration of decedent's estate is being conducted or has been conducted in California.
   b. ☐ Decedent's personal representative's consent to use the procedure provided by Probate Code section 13150 et seq. is attached as Attachment 6b.
7. Proceedings for the administration of decedent's estate in another jurisdiction
   a. ☐ have **not** been commenced.
   b. ☐ have been commenced ☐ and completed.
      (Specify state, county, court, and case number):

8. The **gross value** of all real and personal property in decedent's estate located in California as shown by the *Inventory and Appraisal* attached to this petition, excluding the property described in Probate Code section 13050 (joint tenancy, property passing to decedent's spouse, etc.), does not exceed $100,000. *(Attach an* Inventory and Appraisal *(form DE-160) as Attachment 8.)*
9. a. The decedent is survived by *(check at least one box in each of items (1)-(3))*
   (1) ☐ spouse ☐ no spouse as follows: ☐ divorced or never married ☐ spouse deceased
   (2) ☐ child as follows: ☐ natural or adopted ☐ natural adopted by a third party ☐ no child
   (3) ☐ issue of a predeceased child ☐ no issue of a predeceased child
   b. Decedent ☐ is ☐ is not   survived by a stepchild or foster child or children who would have been adopted by decedent but for a legal barrier. *(See Prob. Code, § 6454.)*
10. *(Complete if decedent was survived by (1) a spouse but no issue (only a or b apply); or (2) no spouse or issue. Check the* **first** *box that applies.)*
    a. ☐ Decedent is survived by a parent or parents who are listed in item 14.
    b. ☐ Decedent is survived by a brother, sister, or issue of a deceased brother or sister, all of whom are listed in item 14.
    c. ☐ Decedent is survived by other heirs under Probate Code section 6400 et seq., all of whom also listed in item 14.
    d. ☐ Decedent is survived by no known next of kin.

11. Attachment 11 contains (1) the **legal description** of decedent's real property and its Assessor's Parcel Number (APN)
    ☐ and personal property   in California passing to petitioner and (2) decedent's interest in the property. *(Attach the legal description of the real and personal property and state decedent's interest.)*

(Continued on reverse)

Form Approved by the Judicial Council of California DE-310 [Rev. January 1, 1998] Mandatory Form [1/1/2000]	**PETITION TO DETERMINE SUCCESSION TO REAL PROPERTY** (Probate)	Probate Code, § 13151

MATTER OF *(Name)*:	CASE NUMBER:
DECEDENT	

12. Each petitioner is a successor of decedent (as defined in Probate Code section 13006) and a successor to decedent's interest
in the real property ☐ and personal property described in item 11 because each petitioner is
   a. ☐ (will) a beneficiary who succeeded to the property under decedent's will.[1]
   b. ☐ (no will) a person who succeeded to the property under Probate Code sections 6401 and 6402.

13. The specific property interest claimed by each petitioner in the real property ☐ and personal property described in item 11
   ☐ is stated in Attachment 13 ☐ is as follows *(specify)*:

14. The names, relationships, ages, and residence or mailing addresses so far as known to or reasonably ascertainable by petitioner
of (1) all persons named or checked in items 1, 9, and 10, (2) all other heirs of decedent, and (3) all devisees of decedent (persons
designated in the will to receive any property)
   ☐ are listed below ☐ are listed in Attachment 14.

Name and relationship	Age	Residence or mailing address

15. The names and addresses of all persons named as executors in decedent's will
   ☐ are listed below ☐ are listed in Attachment 15 ☐ none named ☐ no will.

16. ☐ Petitioner is the trustee of a trust that is a devisee under decedent's will. The names and addresses of all persons
   interested in the trust, as determined in cases of future interests under paragraphs (1), (2), or (3) of subdivision (a) of
   Probate Code section 15804 are listed in Attachment 16.

17. ☐ Decedent's estate was under a ☐ guardianship ☐ conservatorship at decedent's death. The names and
   addresses of all persons serving as guardian or conservator ☐ are listed below ☐ are listed in Attachment 17.

18. Number of pages attached: _____

Date:

* (Signature of all petitioners also required (Prob. Code, § 1020).)

▶ _____
(SIGNATURE OF ATTORNEY *)

I declare under penalty of perjury under the laws of the State of California that the foregoing is true and correct.

Date:

. . . .
(TYPE OR PRINT NAME)

▶ _____
(SIGNATURE OF PETITIONER[2])

. . . .
(TYPE OR PRINT NAME)

▶ _____
(SIGNATURE OF PETITIONER[2])

[1] See Probate Code section 13152(c) for the requirement that a copy of the will be attached in certain instances. If required, include as Attachment 5 or 12a.

[2] Each person named in item 1 must sign.

DE-310 [Rev. January 1, 1998]	**PETITION TO DETERMINE SUCCESSION TO REAL PROPERTY** (Probate)	Page two

DE-315

ATTORNEY OR PARTY WITHOUT ATTORNEY *(Name, state bar number, and address)*:

After recording return to:

TELEPHONE NO.:
FAX NO. *(Optional)*:
E-MAIL ADDRESS *(Optional)*:
ATTORNEY FOR *(Name)*:

SUPERIOR COURT OF CALIFORNIA, COUNTY OF

STREET ADDRESS:
MAILING ADDRESS:
CITY AND ZIP CODE:
BRANCH NAME:

MATTER OF *(Name)*:

FOR RECORDER'S USE ONLY

DECEDENT

CASE NUMBER:

ORDER DETERMINING SUCCESSION TO REAL PROPERTY
(Estates $100,000 or Less)
[ ] **And Personal Property**

FOR COURT USE ONLY

1. Date of hearing: Time:
   Dept./Room: Judge:

THE COURT FINDS

2. All notices required by law have been given.

3. Decedent died on *(date)*:
   a. [ ] a resident of the California county named above.
   b. [ ] a nonresident of California and left an estate in the county named above.
   c. [ ] intestate [ ] testate.

4. At least 40 days have elapsed since the date of decedent's death.

5. a. [ ] No proceeding for the administration of decedent's estate is being conducted
      or has been conducted in California.
   b. [ ] Decedent's personal representative has filed a consent to use the procedure
      provided in Probate Code section 13150 et seq.

6. The gross value of decedent's real and personal property in California, excluding
   property described in Probate Code section 13050, does not exceed $100,000.

7. Each petitioner is a successor of decedent (as defined in Probate Code section 13006) and a successor to decedent's interest in
   the real [ ] and personal   property described in item 9a because each petitioner is
   a. [ ] **(will)** a beneficiary who succeeded to the property under decedent's will.
   b. [ ] **(no will)** a person who succeeded to the property under Probate Code sections 6401 and 6402.

THE COURT FURTHER FINDS AND ORDERS

8. No administration of decedent's estate is necessary in California.

9. a. The following described real   [ ] and personal   property is property of decedent passing to each petitioner *(give legal
      description of real property)*:   [ ] described in Attachment 9a.

   b. Each petitioner's **name** and specific property interest   [ ] is stated in Attachment 9b   [ ] is as follows *(specify)*:

10. [ ] Other *(specify)*:

Date: _____

_____
JUDGE OF THE SUPERIOR COURT

11. Number of pages attached: _____

[ ] SIGNATURE FOLLOWS LAST ATTACHMENT

Page 1 of 1

Form Adopted for Mandatory Use
Judicial Council of California
DE-315 [Rev. January 1, 2003]

**ORDER DETERMINING SUCCESSION
TO REAL PROPERTY**
(Probate)

Probate Code, § 13154

This page intentionally left blank.

DE-111

ATTORNEY OR PARTY WITHOUT ATTORNEY *(Name, State Bar number, and address)*:	*FOR COURT USE ONLY*
TELEPHONE NO.: FAX NO. *(Optional)* E-MAIL ADDRESS *(Optional)*: ATTORNEY FOR *(Name)*:	

SUPERIOR COURT OF CALIFORNIA, COUNTY OF
    STREET ADDRESS:
    MAILING ADDRESS:
    CITY AND ZIP CODE:
    BRANCH NAME:

ESTATE OF *(Name)*:

                                            DECEDENT

PETITION FOR □	**Probate of Will and for Letters Testamentary**	CASE NUMBER:
□	**Probate of Will and for Letters of Administration with Will Annexed**	
□	**Letters of Administration**	HEARING DATE:
□	**Letters of Special Administration** □ **with general powers**	
□	**Authorization to Administer Under the Independent Administration of Estates Act** □ **with limited authority**	DEPT.: TIME:

1. Publication will be in *(specify name of newspaper)*:
   a. □ Publication requested.
   b. □ Publication to be arranged.

2. **Petitioner** *(name each)*:   **requests that**
   a. □ decedent's will and codicils, if any, be admitted to probate.
   b. □ *(name)*:
      be appointed
      (1) □ executor
      (2) □ administrator with will annexed
      (3) □ administrator
      (4) □ special administrator □ with general powers
      and Letters issue upon qualification.
   c. □ full □ limited authority be granted to administer under the Independent Administration of Estates Act.
   d. (1) □ bond not be required for the reasons stated in item 4d.
      (2) □ $ bond be fixed. The bond will be furnished by an admitted surety insurer or as otherwise provided by law. *(Specify reasons in Attachment 2 if the amount is different from the maximum required by Prob. Code, § 8482.)*
      (3) □ $ in deposits in a blocked account be allowed. Receipts will be filed. *(Specify institution and location)*:

3. a. **Estimated value of the estate for filing fee purposes** *(Complete in all cases. The estimated value of the estate is the fair market value of the real and personal property of the estate at the date of the decedent's death, without reduction for encumbrances. See Gov. Code, § 26827.)*:

    (1) □ Less than $250,000   (6) □ At least $1.5 million and less than $2 million
    (2) □ At least $250,000 and less than $500,000   (7) □ At least $2 million and less than $2.5 million
    (3) □ At least $500,000 and less than $750,000   (8) □ At least $2.5 million and less than $3.5 million
    (4) □ At least $750,000 and less than $1 million   (9) □ $ *
    (5) □ At least $1 million and less than $1.5 million   *(For estates of $3.5 million or more, specify total estimated value of estate.)*

   b. □ This petition is not the first petition for appointment of a personal representative with general powers filed in this proceeding. The first petition was filed on *(date)*:

Page 1 of 4

Form Adopted for Mandatory Use Judicial Council of California DE-111 [Rev. January 1, 2005]	**PETITION FOR PROBATE** **(Probate—Decedents Estates)**	Probate Code, §§ 8002, 10450, Government Code, § 26827

ESTATE OF *(Name):*	CASE NUMBER:
DECEDENT	

4. a. Decedent died on *(date):*   at *(place):*

   (1) ☐ a resident of the county named above.

   (2) ☐ a nonresident of California and left an estate in the county named above located at *(specify location permitting publication in the newspaper named in item 1):*

   b. Street address, city, and county of decedent's residence at time of death *(specify):*

   c. **Character and estimated value of the property of the estate** *(complete in all cases):*

   (1) Personal property: $

   (2) Annual gross income from

       (a) real property: $

       (b) personal property: $ _____

   (3) **Subtotal** *(add (1) and (2)):* $ _____

   (4) Gross fair market value of real property: $

   (5) (Less) Encumbrances: $ (_____)

   (6) Net value of real property: $ _____

   (7) **Total** *(add (3) and (6)):* $ _____

   d. (1) ☐ Will waives bond. ☐ Special administrator is the named executor, and the will waives bond.

      (2) ☐ All beneficiaries are adults and have waived bond, and the will does not require a bond.
   (Affix waiver as Attachment 4d(2).)

      (3) ☐ All heirs at law are adults and have waived bond. *(Affix waiver as Attachment 4d(3).)*

      (4) ☐ Sole personal representative is a corporate fiduciary or an exempt government agency.

   e. (1) ☐ Decedent died intestate.

      (2) ☐ Copy of decedent's will dated: ☐ codicil dated *(specify for each):*

                                                        are affixed as Attachment 4e(2).

       (Include typed copies of handwritten documents and English translations of foreign-language documents.)

       ☐ The will and all codicils are self-proving (Prob. Code, § 8220).

   f. **Appointment of personal representative** *(check all applicable boxes):*

   (1) Appointment of executor or administrator with will annexed:

      (a) ☐ Proposed executor is named as executor in the will and consents to act.

      (b) ☐ No executor is named in the will.

      (c) ☐ Proposed personal representative is a nominee of a person entitled to Letters.
   (Affix nomination as Attachment 4f(1)(c).)

      (d) ☐ Other named executors will not act because of   ☐ death   ☐ declination
   ☐ other reasons *(specify):*

           ☐ Continued in Attachment 4f(1)(d).

   (2) Appointment of administrator:

      (a) ☐ Petitioner is a person entitled to Letters. *(If necessary, explain priority in Attachment 4f(2)(a).)*

      (b) ☐ Petitioner is a nominee of a person entitled to Letters. *(Affix nomination as Attachment 4f(2)(b).)*

      (c) ☐ Petitioner is related to the decedent as *(specify):*

   (3) ☐ Appointment of special administrator requested. *(Specify grounds and requested powers in Attachment 4f(3).)*

PETITION FOR PROBATE
(Probate—Decedents Estates)

ESTATE OF (Name):	CASE NUMBER:
DECEDENT	

4. g. Proposed personal representative is a

  ☐ resident of California.

  ☐ nonresident of California (specify permanent address):

  ☐ resident of the United States.

  ☐ nonresident of the United States.

5. ☐ Decedent's will does not preclude administration of this estate under the Independent Administration of Estates Act.

6. a. Decedent is survived by (check items (1) or (2), and (3) or (4), and (5) or (6), and (7) or (8))

  (1) ☐ spouse.

  (2) ☐ no spouse as follows:

    (a) ☐ divorced or never married.

    (b) ☐ spouse deceased.

  (3) ☐ registered domestic partner.

  (4) ☐ no registered domestic partner.

    (See Fam. Code, § 297.5(c); Prob. Code, §§ 37(b), 6401(c), and 6402.)

  (5) ☐ child as follows:

    (a) ☐ natural or adopted.

    (b) ☐ natural adopted by a third party.

  (6) ☐ no child.

  (7) ☐ issue of a predeceased child.

  (8) ☐ no issue of a predeceased child.

  b. Decedent ☐ is ☐ is not survived by a stepchild or foster child or children who would have been adopted by decedent but for a legal barrier. (See Prob. Code, § 6454.)

7. (Complete if decedent is survived by (1) a spouse or registered domestic partner but no issue (only a or b apply), or (2) no spouse, registered domestic partner, or issue. (Check the **first** box that applies):

  a. ☐ Decedent is survived by a parent or parents who are listed in item 9.

  b. ☐ Decedent is survived by issue of deceased parents, all of whom are listed in item 9.

  c. ☐ Decedent is survived by a grandparent or grandparents who are listed in item 9.

  d. ☐ Decedent is survived by issue of grandparents, all of whom are listed in item 9.

  e. ☐ Decedent is survived by issue of a predeceased spouse, all of whom are listed in item 9.

  f. ☐ Decedent is survived by next of kin, all of whom are listed in item 9.

  g. ☐ Decedent is survived by parents of a predeceased spouse or issue of those parents, if both are predeceased, all of whom are listed in item 9.

  h. ☐ Decedent is survived by no known next of kin.

8. (Complete only if no spouse or issue survived decedent.)

  a. ☐ Decedent had no predeceased spouse.

  b. ☐ Decedent had a predeceased spouse who

    (1) ☐ died not more than 15 years before decedent and who owned an interest in **real property** that passed to decedent,

    (2) ☐ died not more than five years before decedent and who owned **personal property** valued at $10,000 or more that passed to decedent,

      (If you checked (1) or (2), check only the **first** box that applies):

      (a) ☐ Decedent is survived by issue of a predeceased spouse, all of whom are listed in item 9.

      (b) ☐ Decedent is survived by a parent or parents of the predeceased spouse who are listed in item 9.

      (c) ☐ Decedent is survived by issue of a parent of the predeceased spouse, all of whom are listed in item 9.

      (d) ☐ Decedent is survived by next of kin of the decedent, all of whom are listed in item 9.

      (e) ☐ Decedent is survived by next of kin of the predeceased spouse, all of whom are listed in item 9.

    (3) ☐ neither (1) nor (2) apply.

PETITION FOR PROBATE
(Probate—Decedents Estates)

ESTATE OF *(Name)*:		CASE NUMBER:
	DECEDENT	

9. Listed below are the names, relationships to decedent, ages, and addresses, so far as known to or reasonably ascertainable by petitioner, of (1) all persons mentioned in decedent's will or any codicil, whether living or deceased; (2) all persons named or checked in items 2, 6, 7, and 8; and (3) all beneficiaries of a trust named in decedent's will or any codicil in which the trustee and personal representative are the same person.

<u>Name and relationship to decedent</u>   <u>Age</u>   <u>Address</u>

☐ Continued on Attachment 9.

10. Number of pages attached: _____

Date:

_____   ▶ _____
(TYPE OR PRINT NAME OF ATTORNEY)   (SIGNATURE OF ATTORNEY)*

* (Signatures of all petitioners are also required. All petitioners must sign, but the petition may be verified by any one of them (Prob. Code, §§ 1020, 1021, Cal. Rules of Court, rule 7.103).)

I declare under penalty of perjury under the laws of the State of California that the foregoing is true and correct.

Date:

_____   ▶ _____
(TYPE OR PRINT NAME OF PETITIONER)   (SIGNATURE OF PETITIONER)

                                                 ▶ _____
_____
(TYPE OR PRINT NAME OF PETITIONER)   (SIGNATURE OF PETITIONER)

☐ Signatures of additional petitioners follow last attachment.

DE-111 [Rev January 1, 2005]   **PETITION FOR PROBATE**   Page 4 of 4
                                              (Probate—Decedents Estates)

DE-121

ATTORNEY OR PARTY WITHOUT ATTORNEY *(Name, State Bar number, and address)*:	*FOR COURT USE ONLY*

TELEPHONE NO.:   FAX NO. *(Optional)*:

E-MAIL ADDRESS *(Optional)*:

ATTORNEY FOR *(Name)*:

SUPERIOR COURT OF CALIFORNIA, COUNTY OF

STREET ADDRESS:

MAILING ADDRESS:

CITY AND ZIP CODE:

BRANCH NAME:

ESTATE OF *(Name)*:

DECEDENT

NOTICE OF PETITION TO ADMINISTER ESTATE OF *(Name)*:	CASE NUMBER:

1. To all heirs, beneficiaries, creditors, contingent creditors, and persons who may otherwise be interested in the will or estate, or both, of *(specify all names by which the decedent was known)*:

2. A **Petition for Probate** has been filed by *(name of petitioner)*:
   in the Superior Court of California, County of *(specify)*:

3. The Petition for Probate requests that *(name)*:
   be appointed as personal representative to administer the estate of the decedent.

4. ☐ The petition requests the decedent's will and codicils, if any, be admitted to probate. The will and any codicils are available for examination in the file kept by the court.

5. ☐ The petition requests authority to administer the estate under the Independent Administration of Estates Act. (This authority will allow the personal representative to take many actions without obtaining court approval. Before taking certain very important actions, however, the personal representative will be required to give notice to interested persons unless they have waived notice or consented to the proposed action.) The independent administration authority will be granted unless an interested person files an objection to the petition and shows good cause why the court should not grant the authority.

6. **A hearing on the petition will be held in this court as follows:**

a. Date:	Time:	Dept.:	Room:

   b. Address of court: ☐ same as noted above   ☐ other *(specify)*:

7. **If you object** to the granting of the petition, you should appear at the hearing and state your objections or file written objections with the court before the hearing. Your appearance may be in person or by your attorney.

8. **If you are a creditor or a contingent creditor of the decedent,** you must file your claim with the court and mail a copy to the personal representative appointed by the court within four months from the date of first issuance of letters as provided in Probate Code section 9100. The time for filing claims will not expire before four months from the hearing date noticed above.

9. **You may examine the file kept by the court.** If you are a person interested in the estate, you may file with the court a *Request for Special Notice* (form DE-154) of the filing of an inventory and appraisal of estate assets or of any petition or account as provided in Probate Code section 1250. A *Request for Special Notice* form is available from the court clerk.

10. ☐ Petitioner   ☐ Attorney for petitioner *(name)*:

(Address):

(Telephone):

NOTE: If this notice is published, print the caption, beginning with the words NOTICE OF PETITION TO ADMINISTER ESTATE, and do not print the information from the form above the caption. The caption and the decedent's name must be printed in at least 8-point type and the text in at least 7-point type. Print the case number as part of the caption. Print items preceded by a box only if the box is checked. Do not print the italicized instructions in parentheses, the paragraph numbers, the mailing information, or the material on page 2.

Page 1 of 2

Form Adopted for Mandatory Use
Judicial Council of California
DE-121 [Rev. January 1, 2006]
NOTICE OF PETITION TO ADMINISTER ESTATE
(Probate—Decedents' Estates)
Probate Code, § 8100
www.courtinfo.ca.gov

DE-121

ESTATE OF (Name):		CASE NUMBER:
	DECEDENT	

PROOF OF SERVICE BY MAIL

1. I am over the age of 18 and not a party to this cause. I am a resident of or employed in the county where the mailing occurred.

2. My residence or business address is (specify):

3. I served the foregoing *Notice of Petition to Administer Estate* on each person named below by enclosing a copy in an envelope addressed as shown below **AND**

    a. ☐ **depositing** the sealed envelope with the United States Postal Service on the date and at the place shown in item 4, with the postage fully prepaid.

    b. ☐ **placing** the envelope for collection and mailing on the date and at the place shown in item 4 following our ordinary business practices. I am readily familiar with this business's practice for collecting and processing correspondence for mailing. On the same day that correspondence is placed for collection and mailing, it is deposited in the ordinary course of business with the United States Postal Service, in a sealed envelope with postage fully prepaid.

4. a. Date mailed: b. Place mailed (city, state):

5. ☐ I served, with the *Notice of Petition to Administer Estate,* a copy of the petition or other document referred to in the notice.

I declare under penalty of perjury under the laws of the State of California that the foregoing is true and correct.

Date:

▶

_____
(TYPE OR PRINT NAME OF PERSON COMPLETING THIS FORM)

_____
(SIGNATURE OF PERSON COMPLETING THIS FORM)

NAME AND ADDRESS OF EACH PERSON TO WHOM NOTICE WAS MAILED

	Name of person served	Address (number, street, city, state, and zip code)
1.		
2.		
3.		
4.		
5.		
6.		

☐ Continued on an attachment. (You may use form DE-121(MA) to show additional persons served.)

Assistive listening systems, computer-assisted real-time captioning, or sign language interpreter services are available upon request if at least 5 days notice is provided. Contact the clerk's office for *Request for Accommodations by Persons With Disabilities and Order* (form MC-410). (Civil Code section 54.8.)

NOTICE OF PETITION TO ADMINISTER ESTATE (Probate—Decedents' Estates)

DE-147

ATTORNEY OR PARTY WITHOUT ATTORNEY *(Name, state bar number, and address)*:	*FOR COURT USE ONLY*
TELEPHONE NO.: FAX NO. *(Optional)*: E–MAIL ADDRESS *(Optional)*: ATTORNEY FOR *(Name)*:	

SUPERIOR COURT OF CALIFORNIA, COUNTY OF
STREET ADDRESS:
MAILING ADDRESS:
CITY AND ZIP CODE:
BRANCH NAME:

ESTATE OF *(Name)*: DECEDENT	
DUTIES AND LIABILITIES OF PERSONAL REPRESENTATIVE **and Acknowledgment of Receipt**	CASE NUMBER:

DUTIES AND LIABILITIES OF PERSONAL REPRESENTATIVE

When the court appoints you as personal representative of an estate, you become an officer of the court and assume certain duties and obligations. An attorney is best qualified to advise you about these matters. You should understand the following:

1. MANAGING THE ESTATE'S ASSETS

a. Prudent investments
You must manage the estate assets with the care of a prudent person dealing with someone else's property. This means that you must be cautious and may not make any speculative investments.

b. Keep estate assets separate
You must keep the money and property in this estate separate from anyone else's, including your own. When you open a bank account for the estate, the account name must indicate that it is an estate account and not your personal account. Never deposit estate funds in your personal account or otherwise mix them with your or anyone else's property. Securities in the estate must also be held in a name that shows they are estate property and not your personal property.

c. Interest-bearing accounts and other investments
Except for checking accounts intended for ordinary administration expenses, estate accounts must earn interest. You may deposit estate funds in insured accounts in financial institutions, but you should consult with an attorney before making other kinds of investments.

d. Other restrictions
There are many other restrictions on your authority to deal with estate property. You should not spend any of the estate's money unless you have received permission from the court or have been advised to do so by an attorney. You may reimburse yourself for official court costs paid by you to the county clerk and for the premium on your bond. Without prior order of the court, you may not pay fees to yourself or to your attorney, if you have one. If you do not obtain the court's permission when it is required, you may be removed as personal representative or you may be required to reimburse the estate from your own personal funds, or both. You should consult with an attorney concerning the legal requirements affecting sales, leases, mortgages, and investments of estate property.

2. INVENTORY OF ESTATE PROPERTY

a. Locate the estate's property
You must attempt to locate and take possession of all the decedent's property to be administered in the estate.

b. Determine the value of the property
You must arrange to have a court-appointed referee determine the value of the property unless the appointment is waived by the court. You, rather than the referee, must determine the value of certain "cash items." An attorney can advise you about how to do this.

c. File an inventory and appraisal
Within four months after Letters are first issued to you as personal representative, you must file with the court an inventory and appraisal of all the assets in the estate.

Page 1 of 2

ESTATE OF (Name):	CASE NUMBER:
DECEDENT	

d. File a change of ownership

At the time you file the inventory and appraisal, you must also file a change of ownership statement with the county recorder or assessor in each county where the decedent owned real property at the time of death, as provided in section 480 of the California Revenue and Taxation Code.

3. NOTICE TO CREDITORS

You must mail a notice of administration to each known creditor of the decedent within four months after your appointment as personal representative. If the decedent received Medi-Cal assistance, you must notify the State Director of Health Services within 90 days after appointment.

4. INSURANCE

You should determine that there is appropriate and adequate insurance covering the assets and risks of the estate. Maintain the insurance in force during the entire period of the administration.

5. RECORD KEEPING

a. Keep accounts

You must keep complete and accurate records of each financial transaction affecting the estate. You will have to prepare an account of all money and property you have received, what you have spent, and the date of each transaction. You must describe in detail what you have left after the payment of expenses.

b. Court review

Your account will be reviewed by the court. Save your receipts because the court may ask to review them. If you do not file your accounts as required, the court will order you to do so. You may be removed as personal representative if you fail to comply.

6. CONSULTING AN ATTORNEY

If you have an attorney, you should cooperate with the attorney at all times. You and your attorney are responsible for completing the estate administration as promptly as possible. **When in doubt, contact your attorney.**

NOTICE: **1. This statement of duties and liabilities is a summary and is not a complete statement of the law. Your conduct as a personal representative is governed by the law itself and not by this summary.**
2. If you fail to perform your duties or to meet the deadlines, the court may reduce your compensation, remove you from office, and impose other sanctions.

ACKNOWLEDGMENT OF RECEIPT

1. I have petitioned the court to be appointed as a personal representative.

2. My address and telephone number are (specify):

3. I acknowledge that I have received a copy of this statement of the duties and liabilities of the office of personal representative.

Date:

_____
(TYPE OR PRINT NAME)

▶ _____
(SIGNATURE OF PETITIONER)

Date:

_____
(TYPE OR PRINT NAME)

▶ _____
(SIGNATURE OF PETITIONER)

CONFIDENTIAL INFORMATION: If required to do so by local court rule, you must provide your date of birth and driver's license number on supplemental Form DE-147S. (Prob. Code, § 8404(b).)

DE-147 [Rev. January 1, 2002]   **DUTIES AND LIABILITIES OF PERSONAL REPRESENTATIVE**   Page 2 of 2
(Probate)

CONFIDENTIAL   **DE-147S**

ESTATE OF *(Name):*	CASE NUMBER:
DECEDENT	

CONFIDENTIAL STATEMENT OF BIRTH DATE
AND DRIVER'S LICENSE NUMBER

(Supplement to *Duties and Liabilities of Personal Representative* (Form DE-147))

*(NOTE: This supplement is to be used if the court by local rule requires the personal representative to provide a birth date and driver's license number. Do **not** attach this supplement to Form DE-147.)*

This separate *Confidential Statement of Birth Date and Driver's License Number* contains confidential information relating to the personal representative in the case referenced above. This supplement shall be kept separate from the *Duties and Liabilities of Personal Representative* filed in this case and shall not be a public record.

INFORMATION ON THE PERSONAL REPRESENTATIVE:

1. Name:

2. Date of birth:

3. Driver's license number: State:

> **TO COURT CLERK:**
> THIS STATEMENT IS **CONFIDENTIAL**. DO NOT FILE
> THIS CONFIDENTIAL STATEMENT IN A PUBLIC COURT FILE.

Form Adopted for Mandatory Use
Judicial Council of California
DE-147S [New January 1, 2001]

**CONFIDENTIAL SUPPLEMENT TO DUTIES AND
LIABILITIES OF PERSONAL REPRESENTATIVE**
(Probate)

Probate Code, § 8404

This page intentionally left blank.

DE-131

ATTORNEY OR PARTY WITHOUT ATTORNEY *(Name, state bar number, and address)* :	TELEPHONE AND FAX NOS.:	*FOR COURT USE ONLY*
ATTORNEY FOR *(Name)*:		

SUPERIOR COURT OF CALIFORNIA, COUNTY OF

STREET ADDRESS:

MAILING ADDRESS:

CITY AND ZIP CODE:

BRANCH NAME:

ESTATE OF *(Name)*:

DECEDENT

PROOF OF SUBSCRIBING WITNESS	CASE NUMBER:

1. I am one of the attesting witnesses to the instrument of which Attachment 1 is a photographic copy. I have examined Attachment 1 and my signature is on it.
   a. ☐ The name of the decedent was signed in the presence of the attesting witnesses present at the same time by
      (1) ☐ the decedent personally.
      (2) ☐ another person in the decedent's presence and by the decedent's direction.
   b. ☐ The decedent acknowledged in the presence of the attesting witnesses present at the same time that the decedent's name was signed by
      (1) ☐ the decedent personally.
      (2) ☐ another person in the decedent's presence and by the decedent's direction.
   c. ☐ The decedent acknowledged in the presence of the attesting witnesses present at the same time that the instrument signed was decedent's
      (1) ☐ will.
      (2) ☐ codicil.

2. When I signed the instrument, I understood that it was decedent's ☐ will ☐ codicil.

3. I have no knowledge of any facts indicating that the instrument, or any part of it, was procured by duress, menace, fraud, or undue influence.

I declare under penalty of perjury under the laws of the State of California that the foregoing is true and correct.

Date:

▶

....
(TYPE OR PRINT NAME)

(SIGNATURE OF WITNESS)

....
(ADDRESS)

ATTORNEY'S CERTIFICATION
(Check local court rules for requirements for certifying copies of wills and codicils)

I am an active member of The State Bar of California. I declare under penalty of perjury under the laws of the State of California that Attachment 1 is a photographic copy of every page of the ☐ will ☐ codicil presented for probate.

Date:

▶

....
(TYPE OR PRINT NAME)

(SIGNATURE OF ATTORNEY)

Form Approved by the
Judicial Council of California
DE-131 [Rev. January 1, 1998]
Mandatory Form [1/1/2000]

PROOF OF SUBSCRIBING WITNESS
(Probate)

Probate Code, § 8220

This page intentionally left blank.

DE-135

ATTORNEY OR PARTY WITHOUT ATTORNEY (Name, state bar number, and address): TELEPHONE AND FAX NOS.:	For Court Use Only:

ATTORNEY FOR (Name):

SUPERIOR COURT OF CALIFORNIA, COUNTY OF

STREET ADDRESS:

MAILING ADDRESS:

CITY AND ZIP CODE:

BRANCH NAME:

ESTATE OF (Name):

                                  DECEDENT

PROOF OF HOLOGRAPHIC INSTRUMENT	CASE NUMBER:

1. I was acquainted with the decedent for the following number of years (specify):

2. ☐ I was related to the decedent as (specify):

3. I have personal knowledge of the decedent's handwriting which I acquired as follows:
   a. ☐ I saw the decedent write.
   b. ☐ I saw a writing purporting to be in the decedent's handwriting and upon which decedent acted or was charged. It was (specify):

   c. ☐ I received letters in the due course of mail purporting to be from the decedent in response to letters I addressed and mailed to the decedent.
   d. ☐ Other (specify other means of obtaining knowledge):

4. I have examined the attached copy of the instrument, and its handwritten provisions were written by and the instrument was signed by the hand of the decedent. (Affix a copy of the instrument as Attachment 4.)

I declare under penalty of perjury under the laws of the State of California that the foregoing is true and correct.
Date:

▶

. . . .
(TYPE OR PRINT NAME)   (SIGNATURE)

. . . .
(ADDRESS)

ATTORNEY'S CERTIFICATION

(Check local court rules for requirements for certifying copies of wills and codicils)

I am an active member of The State Bar of California. I declare under penalty of perjury under the laws of the State of California that Attachment 4 is a photographic copy of every page of the holographic instrument presented for probate.

Date:

▶

. . . .
(TYPE OR PRINT NAME)   (SIGNATURE OF ATTORNEY)

Form Approved by the
Judicial Council of California
DE-135 [Rev. January 1, 1998]
PROOF OF HOLOGRAPHIC INSTRUMENT
(PROBATE)
Probate Code, § 8222

This page intentionally left blank.

DE-140

ATTORNEY OR PARTY WITHOUT ATTORNEY *(Name, state bar number, and address):*	TELEPHONE AND FAX NOS.:	*FOR COURT USE ONLY*

ATTORNEY FOR *(Name):*

SUPERIOR COURT OF CALIFORNIA, COUNTY OF

STREET ADDRESS:

MAILING ADDRESS:

CITY AND ZIP CODE:

BRANCH NAME:

ESTATE OF *(Name):*

DECEDENT

ORDER FOR PROBATE

ORDER APPOINTING

☐ Executor
☐ Administrator with Will Annexed
☐ Administrator   ☐ Special Administrator
☐ Order Authorizing Independent Administration of Estate
    ☐ with full authority   ☐ with limited authority

CASE NUMBER:

WARNING: THIS APPOINTMENT IS NOT EFFECTIVE UNTIL LETTERS HAVE ISSUED.

1. Date of hearing: Time: Dept./Room: Judge:

THE COURT FINDS

2. a. All notices required by law have been given.
   b. Decedent died on *(date):*
      (1) ☐ a resident of the California county named above.
      (2) ☐ a nonresident of California and left an estate in the county named above.
   c. Decedent died
      (1) ☐ intestate
      (2) ☐ testate
      and decedent's will dated: and each codicil dated:
      was admitted to probate by Minute Order on *(date):*

THE COURT ORDERS

3. *(Name):*
   is appointed **personal representative:**
   a. ☐ executor of the decedent's will   d. ☐ special administrator
   b. ☐ administrator with will annexed   (1) ☐ with general powers
   c. ☐ administrator   (2) ☐ with special powers as specified in Attachment 3d(2)
                                                      (3) ☐ without notice of hearing
                                                      (4) ☐ letters will expire on *(date):*

   and letters shall issue on qualification.

4. a. ☐ **Full authority** is granted to administer the estate under the Independent Administration of Estates Act.
   b. ☐ **Limited authority** is granted to administer the estate under the Independent Administration of Estates Act (there is no authority, without court supervision, to (1) sell or exchange real property or (2) grant an option to purchase real property or (3) borrow money with the loan secured by an encumbrance upon real property).

5. a. ☐ Bond is not required.
   b. ☐ Bond is fixed at: $ to be furnished by an authorized surety company or as otherwise provided by law.
   c. ☐ Deposits of: $ are ordered to be placed in a blocked account at *(specify institution and location):*
      and receipts shall be filed. No withdrawals shall be made without a court order. ☐ Additional orders in Attachment 5c.
   d. ☐ The personal representative is not authorized to take possession of money or any other property without a specific court order.

6. ☐ *(Name):*   is appointed probate referee.

Date:

_____
JUDGE OF THE SUPERIOR COURT

7. Number of pages attached: _____

☐ SIGNATURE FOLLOWS LAST ATTACHMENT

Form Approved by the
Judicial Council of California
DE-140 (Rev. January 1, 1998)

ORDER FOR PROBATE

Probate Code, §§ 8006, 8400

This page intentionally left blank.

Form **SS-4**
(Rev. February 2006)
Department of the Treasury
Internal Revenue Service

Application for Employer Identification Number

(For use by employers, corporations, partnerships, trusts, estates, churches, government agencies, Indian tribal entities, certain individuals, and others.)

▶ See separate instructions for each line.   ▶ Keep a copy for your records.

OMB No. 1545-0003

EIN

1 Legal name of entity (or individual) for whom the EIN is being requested	

Type or print clearly.

2 Trade name of business (if different from name on line 1)	**3** Executor, administrator, trustee, "care of" name
4a Mailing address (room, apt., suite no. and street, or P.O. box)	**5a** Street address (if different) (Do not enter a P.O. box.)
4b City, state, and ZIP code	**5b** City, state, and ZIP code

6 County and state where principal business is located

7a Name of principal officer, general partner, grantor, owner, or trustor	**7b** SSN, ITIN, or EIN

8a **Type of entity** (check only one box)

☐ Sole proprietor (SSN) _____
☐ Partnership
☐ Corporation (enter form number to be filed) ▶ _____
☐ Personal service corporation
☐ Church or church-controlled organization
☐ Other nonprofit organization (specify) ▶ _____
☐ Other (specify) ▶

☐ Estate (SSN of decedent) _____
☐ Plan administrator (SSN) _____
☐ Trust (SSN of grantor) _____
☐ National Guard   ☐ State/local government
☐ Farmers' cooperative   ☐ Federal government/military
☐ REMIC   ☐ Indian tribal governments/enterprises
Group Exemption Number (GEN) ▶ _____

8b If a corporation, name the state or foreign country (if applicable) where incorporated

State	Foreign country

9 **Reason for applying** (check only one box)

☐ Started new business (specify type) ▶ _____
☐ Hired employees (Check the box and see line 12.)
☐ Compliance with IRS withholding regulations
☐ Other (specify) ▶

☐ Banking purpose (specify purpose) ▶ _____
☐ Changed type of organization (specify new type) ▶ _____
☐ Purchased going business
☐ Created a trust (specify type) ▶ _____
☐ Created a pension plan (specify type) ▶ _____

10 Date business started or acquired (month, day, year). See instructions.	**11** Closing month of accounting year

12 First date wages or annuities were paid (month, day, year). **Note.** If applicant is a withholding agent, enter date income will first be paid to nonresident alien. (month, day, year) . . . . ▶

13 Highest number of employees expected in the next 12 months (enter -0- if none).

Do you expect to have $1,000 or less in employment tax liability for the calendar year? ☐ **Yes** ☐ **No.** (If you expect to pay $4,000 or less in wages, you can mark yes.)

Agricultural	Household	Other

14 Check **one** box that best describes the principal activity of your business.
☐ Construction ☐ Rental & leasing ☐ Transportation & warehousing
☐ Real estate ☐ Manufacturing ☐ Finance & insurance
☐ Health care & social assistance ☐ Wholesale–agent/broker
☐ Accommodation & food service ☐ Wholesale–other ☐ Retail
☐ Other (specify)

15 Indicate principal line of merchandise sold, specific construction work done, products produced, or services provided.

16a Has the applicant ever applied for an employer identification number for this or any other business? . . . . ☐ **Yes** ☐ **No**
Note. If "Yes," please complete lines 16b and 16c.

16b If you checked "Yes" on line 16a, give applicant's legal name and trade name shown on prior application if different from line 1 or 2 above.
Legal name ▶ _____   Trade name ▶ _____

16c Approximate date when, and city and state where, the application was filed. Enter previous employer identification number if known.

Approximate date when filed (mo., day, year)	City and state where filed	Previous EIN

Third Party Designee

Complete this section **only** if you want to authorize the named individual to receive the entity's EIN and answer questions about the completion of this form.

Designee's name	Designee's telephone number (include area code) ( )
Address and ZIP code	Designee's fax number (include area code) ( )

Under penalties of perjury, I declare that I have examined this application, and to the best of my knowledge and belief, it is true, correct, and complete.

	Applicant's telephone number (include area code) ( )
Name and title (type or print clearly) ▶	
Signature ▶ Date ▶	Applicant's fax number (include area code) ( )

For Privacy Act and Paperwork Reduction Act Notice, see separate instructions.   Cat. No. 16055N   Form **SS-4** (Rev. 2-2006)

Do I Need an EIN?

File Form SS-4 if the applicant entity does not already have an EIN but is required to show an EIN on any return, statement, or other document.[1] See also the separate instructions for each line on Form SS-4.

IF the applicant...	AND...	THEN...
Started a new business	Does not currently have (nor expect to have) employees	Complete lines 1, 2, 4a–8a, 8b (if applicable), and 9–16c.
Hired (or will hire) employees, including household employees	Does not already have an EIN	Complete lines 1, 2, 4a–6, 7a–b (if applicable), 8a, 8b (if applicable), and 9–16c.
Opened a bank account	Needs an EIN for banking purposes only	Complete lines 1–5b, 7a–b (if applicable), 8a, 9, and 16a–c.
Changed type of organization	Either the legal character of the organization or its ownership changed (for example, you incorporate a sole proprietorship or form a partnership)[2]	Complete lines 1–16c (as applicable).
Purchased a going business[3]	Does not already have an EIN	Complete lines 1–16c (as applicable).
Created a trust	The trust is other than a grantor trust or an IRA trust[4]	Complete lines 1–16c (as applicable).
Created a pension plan as a plan administrator[5]	Needs an EIN for reporting purposes	Complete lines 1, 3, 4a–b, 8a, 9, and 16a–c.
Is a foreign person needing an EIN to comply with IRS withholding regulations	Needs an EIN to complete a Form W-8 (other than Form W-8ECI), avoid withholding on portfolio assets, or claim tax treaty benefits[6]	Complete lines 1–5b, 7a–b (SSN or ITIN optional), 8a–9, and 16a–c.
Is administering an estate	Needs an EIN to report estate income on Form 1041	Complete lines 1, 2, 3, 4a–6, 8a, 9-11, 12-15 (if applicable), and 16a–c.
Is a withholding agent for taxes on non-wage income paid to an alien (i.e., individual, corporation, or partnership, etc.)	Is an agent, broker, fiduciary, manager, tenant, or spouse who is required to file Form 1042, Annual Withholding Tax Return for U.S. Source Income of Foreign Persons	Complete lines 1, 2, 3 (if applicable), 4a–5b, 7a–b (if applicable), 8a, 9, and 16a–c.
Is a state or local agency	Serves as a tax reporting agent for public assistance recipients under Rev. Proc. 80-4, 1980-1 C.B. 581[7]	Complete lines 1, 2, 4a–5b, 8a, 9, and 16a–c.
Is a single-member LLC	Needs an EIN to file Form 8832, Entity Classification Election, for filing employment tax returns, **or** for state reporting purposes[8]	Complete lines 1–16c (as applicable).
Is an S corporation	Needs an EIN to file Form 2553, Election by a Small Business Corporation[9]	Complete lines 1–16c (as applicable).

[1] For example, a sole proprietorship or self-employed farmer who establishes a qualified retirement plan, or is required to file excise, employment, alcohol, tobacco, or firearms returns, must have an EIN. A partnership, corporation, REMIC (real estate mortgage investment conduit), nonprofit organization (church, club, etc.), or farmers' cooperative must use an EIN for any tax-related purpose even if the entity does not have employees.

[2] However, do not apply for a new EIN if the existing entity only (a) changed its business name, (b) elected on Form 8832 to change the way it is taxed (or is covered by the default rules), or (c) terminated its partnership status because at least 50% of the total interests in partnership capital and profits were sold or exchanged within a 12-month period. The EIN of the terminated partnership should continue to be used. See Regulations section 301.6109-1(d)(2)(iii).

[3] Do not use the EIN of the prior business unless you became the "owner" of a corporation by acquiring its stock.

[4] However, grantor trusts that do not file using Optional Method 1 and IRA trusts that are required to file Form 990-T, Exempt Organization Business Income Tax Return, must have an EIN. For more information on grantor trusts, see the Instructions for Form 1041.

[5] A plan administrator is the person or group of persons specified as the administrator by the instrument under which the plan is operated.

[6] Entities applying to be a Qualified Intermediary (QI) need a QI-EIN even if they already have an EIN. See Rev. Proc. 2000-12.

[7] See also Household employer on page 3. **Note.** State or local agencies may need an EIN for other reasons, for example, hired employees.

[8] Most LLCs do not need to file Form 8832. See Limited liability company (LLC) on page 4 for details on completing Form SS-4 for an LLC.

[9] An existing corporation that is electing or revoking S corporation status should use its previously-assigned EIN.

DE-150

ATTORNEY OR PARTY WITHOUT ATTORNEY *(Name, state bar number, and address):*	TELEPHONE AND FAX NOS.:	*FOR COURT USE ONLY*

ATTORNEY FOR *(Name):*

SUPERIOR COURT OF CALIFORNIA, COUNTY OF

STREET ADDRESS:

MAILING ADDRESS:

CITY AND ZIP CODE:

BRANCH NAME:

ESTATE OF *(Name):*

DECEDENT

LETTERS		CASE NUMBER:
☐ TESTAMENTARY	☐ OF ADMINISTRATION	
☐ OF ADMINISTRATION WITH WILL ANNEXED	☐ SPECIAL ADMINISTRATION	

LETTERS

1. ☐ The last will of the decedent named above having been proved, the court appoints *(name):*

    a. ☐ executor.

    b. ☐ administrator with will annexed.

2. ☐ The court appoints *(name):*

    a. ☐ administrator of the decedent's estate.

    b. ☐ special administrator of decedent's estate

       (1) ☐ with the special powers specified in the *Order for Probate.*

       (2) ☐ with the powers of a general administrator.

       (3) ☐ letters will expire on *(date):*

3. ☐ The personal representative is authorized to administer the estate under the Independent Administration of Estates Act ☐ **with full authority**
☐ **with limited authority** (no authority, without court supervision, to (1) sell or exchange real property or (2) grant an option to purchase real property or (3) borrow money with the loan secured by an encumbrance upon real property).

4. ☐ The personal representative is not authorized to take possession of money or any other property without a specific court order.

WITNESS, clerk of the court, with seal of the court affixed.

(SEAL)	Date:
	Clerk, by
	_____ (DEPUTY)

AFFIRMATION

1. ☐ PUBLIC ADMINISTRATOR: No affirmation required (Prob. Code, § 7621(c)).

2. ☐ INDIVIDUAL: **I solemnly affirm** that I will perform the duties of personal representative according to law.

3. ☐ INSTITUTIONAL FIDUCIARY *(name):*

    I solemnly affirm that the institution will perform the duties of personal representative according to law. I make this affirmation for myself as an individual and on behalf of the institution as an officer. *(Name and title):*

4. Executed on *(date):*
at *(place):* , California.

▶ _____
(SIGNATURE)

CERTIFICATION

I certify that this document is a correct copy of the original on file in my office and the letters issued the personal representative appointed above have not been revoked, annulled, or set aside, and are still in full force and effect.

(SEAL)	Date:
	Clerk, by
	_____ (DEPUTY)

LETTERS
(Probate)

Probate Code, §§1001, 8403,
8405, 8544, 8545;
Code of Civil Procedure, § 2015.6

This page intentionally left blank.

DE-154, GC-035

ATTORNEY OR PARTY WITHOUT ATTORNEY *(Name, state bar number, and address):*	TELEPHONE AND FAX NOS.:	FOR COURT USE ONLY

ATTORNEY FOR *(Name)*:

SUPERIOR COURT OF CALIFORNIA, COUNTY OF

STREET ADDRESS:

MAILING ADDRESS:

CITY AND ZIP CODE:

BRANCH NAME:

MATTER OF *(Name)*:

☐ DECEDENT ☐ CONSERVATEE ☐ MINOR ☐ TRUST

REQUEST FOR SPECIAL NOTICE

CASE NUMBER:

1. a. ☐ I am a person interested in this proceeding.

   b. ☐ I am the attorney for a person interested in this proceeding *(specify name of interested person)*:

2. I REQUEST SPECIAL NOTICE of *(complete only a or b)*

   a. ☐ the following matters *(check applicable boxes)*:

    (1) ☐ **all matters** for which special notice may be requested *(Do not check boxes (2)-(8).)*

    (2) ☐ inventories and appraisals of property, including supplements

    (3) ☐ accountings

    (4) ☐ reports of the status of administration

    (5) ☐ objections to an appraisal

    (6) ☐ petitions for the sale of property

    (7) ☐ *Spousal Property Petition* (form DE-221) (Prob. Code, § 13650)

    (8) ☐ other petitions: ☐ all petitions ☐ the following petitions *(specify)*:

   b. ☐ the following matters *(specify)*:

3. SEND THE NOTICES to

   a. ☐ the interested person at the following address *(specify)*:

   b. ☐ the attorney at the following address *(specify)*:

Date:

. . . .
(TYPE OR PRINT NAME)

▶

_____
(SIGNATURE)

☐ Attorney for person requesting special notice *(client's name)*:

(Continued on reverse)

Form Approved by the
Judicial Council of California
DE-154, GC-035 (Rev. January 1, 1998)

REQUEST FOR SPECIAL NOTICE
(Probate)

Probate Code, §§ 1250,
2700(c), 17204

MATTER OF (Name):	CASE NUMBER:

NOTE: A formal proof of service or a written admission of service must accompany this *Request for Special Notice* when it is filed with the court.

You must have your request served on either the personal representative, conservator, guardian, or trustee, or his or her attorney, or obtain a signed *Admission of Service (see below)*.

PROOF OF SERVICE BY MAIL

1. I am over the age of 18 and not a party to this cause. I am a resident of or employed in the county where the mailing occurred.
2. My residence or business address is (specify):

3. I served the foregoing *Request for Special Notice* on each person named below by enclosing a copy in an envelope addressed as shown below AND
   a. ☐ **depositing** the sealed envelope with the United States Postal Service with the postage fully prepaid.
   b. ☐ **placing** the envelope for collection and mailing on the date and at the place shown in item 4 following our ordinary business practices. I am readily familiar with this business' practice for collecting and processing correspondence for mailing. On the same day that correspondence is place for collection and mailing, it is deposited in the ordinary course of business with the United States Postal Service in a sealed envelope with postage fully prepaid.

4. a. Date of deposit: b. Place of deposit (city and state):

I declare under penalty of perjury under the laws of the State of California that the foregoing is true and correct.
Date:

▶

. . . .   _____
(TYPE OR PRINT NAME)   (SIGNATURE OF DECLARANT)

NAME AND ADDRESS OF EACH PERSON TO WHOM NOTICE WAS MAILED

☐ List of names and addresses continued in attachment.

ADMISSION OF SERVICE

1. I am the ☐ personal representative, conservator, guardian, or trustee   ☐ the attorney.

2. I ACKNOWLEDGE that I was served a copy of the foregoing *Request for Special Notice*.

Date:

▶

. . . .   _____
(TYPE OR PRINT NAME)   (SIGNATURE)

DE-160/GC-040

ATTORNEY OR PARTY WITHOUT ATTORNEY *(Name, state bar number, and address)*:	FOR COURT USE ONLY
TELEPHONE NO.: FAX NO. *(Optional)*: E-MAIL ADDRESS *(Optional)*: ATTORNEY FOR *(Name)*:	

SUPERIOR COURT OF CALIFORNIA, COUNTY OF

STREET ADDRESS:

MAILING ADDRESS:

CITY AND ZIP CODE:

BRANCH NAME:

ESTATE OF *(Name)*:

☐ DECEDENT   ☐ CONSERVATEE   ☐ MINOR

INVENTORY AND APPRAISAL	CASE NUMBER:
☐ **Partial No.:** ☐ **Corrected** ☐ **Final** ☐ **Reappraisal for Sale** ☐ **Supplemental** ☐ **Property Tax Certificate**	Date of Death of Decedent or of Appointment of Guardian or Conservator:

APPRAISALS

1. Total appraisal by representative, guardian, or conservator (Attachment 1): $
2. Total appraisal by referee (Attachment 2): $

TOTAL: $

DECLARATION OF REPRESENTATIVE, GUARDIAN, CONSERVATOR, OR SMALL ESTATE CLAIMANT

3. Attachments 1 and 2 together with all prior inventories filed contain a true statement of
   ☐ all ☐ a portion   of the estate that has come to my knowledge or possession, including particularly all money and all just claims the estate has against me. I have truly, honestly, and impartially appraised to the best of my ability each item set forth in Attachment 1.

4. ☐ No probate referee is required ☐ by order of the court dated *(specify)*:

5. **Property tax certificate.** I certify that the requirements of Revenue and Taxation Code section 480
   a. ☐ are not applicable because the decedent owned no real property in California at the time of death.
   b. ☐ have been satisfied by the filing of a change of ownership statement with the county recorder or assessor of each county in California in which the decedent owned property at the time of death.

I declare under penalty of perjury under the laws of the State of California that the foregoing is true and correct.

Date:

▶

_____   _____
(TYPE OR PRINT NAME; INCLUDE TITLE IF CORPORATE OFFICER)   (SIGNATURE)

STATEMENT ABOUT THE BOND
(Complete in all cases. Must be signed by attorney for fiduciary, or by fiduciary without an attorney.)

6. ☐ Bond is waived, or the sole fiduciary is a corporate fiduciary or an exempt government agency.
7. ☐ Bond filed in the amount of: $ ☐ Sufficient ☐ Insufficient
8. ☐ Receipts for: $ have been filed with the court for deposits in a blocked account at *(specify institution and location)*:

Date:

▶

_____   _____
(TYPE OR PRINT NAME)   (SIGNATURE OF ATTORNEY OR PARTY WITHOUT ATTORNEY)

Page 1 of 2

Form Adopted for Mandatory Use Judicial Council of California DE-160/GC-040 [Rev. January 1, 2003]	**INVENTORY AND APPRAISAL**	Probate Code, §§ 2610–2616, 8800–8980; Cal. Rules of Court, rule 7.501

ESTATE OF *(Name):*	CASE NUMBER:
☐ DECEDENT ☐ CONSERVATEE ☐ MINOR	

DECLARATION OF PROBATE REFEREE

9. I have truly, honestly, and impartially appraised to the best of my ability each item set forth in Attachment 2.
10. A true account of my commission and expenses actually and necessarily incurred pursuant to my appointment is:

  Statutory commission: $
  Expenses *(specify):* $
  TOTAL: $

I declare under penalty of perjury under the laws of the State of California that the foregoing is true and correct.

Date:

_____   ▶   _____
(TYPE OR PRINT NAME)   (SIGNATURE OF REFEREE)

INSTRUCTIONS

(See Probate Code sections 2610–2616, 8801, 8804, 8852, 8905, 8960, 8961, and 8963 for additional instructions.)

1. See Probate Code section 8850 for items to be included in the inventory.

2. If the minor or conservatee is or has been during the guardianship or conservatorship confined in a state hospital under the jurisdiction of the State Department of Mental Health or the State Department of Developmental Services, mail a copy to the director of the appropriate department in Sacramento. (Prob. Code, § 2611.)

3. The representative, guardian, conservator, or small estate claimant shall list on Attachment 1 and appraise as of the date of death of the decedent or the date of appointment of the guardian or conservator, at fair market value, moneys, currency, cash items, bank accounts and amounts on deposit with each financial institution (as defined in Probate Code section 40), and the proceeds of life and accident insurance policies and retirement plans payable upon death in lump sum amounts to the estate, except items whose fair market value is, in the opinion of the representative, an amount different from the ostensible value or specified amount.

4. The representative, guardian, conservator, or small estate claimant shall list in Attachment 2 all other assets of the estate which shall be appraised by the referee.

5. If joint tenancy and other assets are listed for appraisal purposes only and not as part of the probate estate, they must be separately listed on additional attachments and their value excluded from the total valuation of Attachments 1 and 2.

6. Each attachment should conform to the format approved by the Judicial Council. (See *Inventory and Appraisal Attachment* (form DE-161/GC-041) and Cal. Rules of Court, rule 201.)

DE-161, GC-041

ESTATE OF *(Name)*:	CASE NUMBER:

INVENTORY AND APPRAISAL
ATTACHMENT NO.: _____

(In decedents' estates, attachments must conform to Probate
Code section 8850(c) regarding community and separate property.)

Page: _____ of: _____ total pages.
(Add pages as required.)

Item No.   Description   Appraised value

1.

Form Approved by the
Judicial Council of California
DE-161, GC-041 [Rev. January 1, 1998]

INVENTORY AND APPRAISAL ATTACHMENT

Probate Code, §§ 301,
2610-2613, 8800-8920,
10309

DE-161, GC-041

ESTATE OF *(Name):*	CASE NUMBER:

INVENTORY AND APPRAISAL
ATTACHMENT NO: _____

(In decedents' estates, attachments must conform to Probate
Code section 8850(c) regarding community and separate property.)

Page: _____ of: _____ total pages.
(Add pages as required.)

Item No.	Description	Appraised value
1.		
2.		
3.		
4.		

Form Approved by the
Judicial Council of California
DE-161, GC-041 [Rev. January 1, 1998]

INVENTORY AND APPRAISAL ATTACHMENT

Probate Code. §§ 301,
2610-2613, 8800-8920,
10309

FORM

C

CHANGE IN OWNERSHIP STATEMENT
(DEATH OF REAL PROPERTY OWNER)

MAILING ADDRESS (Make corrections, if necessary)	**ASSESSOR'S IDENTIFICATION NUMBER**		
	MAPBOOK	PAGE	PARCEL
	PROPERTY ADDRESS		

Section 480 of the Revenue and Taxation Code States:

(a) Whenever any change in ownership of real property or of a mobilehome subject to local property taxation, and which is assessed by the county assessor, occurs, the transferee shall file a signed change in ownership statement in the county where the real property or mobilehome is located, as provided for in subdivision (c). In the case of a change in ownership where the transferee is not locally assessed, no change in ownership statement is required.

(b) The personal representative shall file a change in ownership statement with the county recorder or assessor in each county where the decedent owned real property at the time of death. The statement shall be filed at the time the inventory and appraisal is filed with the court clerk.

IMPORTANT NOTICE

The law requires any transferee acquiring an interest in real property or mobilehome subject to local property taxation, and which is assessed by the county assessor, to file a change in ownership statement with the county recorder or assessor. The change in ownership statement must be filed at the time of recording or, if the transfer is not recorded, within 45 days of the date of the change in ownership. The failure to file a change in ownership statement within 45 days from the date of a written request by the assessor results in a penalty of either: (1) one hundred dollars ($100), or (2) 10 percent of the taxes applicable to the new base year value reflecting the change in ownership of the real property or mobilehome, whichever is greater but not to exceed two thousand five hundred dollars ($2,500) if such failure to file was not willful. This penalty will be added to the assessment roll and shall be collected like any other delinquent property taxes, and be subject to the same penalties for nonpayment.

This notice is a written request from the Office of the Assessor for the Change in Ownership Statement. Failure to file this Statement will result in the assessment of a penalty as stated above.

The statement will remain confidential as required by § 481 of the Revenue and Taxation Code.

Passage of Decedent's Property: Probate Code §7000 et seq.

"Subject to §7001, title to a decedent's property passes on the decedent's death to the person to whom it is devised in the decedent's last will or, in the absence of such devise, to the decedent's heirs as prescribed in the laws governing intestate succession."

Date of Change in Ownership: California Code of Regulations, Title 18, Rule 462 (n)(3)

". . . (3) Inheritance (by will or intestate succession). The date of death of decedent."

Inventory and Appraisal: Probate Code §8800

"(d) Concurrent with the filing of the inventory and appraisal pursuant to this section, the personal representative shall also file a certification that the requirements of §480 of the Revenue and Taxation Code either:
   (1)   Are not applicable because the decedent owned no real property in California at the time of death.
   (2)   Have been satisfied by the filing of a change in ownership statement with the county recorder or assessor of each county in which the decedent owned property at the time of death."

If you request, the Office of the Assessor will date receipt your statement and return a copy to you for your records. Also, the Probate Division of the Superior Court will forward a copy of the Inventory and Appraisal to the Office of the Assessor. An extra copy should be provided to the Court for this purpose.

Instructions: Complete a separate form for each property. Answer each question. Upon completion, mail this form and a copy of the death certificate to:

1. NAME OF DECEDENT	2. DATE OF DEATH

3. STREET ADDRESS OF REAL PROPERTY	4. ASSESSOR'S IDENTIFICATION NUMBER		
	a. Mapbook	b. Page	c. Parcel

5. DESCRIPTIVE INFORMATION (Check a, b or c, if applicable)

a. ☐ Attached is copy of deed by which decedent acquired title.

b. ☐ Attached is copy of most recent tax bill.

c. ☐ Deed or tax bill are not available; attached is the legal description.

6. DISPOSITION OF REAL PROPERTY WILL BE BY (Check one)

a. ☐ Intestate succession.

b. ☐ PC 13650 distribution of community property to surviving spouse.

c. ☐ Affidavit of death of joint tenant.

d. ☐ Decree of distribution pursuant to will.

e. ☐ Action of trustee pursuant to terms of a trust.

7. TRANSFEREE INFORMATION (Check a, b, c, or d if applicable)

a. ☐ Transfer is to decedent's spouse. (Check even if affidavit of death of joint tenant is to be recorded.) [Article XIIIA (G)]

Name of spouse _____

b. ☐ Transfer is to a trust of which the spouse is the sole beneficiary or the income beneficiary.

Name of spouse _____

c. ☐ Transfer is to decedent's child(ren) or parent(s) and is excluded from reassessment [Article XIIIA (h)]

☐ Property was principal residence of decedent (fully excluded).

☐ Property subject to $1 million limitation to this transferee.

List name(s) of child(ren) or parent(s) in #9 below. **NOTE:** A claim for exclusion must be filed. To obtain application, call (213) 974-3211

Important: A claim must be filed within three years after the date of death or transfer, or prior to the date of transfer to a third party, whichever is earlier.

d. ☐ Transfer is to decedent's other beneficiaries. *(Where known, indicate names of beneficiaries and the percentage of ownership interest each is to receive.)*

_____

_____

8. SALE PRIOR TO DISTRIBUTION

☐ This property has been sold or will be sold prior to distribution. (Where appropriate, attach the conveyance document and/or court order.) **NOTE:** See exclusion, item 7c, above.

9. ADDITIONAL INFORMATION

☐ Additional sheets attached. (Should you wish to explain any of the foregoing or provide additional information, please attach additional sheets.)

NAME (Please print)	TITLE (If corporate officer/partner)	TELEPHONE NO. (8 a.m. - 5 p.m.)

I declare under penalty of perjury that the foregoing is true and correct to the best of my knowledge and belief.

_____
Signature of owner or corporate officer

Signed at, _____ , California, this _____ day of _____ , _____

NOTICE OF ADMINISTRATION
OF THE ESTATE OF

(NAME)

DECEDENT

NOTICE TO CREDITORS

1. *(Name)*:
   (Address):

   (Telephone):
   is the **personal representative** of the **ESTATE OF** *(name)*:   , who is deceased.

2. The personal representative HAS BEGUN ADMINISTRATION of the decedent's estate in the

   a. **SUPERIOR COURT OF CALIFORNIA, COUNTY OF** *(specify)*:
      STREET ADDRESS:
      MAILING ADDRESS:
      CITY AND ZIP CODE:
      BRANCH NAME:

   b. Case number *(specify)*:

3. You must FILE YOUR CLAIM with the court clerk (address in item 2a) AND mail or deliver a copy to the personal representative before the **later** of the following times as provided in Probate Code section 9100:

   a. **four months** after *(date)*: [   ] , the date letters (authority to act for the estate) were first issued to the personal representative, OR

   b. **sixty days** after *(date)*: [   ] , the date this notice was mailed or personally delivered to you.

4. LATE CLAIMS: If you do not file your claim before it is due, you must file a petition with the court for permission to file a late claim as provided in Provate Code section 9103.

WHERE TO GET A CREDITOR'S CLAIM FORM: If a *Creditor's Claim* (form DE-172) did not accompany this notice, you may obtain a copy from any superior court clerk or from the person who sent you this notice. A letter to the court stating your claim is *not* sufficient.

FAILURE TO FILE A CLAIM: Failure to file a claim with the court and serve a copy of the claim on the personal representative will in most instances invalidate your claim.

IF YOU MAIL YOUR CLAIM: If you use the mail to file your claim with the court, for your protection you should send your claim by certified mail, with return receipt requested. If you use the mail to serve a copy of your claim on the personal representative, you should also use certified mail.

Note: To assist the creditor and the court, please send a copy of the *Creditor's Claim* form with this notice.

(Proof of Service on reverse)

Form Approved by the
Judicial Council of California
DE-157 [Rev. January 1, 1998]

NOTICE OF ADMINISTRATION TO CREDITORS
(Probate)

Probate Code, §§ 9050,
9052

[Optional]
PROOF OF SERVICE BY MAIL

1. I am over the age of 18 and not a party to this cause. I am a resident of or employed in the county where the mailing occurred.
2. My residence or business address is *(specify):*

3. I served the foregoing *Notice of Administration to Creditors* ☐ and a blank *Creditor's Claim* form* on each person named below by enclosing a copy in an envelope addressed as shown below AND
   a. ☐ **depositing** the sealed envelope with the United States Postal Service with the postage fully prepaid.
   b. ☐ **placing** the envelope for collection and mailing on the date and at the place shown in item 4 following our ordinary business practices. I am readily familiar with the business' practice for collecting and processing correspondence for mailing. On the same day that correspondence is placed for collection and mailing, it is deposited in the ordinary course of business with the United States Postal Service in a sealed envelope with postage fully prepaid.

4. a. Date of deposit: b. Place of deposit *(city and state):*

I declare under penalty of perjury under the laws of the State of California that the foregoing is true and correct.

Date:

· ·

        (TYPE OR PRINT NAME) ▶   (SIGNATURE OF DECLARANT)

NAME AND ADDRESS OF EACH PERSON TO WHOM NOTICE WAS MAILED

☐ List of names and addresses continued in attachment.

*NOTE: *To assist the creditor and the court, please send a copy of the* Creditor's Claim *(form DE-172) with the notice.*

DE-157 [Rev. January 1, 1998]   **NOTICE OF ADMINISTRATION TO CREDITORS**   **Page two**
(Probate)

DE-172

ATTORNEY OR PARTY WITHOUT ATTORNEY *(Name, state bar number, and address)*:	TELEPHONE AND FAX NOS.:	*FOR COURT USE ONLY*

ATTORNEY FOR *(Name)*:

SUPERIOR COURT OF CALIFORNIA, COUNTY OF

STREET ADDRESS:

MAILING ADDRESS:

CITY AND ZIP CODE:

BRANCH NAME:

ESTATE OF *(Name)*:

DECEDENT

CREDITOR'S CLAIM	CASE NUMBER:

You must file this claim with the court clerk at the court address above before the LATER of (a) four months after the date letters (authority to act for the estate) were first issued to the personal representative, or (b) sixty days after the date the *Notice of Administration* was given to the creditor, if notice was given as provided in Probate Code section 9051. You must also mail or deliver a copy of this claim to the personal representative and his or her attorney. A proof of service is on the reverse.

WARNING: Your claim will in most instances be invalid if you do not properly complete this form, file it on time with the court, and mail or deliver a copy to the personal representative and his or her attorney.

---

1. Total amount of the claim: $
2. Claimant *(name)*:
   a. ☐ an individual
   b. ☐ an individual or entity doing business under the fictitious name of *(specify)*:

   c. ☐ a partnership. The person signing has authority to sign on behalf of the partnership.
   d. ☐ a corporation. The person signing has authority to sign on behalf of the corporation.
   e. ☐ other (specify):
3. Address of claimant *(specify)*:

4. Claimant is ☐ the creditor ☐ a person acting on behalf of creditor *(state reason)*:

5. ☐ Claimant is ☐ the personal representative ☐ the attorney for the personal representative.
6. I am authorized to make this claim which is just and due or may become due. All payments on or offsets to the claim have been credited. Facts supporting the claim are ☐ on reverse ☐ attached.

I declare under penalty of perjury under the laws of the State of California that the foregoing is true and correct.

Date:

▶

· · · · · · · · · · · · · · · · · · · ·
(TYPE OR PRINT NAME AND TITLE)   (SIGNATURE OF CLAIMANT)

INSTRUCTIONS TO CLAIMANT

A. On the reverse, itemize the claim and show the date the service was rendered or the debt incurred. Describe the item or service in detail, and indicate the amount claimed for each item. Do not include debts incurred after the date of death, except funeral claims.

B. If the claim is not due or contingent, or the amount is not yet ascertainable, state the facts supporting the claim.

C. If the claim is secured by a note or other written instrument, the original or a copy must be attached *(state why original is unavailable.)* If secured by mortgage, deed of trust, or other lien on property that is of record, it is sufficient to describe the security and refer to the date or volume and page, and county where recorded. *(See Prob. Code, § 9152.)*

D. Mail or take this original claim to the court clerk's office for filing. If mailed, use certified mail, with return receipt requested.

E. Mail or deliver a copy to the personal representative and his or her attorney. Complete the *Proof of Mailing or Personal Delivery* on the reverse.

F. The personal representative or his or her attorney will notify you when your claim is allowed or rejected.

G. Claims against the estate by the personal representative and the attorney for the personal representative must be filed within the claim period allowed in Probate Code section 9100. See the notice box above.

(Continued on reverse)

Form Approved by the
Judicial Council of California
DE-172 [Rev. January 1, 1998]
Mandatory Form [1/1/2000]

CREDITOR'S CLAIM
(Probate)

Probate Code, §§ 9000 et seq., 9153

ESTATE OF *(Name)*:	CASE NUMBER:
DECEDENT	

FACTS SUPPORTING THE CREDITOR'S CLAIM
☐ See attachment *(if space is insufficient)*

Date of item	Item and supporting facts	Amount claimed
	TOTAL:	$

PROOF OF ☐ MAILING ☐ PERSONAL DELIVERY TO PERSONAL REPRESENTATIVE
(Be sure to mail or take the original to the court clerk's office for filing)

1. I am the creditor or a person acting on behalf of the creditor. At the time of mailing or delivery I was at least 18 years of age.
2. My residence or business address is *(specify)*:

3. I mailed or personally delivered a copy of this *Creditor's Claim* to the personal representative as follows *(check either a or b below)*:
   a. ☐ **Mail.** I am a resident of or employed in the county where the mailing occurred.
      (1) I enclosed a copy in an envelope AND
         (a) ☐ **deposited** the sealed envelope with the United States Postal Service with the postage fully prepaid.
         (b) ☐ **placed** the envelope for collection and mailing on the date and at the place shown in items below following our ordinary business practices. I am readily familiar with this business' practice for collecting and processing correspondence for mailing. On the same day that correspondence is placed for collection and mailing, it is deposited in the ordinary course of business with the United States Postal Service in a sealed envelope with postage fully prepaid.
      (2) The envelope was addressed and mailed first-class as follows:
         (a) Name of personal representative served:
         (b) Address on envelope:

         (c) Date of mailing:
         (d) Place of mailing *(city and state)*:
   b. ☐ **Personal delivery.** I personally delivered a copy of the claim to the personal representative as follows:
      (1) Name of personal representative served:
      (2) Address where delivered:

      (3) Date delivered:
      (4) Time delivered:

I declare under penalty of perjury under the laws of the State of California that the foregoing is true and correct.
Date:

▶

_____   _____
(TYPE OR PRINT NAME OF CLAIMANT)   (SIGNATURE OF CLAIMANT)

DE-172 [Rev. January 1,1998]

CREDITOR'S CLAIM
(Probate)

Page two

DE-174

ATTORNEY OR PARTY WITHOUT ATTORNEY *(Name, state bar number, and address)*:	FOR COURT USE ONLY
TELEPHONE NO.: FAX NO.:	
ATTORNEY FOR *(Name)*:	

SUPERIOR COURT OF CALIFORNIA, COUNTY OF
STREET ADDRESS:
MAILING ADDRESS:
CITY AND ZIP CODE:
BRANCH NAME:

ESTATE OF *(Name)*:

                                                                    DECEDENT

ALLOWANCE OR REJECTION OF CREDITOR'S CLAIM	CASE NUMBER:

NOTE: Attach a copy of the creditor's claim. If allowance or rejection by the court is not required, do not include any pages attached to the creditor claim form.

PERSONAL REPRESENTATIVE'S ALLOWANCE OR REJECTION

1. Name of creditor *(specify)*:
2. The claim was filed on *(date)*:
3. Date of first issuance of letters:
4. Date of *Notice of Administration*:
5. Date of decedent's death:
6. Estimated value of estate: $
7. Total amount of the claim: $
8. ☐ Claim is allowed for: $ *(The court must approve certain claims before they are paid.)*
9. ☐ Claim is rejected for: $ *(A creditor has three months to act on a rejected claim. See box below.)*
10. Notice of allowance or rejection given on *(date)*:
11. ☐ The personal representative is authorized to administer the estate under the Independent Administration of Estates Act.

Date:

▶

. . . .
(TYPE OR PRINT NAME)   (SIGNATURE OF PERSONAL REPRESENTATIVE)

REJECTED CLAIMS: From the date notice of rejection is given, the creditor must act on the rejected claim (e.g., file a lawsuit) as follows:
a. **Claim due:** within three months after the notice of rejection.
b. **Claim not due:** within three months after the claim becomes due.

COURT'S APPROVAL OR REJECTION

12. ☐ Approved for: $

13. ☐ Rejected for: $

Date:

14. Number of pages attached: _____

SIGNATURE OF ☐ JUDGE ☐ COMMISSIONER
☐ SIGNATURE FOLLOWS LAST ATTACHMENT

(Proof of Service on reverse)

Form Adopted for Mandatory Use
Judicial Council of California
DE-174 [Rev. January 1, 2000]

ALLOWANCE OR REJECTION OF CREDITOR'S CLAIM
(Probate)

Probate Code, § 9000 et seq.,
9250–9256, 9353

ESTATE OF *(Name)*:	CASE NUMBER:
DECEDENT	

PROOF OF ☐ MAILING ☐ PERSONAL DELIVERY TO CREDITOR

1. At the time of mailing or personal delivery I was at least 18 years of age and **not a party** to this proceeding.

2. My residence or business address is *(specify)*:

3. I mailed or personally delivered a copy of the *Allowance or Rejection of Creditor's Claim* as follows *(complete either a or b)*:

   a. ☐ **Mail.** I am a resident of or employed in the county where the mailing occurred.
      (1) I enclosed a copy in an envelope AND
         (a) ☐ **deposited** the sealed envelope with the United States Postal Service with the postage fully prepaid.
         (b) ☐ **placed** the envelope for collection and mailing on the date and at the place shown in items below following our ordinary business practices. I am readily familiar with this business's practice for collecting and processing correspondence for mailing. On the same day that correspondence is placed for collection and mailing, it is deposited in the ordinary course of business with the United States Postal Service in a sealed envelope with postage fully prepaid.
      (2) The envelope was addressed and mailed first-class as follows:
         (a) Name of creditor served:
         (b) Address on envelope:

         (c) Date of mailing:
         (d) Place of mailing *(city and state)*:

   b. ☐ **Personal delivery.** I personally delivered a copy to the creditor as follows:
      (1) Name of creditor served:
      (2) Address where delivered:

      (3) Date delivered:
      (4) Time delivered:

I declare under penalty of perjury under the laws of the State of California that the foregoing is true and correct.

Date:

. . . .
(TYPE OR PRINT NAME OF DECLARANT)

▶ _____
(SIGNATURE OF DECLARANT)

ALLOWANCE OR REJECTION OF CREDITOR'S CLAIM
(Probate)

DE-165

ATTORNEY OR PARTY WITHOUT ATTORNEY (Name, state bar number, and address):	TELEPHONE AND FAX NOS.:	FOR COURT USE ONLY

ATTORNEY FOR (Name):

SUPERIOR COURT OF CALIFORNIA, COUNTY OF

STREET ADDRESS:

MAILING ADDRESS:

CITY AND ZIP CODE:

BRANCH NAME:

ESTATE OF (Name):

                                                                DECEDENT

NOTICE OF PROPOSED ACTION Independent Administration of Estates Act ☐ Objection ☐ Consent	CASE NUMBER:

NOTICE: If you do not object in writing or obtain a court order preventing the action proposed below, you will be treated as if you consented to the proposed action and you may not object after the proposed action has been taken. If you object, the personal representative may take the proposed action only under court supervision. An objection form is on the reverse. If you wish to object, you may use the form or prepare your own written objection.

1. The personal representative (executor or administrator) of the estate of the deceased is (names):

2. The personal representative has authority to administer the estate without court supervision under the Independent Administration of Estates Act (Prob. Code, § 10400 et seq.)
   a. ☐ with **full authority** under the act.
   b. ☐ with **limited authority** under the act (there is no authority, without court supervision, to (1) sell or exchange real property or (2) grant an option to purchase real property or (3) borrow money with the loan secured by an encumbrance upon real property).

3. **On or after** (date): _____ , the personal representative will take the following action without court supervision (describe in specific terms here or in Attachment 3):
   ☐ The proposed action is described in an attachment labeled Attachment 3.

4. ☐ **Real property transaction** (Check this box and complete item 4b if the proposed action involves a sale or exchange or a grant of an option to purchase real property.)
   a. The material terms of the transaction are specified in item 3, including any sale price and the amount of or method of calculating any commission or compensation to an agent or broker.
   b. $ _____ is the value of the subject property in the probate inventory.   ☐ No inventory yet.

NOTICE: A sale of real property without court supervision means that the sale will NOT be presented to the court for confirmation at a hearing at which higher bids for the property may be presented and the property sold to the highest bidder.

(Continued on reverse)

NOTICE OF PROPOSED ACTION
Objection - Consent
(Probate)
Probate Code, § 10580 et seq.

ESTATE OF *(Name):*	CASE NUMBER:
DECEDENT	

5. **If you OBJECT to the proposed action**
   a. **Sign** the objection form below and deliver or mail it to the personal representative at the following address *(specify name and and address)*:

   OR

   b. **Send** your own written objection to the address in item 5a. *(Be sure to identify the proposed action and state that you object to it.)*
   OR

   c. **Apply** to the court for an order preventing the personal representative from taking the proposed action without court supervision.

   d. **NOTE:** Your written objection or the court order must be received by the personal representative before the date in the box in item 3, or before the proposed action is taken, whichever is later. If you object, the personal representative may take the proposed action only under court supervision.

6. **If you APPROVE the proposed action,** you may sign the consent form below and return it to the address in item 5a. If you do not object in writing or obtain a court order, you will be treated as if you consented to the proposed action.

7. **If you need more INFORMATION, call** *(name):*

   (telephone): ( )

Date:

▶ _____
(TYPE OR PRINT NAME)   (SIGNATURE OF PERSONAL REPRESENTATIVE OR ATTORNEY)

OBJECTION TO PROPOSED ACTION

☐ **I OBJECT** to the action proposed in item 3.

NOTICE:	**Sign and return this form (both sides) to the address in item 5a. The form must be received before the date in the box in item 3, or before the proposed action is taken, whichever is later.** *(You may want to use certified mail, with return receipt requested. Make a copy of this form for your records.)*

Date:

▶ _____
(TYPE OR PRINT NAME)   (SIGNATURE OF OBJECTOR)

CONSENT TO PROPOSED ACTION

☐ **I CONSENT** to the action proposed in item 3.

NOTICE:	**You may indicate your *consent* by signing and returning this form (both sides) to the address in item 5a.** If you do not object in writing or obtain a court order, you will be treated as if you consented to the proposed action.

Date:

▶ _____
(TYPE OR PRINT NAME)   (SIGNATURE OF CONSENTER)

NOTICE OF PROPOSED ACTION
Objection - Consent
(Probate)

DE-165

ATTORNEY OR PARTY WITHOUT ATTORNEY (Name, state bar number, and address):	TELEPHONE AND FAX NOS.:	FOR COURT USE ONLY

ATTORNEY FOR (Name):

SUPERIOR COURT OF CALIFORNIA, COUNTY OF

STREET ADDRESS:

MAILING ADDRESS:

CITY AND ZIP CODE:

BRANCH NAME:

ESTATE OF (Name):

DECEDENT

NOTICE OF PROPOSED ACTION
Independent Administration of Estates Act
☐ Objection   ☐ Consent

CASE NUMBER:

NOTICE: If you do not object in writing or obtain a court order preventing the action proposed below, you will be treated as if you consented to the proposed action and you may not object after the proposed action has been taken. If you object, the personal representative may take the proposed action only under court supervision. An objection form is on the reverse. If you wish to object, you may use the form or prepare your own written objection.

1. The personal representative (executor or administrator) of the estate of the deceased is (names):

2. The personal representative has authority to administer the estate without court supervision under the Independent Administration of Estates Act (Prob. Code, § 10400 et seq.)
   a. ☐ with **full authority** under the act.
   b. ☐ with **limited authority** under the act (there is no authority, without court supervision, to (1) sell or exchange real property or (2) grant an option to purchase real property or (3) borrow money with the loan secured by an encumbrance upon real property).

3. **On or after** (date): _____ , the personal representative will take the following action without court supervision (describe in specific terms here or in Attachment 3):
   ☐ The proposed action is described in an attachment labeled Attachment 3.

4. ☐ **Real property transaction** (Check this box and complete item 4b if the proposed action involves a sale or exchange or a grant of an option to purchase real property.)
   a. The material terms of the transaction are specified in item 3, including any sale price and the amount of or method of calculating any commission or compensation to an agent or broker.
   b. $ _____ is the value of the subject property in the probate inventory.   ☐ No inventory yet.

NOTICE: A sale of real property without court supervision means that the sale will NOT be presented to the court for confirmation at a hearing at which higher bids for the property may be presented and the property sold to the highest bidder.

(Continued on reverse)

NOTICE OF PROPOSED ACTION
Objection - Consent
(Probate)
Probate Code, § 10580 et seq.

ESTATE OF *(Name)*:	CASE NUMBER:
DECEDENT	

5. **If you OBJECT to the proposed action**

   a. **Sign** the objection form below and deliver or mail it to the personal representative at the following address *(specify name and and address)*:

     OR

   b. **Send** your own written objection to the address in item 5a. *(Be sure to identify the proposed action and state that you object to it.)*
     OR

   c. **Apply** to the court for an order preventing the personal representative from taking the proposed action without court supervision.

   d. **NOTE:** Your written objection or the court order must be received by the personal representative before the date in the box in item 3, or before the proposed action is taken, whichever is later. If you object, the personal representative may take the proposed action only under court supervision.

6. **If you APPROVE the proposed action**, you may sign the consent form below and return it to the address in item 5a. If you do not object in writing or obtain a court order, you will be treated as if you consented to the proposed action.

7. **If you need more INFORMATION, call** *(name)*:

               (telephone):   (   )

Date:

_____   ▶ _____
(TYPE OR PRINT NAME)   (SIGNATURE OF PERSONAL REPRESENTATIVE OR ATTORNEY)

OBJECTION TO PROPOSED ACTION

☐   **I OBJECT** to the action proposed in item 3.

NOTICE: Sign and return this form (both sides) to the address in item 5a. **The form must be received before the date in the box in item 3, or before the proposed action is taken, whichever is later.** *(You may want to use certified mail, with return receipt requested. Make a copy of this form for your records.)*

Date:

_____   ▶ _____
(TYPE OR PRINT NAME)   (SIGNATURE OF OBJECTOR)

CONSENT TO PROPOSED ACTION

☐   **I CONSENT** to the action proposed in item 3.

NOTICE: You may indicate your *consent* by signing and returning this form (both sides) to the address in item 5a. If you do not object in writing or obtain a court order, you will be treated as if you consented to the proposed action.

Date:

_____   ▶ _____
(TYPE OR PRINT NAME)   (SIGNATURE OF CONSENTER)

DE-166

ATTORNEY OR PARTY WITHOUT ATTORNEY *(Name, state bar number, and address):*	TELEPHONE AND FAX NOS.:	*FOR COURT USE ONLY*

ATTORNEY FOR *(Name):*

SUPERIOR COURT OF CALIFORNIA, COUNTY OF

STREET ADDRESS:

MAILING ADDRESS:

CITY AND ZIP CODE:

BRANCH NAME:

ESTATE OF *(Name):*

DECEDENT

WAIVER OF NOTICE OF PROPOSED ACTION
(Probate Code section 10583)
(Revocation of Waiver)

CASE NUMBER:

WARNING
READ BEFORE YOU SIGN

A. The law requires the personal representative to give you notice of certain actions he or she proposes to take to administer the estate. If you sign this form, the personal representative will NOT have to give you notice.

B. You have the right (1) to object to a proposed action and (2) to require the court to supervise the proposed action. If you do not object before the personal representative acts, you lose your right and you cannot object later.

C. IF YOU SIGN THIS FORM, YOU GIVE UP YOUR RIGHT TO RECEIVE NOTICE. This means you give the personal representative the right to take actions concerning the estate without first giving you the notice otherwise required by law. You cannot object after the action is taken.

D. You have the right to revoke (cancel) this waiver at any time. Your revocation must be in writing and is not effective until it is actually received by the personal representative. *(A form to revoke your waiver is on the reverse. You may want to revoke this waiver later. Keep a copy of this form so you can.)*

E. If you do not understand this form, ask a lawyer to explain it to you.

WAIVER OF RIGHT TO NOTICE

1. **I understand** that the **personal representative** named here has authority to administer the estate of the decedent without court supervision under the Independent Administration of Estates Act (California Probate Code sections 10400-10592).
   a. *(name):*
   b. *(address):*

(Mail or deliver notices to the personal representative at this address.)

2. **I understand** I have the right to receive notice of certain actions the personal representative may propose to take. I understand that those actions may affect my interest in the estate.

3. **I understand** that by signing this waiver form I give up my right to receive notices from the personal representative of actions he or she may decide to take.

(Continued on reverse)

Form Adopted by the Judicial Council of California DE-166 [Rev. January 1, 1998]	**WAIVER OF NOTICE OF PROPOSED ACTION** (Probate)	Probate Code, §§ 10583, 10584

ESTATE OF *(Name)*:	CASE NUMBER:
DECEDENT	

4. By signing below, **I WAIVE MY RIGHT** to receive prior notice of *(CHECK ONLY ONE BOX to indicate your choice)*:
    a. ☐   Any and all actions the personal representative is authorized to take under the Independent Administration of Estates Act.
    b. ☐   Any of the kinds of transactions I have listed below that the personal representative is authorized to take under the
         Independent Administration of Estates Act *(specify which actions you are waiving your right to receive notice of)*:
            ☐   See Attachment 4.

Date:

....
(TYPE OR PRINT NAME)   ▶ _____
                                                                  (SIGNATURE)

My address is *(type or print)*:

_____

(Keep a copy for your records.)

REVOCATION OF WAIVER OF NOTICE OF PROPOSED ACTION

1. I previously signed a waiver of my right to receive notices of proposed actions by the personal representative under the Independent Administration of Estates Act.

2. **I revoke** (cancel) any previous waiver of my right to receive notices of proposed actions by the personal representative of the estate of the decedent.

3. I request the personal representative to send me all notices required by law.
Date:

....
(TYPE OR PRINT NAME)   ▶ _____
                                                                  (SIGNATURE)

My address is *(type or print)*:

(Mail or deliver this revocation to the personal representative at the address in item 1 on the reverse. Keep a copy for your records.)

PROOF OF SERVICE BY MAIL

1. I mailed a copy of the ☐ *Waiver of Notice of Proposed Action* ☐ *Revocation*   to the personal representative by
☐ depositing a copy of the revocation with the United States Postal Service, in a sealed envelope with postage fully prepaid by first-class mail or ☐ placing the envelope for collection and mailing on the date and place below following our ordinary business practices. I am readily familiar with this business' practice for collecting and processing correspondence for mailing. On the same day that correspondence is placed for collection and mailing, it is deposited in the ordinary course of business with the Untied States Postal Service in a sealed envelope with postage fully prepaid.
I am a resident of or employed in the county where the mailing occurred.

2. The envelope was addressed and mailed as follows:
    a. Name of personal representative served:
    b. Address on envelope:

    c. Date of mailing:
    d. Place of mailing *(city and state)*:
I declare under penalty of perjury under the laws of the State of California that the foregoing is true and correct.
Date:

☐
....
(TYPE OR PRINT NAME)   ▶ _____
                                                                   (SIGNATURE)

    WAIVER OF NOTICE OF PROPOSED ACTION
(Probate)

DE-270, GC-070

ATTORNEY OR PARTY WITHOUT ATTORNEY (Name, state bar number, and address):	TELEPHONE AND FAX NOS.:	FOR COURT USE ONLY

ATTORNEY FOR (Name):

SUPERIOR COURT OF CALIFORNIA, COUNTY OF

STREET ADDRESS:

MAILING ADDRESS:

CITY AND ZIP CODE:

BRANCH NAME:

ESTATE OF (Name):

☐ DECEDENT   ☐ CONSERVATEE   ☐ MINOR

EX PARTE PETITION FOR AUTHORITY TO SELL SECURITIES AND ORDER	CASE NUMBER:

1. **Petitioner** (name of each. See footnote[1] before completing):

   is the ☐ personal representative ☐ conservator ☐ guardian of the estate and requests a court order authorizing sale of estate securities.

2. a. The estate's securities described on the reverse should be sold for cash at the market price at the time of sale on an established stock or bond exchange, or, if unlisted, the sale will be made for not less than the minimum price stated on the reverse.

   b. ☐ Authority is given in decedent's will to sell property; **or**

   c. ☐ The sale is necessary to raise cash to pay
      (1) ☐ debts
      (2) ☐ legacies
      (3) ☐ family allowance
      (4) ☐ expenses
      (5) ☐ support of ward
      (6) ☐ other (specify):

   d. ☐ The sale is for the advantage, benefit, and best interests of the estate, and those interested in the estate.

   e. Other facts pertinent to this petition are as follows:
      (1) ☐ Special notice has not been requested.
      (2) ☐ Waivers of all special notices are presented with this petition.
      (3) ☐ No security to be sold is specifically bequeathed.
      (4) ☐ Other (specify):

Date:

▶ _____
(SIGNATURE OF ATTORNEY*)

* (Signature of all petitioners also required (Prob. Code , § 1020).)

I declare under penalty of perjury under the laws of the State of California that the foregoing is true and correct.

Date:

....
(TYPE OR PRINT NAME)

▶ _____
(SIGNATURE OF PETITIONER)

....
(TYPE OR PRINT NAME)

▶ _____
(SIGNATURE OF PETITIONER)

[1] Each personal representative, guardian, or conservator must sign the petition.

(Continued on reverse)

Form Approved by the Judicial Council of California DE-270, GC-070 [Rev. January 1, 1998]	**EX PARTE PETITION FOR AUTHORITY TO SELL SECURITIES AND ORDER**	Probate Code, §§9630, 10000, 10200, 10201, 10252, 10261

ESTATE OF *(Name):*	CASE NUMBER:

LIST OF SECURITIES

Number of shares or face value of bonds	Name of security	Name of exchange *(when required by local rule)*	Recent bid asked *(when required by local rule)*	Minimum selling price

---

ORDER AUTHORIZING SALE OF SECURITIES

THE COURT FINDS the sale is proper.

THE COURT ORDERS

the ☐ personal representative ☐ guardian ☐ conservator is authorized to sell the securities described above upon the terms and conditions specified. Notice of hearing on the petition is dispensed with.

Date: _____

_____
JUDGE OF THE SUPERIOR COURT

☐ SIGNATURE FOLLOWS LAST ATTACHMENT

DE-270, GC-070 [Rev. January 1, 1998]

**EX PARTE PETITION FOR AUTHORITY
TO SELL SECURITIES AND ORDER**

Page two

DE-260/GC-060

ATTORNEY OR PARTY WITHOUT ATTORNEY *(Name, State Bar number, and address):*	FOR COURT USE ONLY
TELEPHONE NO.: FAX NO. *(Optional):*	
E-MAIL ADDRESS *(Optional):*	
ATTORNEY FOR *(Name):*	

SUPERIOR COURT OF CALIFORNIA, COUNTY OF
STREET ADDRESS:
MAILING ADDRESS:
CITY AND ZIP CODE:
BRANCH NAME:

☐ ESTATE ☐ CONSERVATORSHIP ☐ GUARDIANSHIP OF
(Name):

☐ DECEDENT ☐ CONSERVATEE ☐ MINOR

REPORT OF SALE AND PETITION FOR ORDER CONFIRMING SALE OF REAL PROPERTY ☐ **and Sale of Other Property Sold as a Unit**	CASE NUMBER:
	HEARING DATE AND TIME: DEPT.:

1. **Petitioner** *(name of each):*

   is the ☐ personal representative ☐ conservator ☐ guardian of the estate of the decedent, conservatee, or minor
   ☐ purchaser (30 days have passed since the sale) *(Attach supporting declaration (Prob. Code, § 10308(b).)*

   and **requests** a court order for *(check all that apply):*
   a. confirmation of sale of the estate's interest in the real property described in Attachment 2e
   b. ☐ confirmation of sale of the estate's interest in other property sold as a unit as described in Attachment 2c.
   c. ☐ approval of commission of *(specify):*   % of the amount of: $
   d. additional bond ☐ is fixed at: $ ☐ is not required.

2. **Description of property sold**
   a. Interest sold: ☐ 100% ☐ Undivided *(specify):* %
   b. ☐ Improved ☐ Unimproved
   c. ☐ Real property sold as a unit with other property *(describe in Attachment 2c).*
   d. Street address and location *(specify):*

   e. Legal description is affixed as Attachment 2e.

3. **Appraisal**
   a. Date of death of decedent or appointment of conservator or guardian *(specify):*
   b. Appraised value at above date: $
   c. Reappraised value within one year before the hearing: $ ☐ Amount includes value of other property
   sold as a unit. *(If more than one year has elapsed from the date in item 3a to the date of the hearing, reappraisal is required.)*
   d. Appraisal or reappraisal by probate referee ☐ has been filed ☐ will be filed
   ☐ has been waived by order dated:

4. **Manner and terms of sale**
   a. Name of purchaser and manner of vesting title *(specify):*

   b. ☐ Purchaser is the ☐ personal representative ☐ attorney for the personal representative.
   c. Sale was ☐ private ☐ public on *(date):*
   d. Amount bid: $ Deposit: $
   e. Payment ☐ Cash ☐ Credit *(specify terms on Attachment 4e.)*
   f. ☐ Other terms of sale *(specify terms on Attachment 4f.)*
   g. ☐ Mode of sale specified in will. ☐ Petitioner requests relief from complying for the reasons stated in Attachment 4g.
   h. ☐ Terms comply with Probate Code section 2542 *(guardianships and conservatorships).*

Page 1 of 2

Form Adopted for Mandatory Use
Judicial Council of California
DE-260/GC-060 [Rev. January 1, 2005]

**REPORT OF SALE AND PETITION FOR ORDER
CONFIRMING SALE OF REAL PROPERTY**
(Probate—Decedents' Estates and Guardianships and Conservatorships)

Probate Code, §§ 2540, 10308
www.courtinfo.ca.gov

DE-260/GC-060

☐ ESTATE ☐ CONSERVATORSHIP ☐ GUARDIANSHIP OF	CASE NUMBER:
(Name):	

5. **Commission**
   a. ☐ Sale without broker
   b. ☐ A written ☐ exclusive ☐ nonexclusive   contract for commission was entered into with *(name):*

   c. ☐ Purchaser was procured by *(name):*
      a licensed real estate broker who is not buying for his or her account.
   d. ☐ Commission is to be divided as follows:

6. **Bond**
   a. Amount before sale: $ ☐ none.
   b. Additional amount needed: $ ☐ none.
   c. ☐ Proceeds are to be deposited in a blocked account. Receipts will be filed. *(Specify institution and location):*

7. **Notice of sale**
   a. ☐ Published ☐ Posted as permitted by Probate Code section 10301 ($5,000 or less)
   b. ☐ Will authorizes sale of the property
   c. ☐ Will directs sale of the property

8. **Notice of hearing**
   a. Special devisee:
      (1) ☐ None.
      (2) ☐ Consent to be filed.
      (3) ☐ Written notice will be given.
   b. Special notice:
      (1) ☐ None requested.
      (2) ☐ Has been or will be waived.
      (3) ☐ Required written notice will be given.

   c. Personal representative, conservator of the estate, or guardian of the estate:
      (1) ☐ Petitioner (consent or notice not required).
      (2) ☐ Consent to be filed.
      (3) ☐ Written notice will be given.

9. **Reason for sale** *(need not complete if item 7b or 7c checked)*
   a. ☐ Necessary to pay
      (1) ☐ debts
      (2) ☐ devise
      (3) ☐ family allowance
      (4) ☐ expenses of administration
      (5) ☐ taxes
   b. ☐ The sale is to the advantage of the estate and in the best interest of the interested persons.

10. **Formula for overbids**
    a. Original bid: $ _____
    b. 10% of first $10,000 of original bid: $ _____
    c. 5% of (original bid minus $10,000): $ _____
    d. Minimum overbid (a + b + c): $ _____

11. **Overbid.** Required amount of first overbid *(see item 10):* $ [_____]

12. **Petitioner's efforts** to obtain the highest and best price reasonably attainable for the property were as follows *(specify activities taken to expose the property to the market, e.g., multiple listings, advertising, open houses, etc.):*

13. Number of pages attached: _____

Date:

_____
(TYPE OR PRINT NAME OF ATTORNEY)

▶ _____
(SIGNATURE OF ATTORNEY*)
* (Signature of all petitioners also required (Prob. Code, § 1020))

I declare under penalty of perjury under the laws of the State of California that the foregoing is true and correct.

Date:

_____
(TYPE OR PRINT NAME OF PETITIONER)

▶ _____
(SIGNATURE OF PETITIONER)

DE-260 GC-060 [Rev. January 1, 2006]

**REPORT OF SALE AND PETITION FOR ORDER
CONFIRMING SALE OF REAL PROPERTY**
(Probate—Decedents' Estates and Guardianships and Conservatorships)

Page 2 of 2

DE-120

ATTORNEY OR PARTY WITHOUT ATTORNEY *(Name, State Bar number, and address):*	*FOR COURT USE ONLY*

TELEPHONE NO.:   FAX NO. *(Optional)*:

E-MAIL ADDRESS *(Optional)*:

ATTORNEY FOR *(Name)*:

SUPERIOR COURT OF CALIFORNIA, COUNTY OF

STREET ADDRESS:

MAILING ADDRESS:

CITY AND ZIP CODE:

BRANCH NAME:

☐ ESTATE OF *(Name):*   ☐ IN THE MATTER OF *(Name):*

☐ DECEDENT ☐ TRUST ☐ OTHER

NOTICE OF HEARING—DECEDENT'S ESTATE OR TRUST

CASE NUMBER:

This notice is required by law.
This notice does not require you to appear in court, but you may attend the hearing if you wish.

---

1. NOTICE is given that *(name):*
   (representative capacity, if any):
   has filed *(specify):**

2. You may refer to the filed documents for more information. *(Some documents filed with the court are confidential.)*

3. A HEARING on the matter will be held as follows:

   a. Date: Time: Dept.:   Room:

   b. Address of court ☐ shown above ☐ is *(specify):*

Assistive listening systems, computer-assisted real-time captioning, or sign language interpreter services are available upon request if at least 5 days notice is provided. Contact the clerk's office for *Request for Accommodations by Persons With Disabilities and Order* (form MC-410). (Civil Code section 54.8.)

* Do **not** use this form to give notice of a petition to administer estate (see Prob. Code, § 8100 and form DE-121) or notice of a hearing in a guardianship or conservatorship (see Prob. Code, §§ 1511 and 1822 and form GC-020).

Page 1 of 2

Form Adopted for Mandatory Use
Judicial Council of California
DE-120 [Rev. July 1, 2005]

NOTICE OF HEARING—DECEDENT'S ESTATE OR TRUST
(Probate—Decedents' Estates)

Probate Code §§851, 1211,
1215, 1216, 1230, 17100
www.courtinfo.ca.gov

☐ ESTATE OF (Name): ☐ IN THE MATTER OF (Name):	CASE NUMBER:
☐ DECEDENT ☐ TRUST ☐ OTHER	

CLERK'S CERTIFICATE OF POSTING

1. I certify that I am not a party to this cause.
2. A copy of the foregoing *Notice of Hearing—Decedent's Estate or Trust*
   a. was posted at *(address):*

   b. was posted on *(date):*

Date: _____

Clerk, by _____ , Deputy

PROOF OF SERVICE BY MAIL *

1. I am over the age of 18 and not a party to this cause. I am a resident of or employed in the county where the mailing occurred.
2. My residence or business address is *(specify):*

3. I served the foregoing *Notice of Hearing—Decedent's Estate or Trust* on each person named below by enclosing a copy in an envelope addressed as shown below AND
   a. ☐ **depositing** the sealed envelope on the date and at the place shown in item 4 with the United States Postal Service with the postage fully prepaid.
   b. ☐ **placing** the envelope for collection and mailing on the date and at the place shown in item 4 following our ordinary business practices. I am readily familiar with this business's practice for collecting and processing correspondence for mailing. On the same day that correspondence is placed for collection and mailing, it is deposited in the ordinary course of business with the United States Postal Service in a sealed envelope with postage fully prepaid.

4. a. Date mailed: b. Place mailed *(city, state):*

5. ☐ I served with the *Notice of Hearing—Decedent's Estate or Trust* a copy of the petition or other document referred to in the Notice.

I declare under penalty of perjury under the laws of the State of California that the foregoing is true and correct.

Date: _____

_____   _____
(TYPE OR PRINT NAME OF PERSON COMPLETING THIS FORM)   (SIGNATURE OF PERSON COMPLETING THIS FORM)

NAME AND ADDRESS OF EACH PERSON TO WHOM NOTICE WAS MAILED

	Name of person served	Address *(number, street, city, state, and zip code)*
1.		
2.		
3.		
4.		

☐ Continued on an attachment. *(You may use Attachment to Notice of Hearing Proof of Service by Mail, form DE-120(MA)/GC-020(MA), for this purpose.)*

* Do not use this form for proof of personal service. You may use form DE-120(P) to prove personal service of this Notice.

DE-120 [Rev. July 1, 2005]

NOTICE OF HEARING—DECEDENT'S ESTATE OR TRUST
(Probate—Decedents' Estates)

Page 2 of 2

DE-265/GC-065

ATTORNEY OR PARTY WITHOUT ATTORNEY *(Name, State Bar number, and address)*:

After recording return to:

TELEPHONE NO.:

FAX NO. *(Optional)*:

E-MAIL ADDRESS *(Optional)*:

ATTORNEY FOR *(Name)*:

SUPERIOR COURT OF CALIFORNIA, COUNTY OF

STREET ADDRESS:

MAILING ADDRESS:

CITY AND ZIP CODE:

BRANCH NAME:

FOR RECORDER'S USE

☐ ESTATE OF
☐ CONSERVATORSHIP OF   *(Name)*:
☐ GUARDIANSHIP OF

☐ DECEDENT   ☐ CONSERVATEE   ☐ MINOR

ORDER CONFIRMING SALE OF REAL PROPERTY
☐ **and Confirming Sale of Other Property as a Unit**

CASE NUMBER:

1. Hearing date: Time: Dept.:   Rm.:

FOR COURT USE ONLY

THE COURT FINDS

2. All notices required by law were given and, if required, proof of notice of sale was made.

3. a. ☐ Sale was authorized or directed by the will
   b. ☐ Good reason existed for the sale
   of the property commonly described as *(street address or location)*:

4. The sale was legally made and fairly conducted.

5. The confirmed sale price is not disproportionate to the value of the property.

6. ☐ Private sale: The amount bid is 90% or more of the appraised value of the property as appraised within one year of the date of the hearing.

7. An offer exceeding the amount bid by the statutory percentages ☐ cannot be obtained ☐ was obtained in open court. The offer complies with all applicable law.

8. The ☐ personal representative ☐ conservator ☐ guardian of the estate of the decedent, conservatee, or minor has made reasonable efforts to obtain the highest and best price reasonably attainable for the property.

THE COURT ORDERS

9. The sale of the real property legally described ☐ in item 15 on page 2 ☐ on Attachment 9
   ☐ and other property sold as a unit described ☐ in item 15 on page 2 ☐ on Attachment 9   is confirmed to *(name)*:

   (manner of vesting title):
   for the sale price of: $ on the following terms *(use item 15 on page 2 or Attachment 9 if necessary)*:

   ☐ Continued in item 15 on page 2.   ☐ Continued on Attachment 9.

10. The ☐ personal representative ☐ conservator ☐ guardian of the estate of the decedent, conservatee, or minor
    (name):
    is directed to execute and deliver a conveyance of the estate's interest in the real property described in item 9
    ☐ and other property described in item 9 sold as a unit   upon receipt of the consideration for the sale.

Page 1 of 2

Form Adopted for Mandatory Use
Judicial Council of California
DE-265/GC-065 [Rev. January 1, 2006]

ORDER CONFIRMING SALE OF REAL PROPERTY
(Probate—Decedents' Estates and Guardianships and Conservatorships)

Probate Code, §§ 2543, 10313
www.courtinfo.ca.gov

DE-265/GC-065

☐ ESTATE ☐ CONSERVATORSHIP ☐ GUARDIANSHIP OF	CASE NUMBER:
(Name):	

11. a. ☐ No additional bond is required.
    b. ☐ Additional bond is required in the amount of: $, surety, or otherwise, as provided by law.
    c. ☐ Net sale proceeds must be deposited by escrow holder in a blocked account to be withdrawn only on court order. Receipts must be filed. *(Specify institution and location):*

12. a. ☐ No commission is payable.
    b. ☐ A commission from the proceeds of the sale is approved in the amount of: $
       to be paid as follows *(specify):*

13. Other *(specify, use Attachment 13 if necessary):*

14. Number of pages attached: _____

Date: _____

                              JUDICIAL OFFICER
            ☐ Signature follows last attachment.

15. ☐ *(Check all that apply):* ☐ **Legal description** of the ☐ real property ☐ personal property in item 9:
                                ☐ Additional terms of sale from item 9:

[SEAL]	**CLERK'S CERTIFICATE**
	I certify that the foregoing *Order Confirming Sale of Real Property,* including any attached description of real or personal property, is a true and correct copy of the original on file in my office.
	Date: CLERK, by _____, Deputy

ORDER CONFIRMING SALE OF REAL PROPERTY
(Probate—Decedents' Estates and Guardianships and Conservatorships)

STATE OF CALIFORNIA
FRANCHISE TAX BOARD
Telephone (916) 845-4210

REQUEST FOR ESTATE
INCOME TAX CLEARANCE CERTIFICATE
As required under California Revenue
and Taxation Code Section 19513

☐ **Expedite Request (see Instructions)**

PLEASE READ INSTRUCTIONS ON SIDE 2 BEFORE COMPLETING THIS FORM

MAIL TO: ESTATE INCOME TAX CLEARANCE CERTIFICATE UNIT MS D-7	FILE AT LEAST 30 DAYS PRIOR TO THE COURT
FRANCHISE TAX BOARD PO BOX 1468 SACRAMENTO CA 95812-1468	HEARING ON FINAL ACCOUNT. APPROXIMATE DATE OF COURT HEARING _____

Estate of	Federal Employer Id. No.	Date of Death
Name of Fiduciary	Area Code and Phone No.	Decedent's Social Security No.
Address of Fiduciary (Number and Street)		Probate No.
City or Town, State, and ZIP Code		County of Probate
Name of Attorney		Area Code and Phone No.
Address of Attorney (Number and Street)		Mail Tax Clearance Certificate to:
City or Town, State, and ZIP Code		☐ Attorney ☐ Fiduciary

ANSWER THESE QUESTIONS AND FURNISH THE REQUIRED DOCUMENTS

1. Was decedent a resident of the State of California on the date of death? _____
   (If "no," furnish a copy of the California Estate Tax Return (Form ET-1) and Declaration Concerning Residence (Form IT-2) if filed with the California State Controller).

2. Have probate proceedings been instituted in any other state? _____

3. Value of the assets of this estate on date of death. (Please attach federal Form 706.) _____
   (If not exceeding $1,000,000, you do not need an Estate Income Tax Clearance Certificate. **See instructions on Side 2.**)

4. Are assets exceeding $250,000 distributable to one or more nonresident beneficiaries? _____
   (If "no," you do not need an Estate Income Tax Clearance Certificate. **See instructions on Side 2.**)

5. Has a preliminary distribution been made? _____
   (If "yes," furnish a copy of the court order authorizing the distribution.)

You must file a return for all taxable years that have ended (even if a return is not yet due), or submit a deposit in the form of check or bond in an amount to be determined by this office. We require a Specialized Tax Service Fee for Expedited Estate Income Tax Clearance Certificate Requests. See instructions on Side 2.

DECLARATION REGARDING CALIFORNIA RETURNS FOR DECEDENT AND FOR ESTATE
(To be completed for the four taxable years immediately preceding the date of this request.)

A. DECEDENT
California Individual Income Tax Returns (Form 540, 540A, 540 2EZ, or Long or Short Form 540NR) have been filed by or on behalf of the decedent for the following years: _____ _____ _____ _____ . If the returns were not filed for any of the above years, explain in full: _____

_____

B. ESTATE
California Fiduciary Income Tax Returns (Form 541) have been filed for the following years:
_____ _____ _____ _____ . If fiduciary returns were not filed for any of the last four years during which the estate was in existence, explain in full: _____

_____

I declare, under penalties of perjury, that the information given above is true to the best of my knowledge and belief.

SIGNATURE OF FIDUCIARY OR REPRESENTATIVE	TITLE	DATE

ALLOW AT LEAST 30 DAYS FOR A RESPONSE TO THIS APPLICATION

FTB 3571 C2 (REV 03-2005) SIDE 1

INSTRUCTIONS

A. California Revenue and Taxation Code Section 19513 Estate Income Tax Clearance Certificates

For certain estates, Section 19513 prohibits the probate court from allowing the final account of the fiduciary unless the Franchise Tax Board certifies that all taxes have been paid or secured as required by law.

The Estate Income Tax Clearance Certificate is only required if an estate meets **BOTH** of the following **TWO** requirements:
(1) Had assets with a fair market value exceeding $1,000,000 on the date of death, **AND**
(2) Is to distribute assets exceeding $250,000 to one or more nonresident beneficiaries.

In determining if the assets exceed $1,000,000, include the fair market value of all assets on date of death, wherever situated, for decedents who were California residents. Nonresident decedents should only include the value of those assets located in California.

In determining if assets exceeding $250,000 are distributable to nonresident beneficiaries, the residency of a trust which is a beneficiary of the decedent's estate is determined by the residency of the trust's fiduciaries and beneficiaries.

Before issuing the Estate Income Tax Clearance Certificate, we require payment of all accrued taxes of the decedent and the estate. We may also require a deposit by check, or bond to secure the payment of any taxes which may later become payable.

The Estate Income Tax Clearance Certificate is valid only to the end of the current taxable year. We will only issue a new Estate Income Tax Clearance Certificate extending the expiration date when a return is filed for each subsequent year and the tax for that year, if any, is paid.

The Estate Income Tax Clearance Certificate is issued to the fiduciary or representative designated on the application. THE ACTUAL FILING OF THE ESTATE INCOME TAX CLEARANCE CERTIFICATE WITH THE COURT IS THE RESPONSIBILITY OF THE FIDUCIARY OR REPRESENTATIVE.

B. Effect of the Estate Income Tax Clearance Certificate and Continuing Liability of the Fiduciary

The Estate Income Tax Clearance Certificate issued under California Revenue and Taxation Code Section 19513 does not relieve the estate of liability for any taxes due or which may become due from the decedent or the estate. Neither does the certificate relieve the fiduciary of the personal liability for taxes and other expenses as imposed by California Revenue and Taxation Code Section 19516.

C. Other Information

You do not need to submit a copy of the Final Account of the fiduciary unless we request it.

We may require fiduciaries to withhold tax on California source income distributed to nonresident beneficiaries. Income from intangible personal property such as interest and dividend income or gain from the sale of stocks or bonds is generally not taxable to a nonresident beneficiary and therefore not subject to withholding. Failure to withhold when required may make the fiduciary personally liable for the amount due. For information on determining requirements for withholding, telephone **(888)** 792-4900 (toll free) or write to: Withholding Services and Compliance Section, Franchise Tax Board, PO Box 942867, Sacramento, CA 94267-0651.

Income earned by the estate in the final year in which its assets are distributed pursuant to a decree of final distribution is taxable to the beneficiaries. The estate must file a final return and properly report the income distribution.

You should compute the return for the fractional part of the year prior to death on the basis of the method of accounting followed by the decedent. You can **not** include income and deductions for expenses, interest, taxes, and depletion accrued solely by reason of death in the return of a decedent for the period in which death occurred. Include those items in the return of the estate or beneficiary, as the case may be, upon receipt or payment.

Return filing requirements are in the applicable instructions for the:
- California Individual Income Tax Returns (Form 540, 540A, 540 2EZ, or Long or Short Form 540NR)
- California Fiduciary Income Tax Returns (Form 541)

D. Returns Required

You must file a final fiduciary return (Form 541) for the year in which the estate closes if the filing requirements are met. You should also file a return to establish any excess deductions allowed to beneficiaries in the final year.

The decedents final personal income tax return (Form 540, 540A, 540 2EZ, or Long or Short Form 540NR) must be marked "FINAL" at the top of the return in block letters.

In addition, please furnish copies of any other returns filed for the decedent or the estate within the last 12 months. Write **"COPY – DO NOT PROCESS"** in bold letters on the face of each copy. If you submit original returns with this application, include an additional copy of each return with the words, **"COPY – DO NOT PROCESS"** in bold letters on the face of each copy. Mail the completed Estate Income Tax Request for Clearance Certificate and required returns to:

ESTATE INCOME TAX CLEARANCE CERTIFICATE UNIT
MS D-7
FRANCHISE TAX BOARD
PO BOX 1468
SACRAMENTO CA 95812-1468

Expedited Estate Income Tax Clearance Certificate Request

We charge a non-refundable $100 specialized service fee to process an Expedited Tax Clearance Certificate request. The fee is due and payable at the time you submit the request and **must** be paid by certified funds (cashiers check or money order). (CR&TC section 19591) Submit form FTB 3571, along with all necessary documentation and payment with certified funds (marked "Specialized Tax Service Fee") via overnight private mail service to:

Franchise Tax Board
Estate Income Tax Clearance Unit MS D-7
Sacramento CA 95827

ASSISTANCE

From within the United States, call . . . . (800) 852-5711
From outside the United States, call (not toll-free) . . . . (916) 845-6500

Website at: **www.ftb.ca.gov**

Assistance for persons with disabilities: We comply with the Americans with Disabilities Act. Persons with hearing or speech impairments please call TTY/TDD (800) 822-6268.

NAME, ADDRESS AND TELEPHONE NUMBER OF ATTORNEY(S)

Bar No.:

Attorney(s) for _____

SUPERIOR COURT OF CALIFORNIA, COUNTY OF _____

_____

IN THE MATTER OF THE _____

_____

_____
(Deceased/Minor/Incompetent, Etc.)

CASE NUMBER

DECLARATION FOR FINAL DISCHARGE

I, _____, say:

I am the _____ of the above entitled estate; that I have, under approval, authoriza-
(Executor/Administrator/Guardian, Etc.)

tion and order of the Court, paid all sums of money due from me as such _____
(Executor/Administrator/Guardian, Etc.)

and all required receipts and vouchers for same are on file in said estate; that distribution and delivery has been
made of all the property and assets of said estate in accordance with the decree therefor made and that receipts
from all the respective distributees are on file in said estate and that I have performed all acts lawfully required
of me as such _____
(Executor/Administrator/Guardian, Etc.)

I declare under penalty of perjury that the foregoing is true and correct.

Executed on _____ at _____ , California.
(Date)   (Place)

_____

ORDER OF FINAL DISCHARGE

It appearing from the aforesaid declaration that the above entitled estate has been fully administered and that a final
decree of discharge is in order.

It is therefore ORDERED, ADJUDGED AND DECREED that _____
(Name)

as _____ of the above entitled estate is hereby released and discharged
(Executor/Administrator/Guardian, Etc.)

and that _____ and _____ sureties are discharged and released from all liability to be incurred hereafter.
(He/She)   (His/Her)

Dated: _____   _____
                                           JUDGE OF THE SUPERIOR COURT

DECLARATION AND ORDER OF FINAL DISCHARGE

LS-1327

This page intentionally left blank.

DECLARATION FOR TRANSFER OF DECEDENT'S PROPERTY
TO SURVIVING SPOUSE OR DOMESTIC PARTNER
UNDER CALIFORNIA PROBATE CODE SECTION 13500

The decedent,   (ss#   ), a resident of   CA, died on   , in

At least 40 days have elapsed since the date of the decedent's death as shown in a certified copy of the decedent's death certificate attached to this declaration.

The property of the decedent that is to be paid, transferred or delivered to the declarant is:

The declarant is the surviving spouse or domestic partner of the decedent. The declarant is entitled to the above referenced property under the decedent's will or under the laws of intestate succession.

Under California Probate Code Section 13500 said property is to be paid, delivered or transferred to declarant without probate.

No other person has a superior right to the interest of the decedent in the described property.

The declarant requests that the described property be paid, delivered, or transferred to the declarant.

The declarant herein declares under penalty of perjury under the laws of the State of California that the foregoing is true and correct.

Dated:

_____

Surviving Spouse

Index

Receipts, 56, 57, 61, 118, 119, 125, 128
Report of Sale and Petition for Order Confirming
    Sale, 90, 93, 94, 97, 98, 99, 101, 102, 104
Request for Special Notice, 58, 81, 116, 122, 126
residence, 11, 16, 22, 26, 28, 30, 33, 34, 38, 54, 64,
    65, 66, 78, 79, 84, 94, 102

S

safe-deposit box, 56
securities, 38, 51, 83, 85, 86, 89, 90, 92, 93
separate property, 3, 4, 19, 63
small estate, 25, 80
Social Security, 8, 10, 11, 56
solvent estate, 70, 120
special administrator, 5, 35, 37, 41
special notice, 58, 81, 84, 101, 102, 116, 122, 126
specific bequest, 107, 118
Spousal/Domestic Partner Property Order, 23, 24
Spousal/Domestic Partner Property Petition, 19-
    20, 22, 23, 32, 49, 52, 60, 74, 84, 98, 104
spouse, 3, 4, 6, 8, 10, 14, 16, 17, 18, 19, 20, 21, 23,
    24, 41, 42, 43, 53, 57, 72, 77, 78, 79, 80, 106,
    108, 110, 111, 112, 113, 122
status report, 115
statutory fee, 123
stock, 7, 11, 19, 24, 54, 64, 92, 108, 111, 118, 119
stocks, 11, 63, 92

T

tax identification number, 53, 56
title, 1, 3, 4, 5, 9, 10, 12, 13, 14, 18, 19, 20, 24, 25,
    26, 27, 28, 34, 40, 48, 51, 56, 66, 97, 98, 99, 100,
    103, 109, 117, 127
transfer agent, 11
transfer on death (T.O.D.) accounts, 5, 16, 17
trustee, 5, 18, 22, 31, 47
trusts, 112

W

Waxman-Duffy Prepaid Health Care Plan, 72
wills, 6, 9, 29, 33, 34, 35, 37, 38, 39, 40, 41, 50, 52,
    77, 78, 89, 117, 121, 124
    self-proving, 39, 40
witnesses, 39, 40, 43, 44